The Welfare State in Israel

The Welfare State in Israel

The Evolution of Social Security Policy and Practice

Abraham Doron
and
Ralph M. Kramer

Westview Press
BOULDER • SAN FRANCISCO • OXFORD

Westview Special Studies on the Middle East

Copyright © 1991 by Westview Press, Inc.

Published in 1991 in the United States of America by Westview Press, Inc., 5500 Central Avenue, Boulder, Colorado 80301-2847, and in the United Kingdom by Westview Press, 36 Lonsdale Road, Summertown, Oxford OX2 7EW

Library of Congress Cataloging-in-Publication Data
Doron, Abraham.
  The welfare state in Israel : the evolution of social security
policy and practice / Abraham Doron and Ralph M. Kramer.
    p.   cm.—(Westview special studies on the Middle East)
  Includes index.
  ISBN 0-8133-8055-3
  1. Social security—Israel.   2. Public welfare—Israel.
I. Kramer, Ralph M.   II. Title.   III. Series.
HD7212.2.D67   1991
368.4′0095694—dc20
                                                             91-22137
                                                                  CIP

Printed and bound in the United States of America

10   9   8   7   6   5   4   3   2   1

Contents

Tables

Preface and Acknowledgments

This book presents a perspective on the State of Israel that is quite different from the one familiar to most readers. Since Israel gained independence in 1948, public and scholarly interest has been concentrated almost exclusively on the Arab-Israeli conflict. We have chosen, however, to tell the story for the first time of one of the overlooked features of Israeli society: namely, the development of those social and political institutions that transformed Israel into a modern welfare state during a rather short period of time.

Israel has a unique history, but it also shares with most European and North American countries many features of its social security programs and administration. As in other countries, the evolution of the Israeli welfare state is a story of conflicting ideologies: traditionalism versus modernism; voluntary associations versus corporatism; state versus market, in the context of a struggle to achieve social protection, social integration, and equity in a rapidly changing society in the midst of unprecedented mass immigration and wars.

Apart from its many dramatic features, the process we describe here is a reminder that the development of welfare states, their modes of operation, and what is perceived as the "crisis of the welfare state" may also be understood in terms of case studies of small states as well as cross-national surveys of mostly large countries. The study of the development of the welfare state in Israel can serve as a microcosm of the key social policy issues and trends found in all modern industrial societies. At the same time, the unique history of Israel shows how a social security system can contribute to the transformation of society.

We embarked on this study with a shared interest in public policy. Our first collaboration occurred in 1975 during a research visit to Israel by Professor Kramer, who had been studying the role of voluntary organizations in welfare states. We were both struck by the similarity of public assistance programs in Israel with those of much older and larger countries that have entirely different sociopolitical traditions. This realization led us to an analysis of the influence of ideology on income-support policy in

Israel, which was subsequently published in the *Journal of Social Policy* in 1976.

Ten years later we again met in Jerusalem when Professor Kramer returned for a two-year stay at the Hebrew University in Jerusalem where he directed the University of California's Education Abroad Program from 1986–1988. We resumed our collaboration and prepared the first comprehensive account of the development of the social security core of the welfare state in Israel. We wanted to illuminate the ways in which social security policy was influenced by such factors as ideology, politics, economic development, demography, and public opinion in a society changing rapidly through mass immigration.

Although considerable research on social security had been published in Israel, little of it was comparative or available to nonreaders of Hebrew. Our book is thus an attempt to open this side of Israeli society to a broader international readership. Our primary interest is in the income-maintenance functions of the welfare state, and hence it constitutes the main focus of our study. Because of their complexity—which would require separate and extensive treatment—housing, education, health, and labor policy are considered only as they impinge directly on the emergence of social security policy.

Another boundary of the study is its focus on the State of Israel within its 1967 borders, which do not include the administered territories on the West Bank and Gaza—where Israeli law and institutions do not apply.

We want to acknowledge with gratitude the generous grants we received that made this study possible. These include research grants from the National Insurance Institute in Israel, the Paul Baerwald School of Social Work of the Hebrew University of Jerusalem, and the Institute of International Studies of the University of California at Berkeley. Portions of the study were completed while Professor Doron was on sabbatical leave during the academic year 1988–1989 at the University of Maryland in Baltimore, and Professor Kramer was a Lady Davis Scholar at the Hebrew University.

The cooperation and support of Yossi Tamir and Leah Achdut of the National Insurance Institute in Israel is much appreciated. In the preparation of the manuscript for publication, the technical assistance of Dr. Michael Shalev and Menachem Birnbaum of the Hebrew University and Sara Lemann of Jerusalem is gratefully acknowledged.

Abraham Doron
Ralph M. Kramer

1

Introduction

The welfare state in Israel has its roots in the millennial history of the Jewish people and in the development of political Zionism in the latter part of the nineteenth century, which led to the reestablishment of the Jewish state in 1948.[1] The experience of Israel in developing its welfare state is noteworthy because of its similarity to the history of the welfare state in larger, older, and more advanced nations and because of the unique circumstances attending Israel's precarious establishment and growth. A post-World War II latecomer to the ranks of social democratic welfare states, Israel developed a modern system of social security that compressed into three decades a process that originated in England's seventeenth-century Poor Laws.

Yet there are many variations in the type, form, and scope of welfare states that have developed in capitalist and socialist economies, in advanced industrialized societies and developing nations, and in democratic and totalitarian societies. There are also a great many similarities; however, no single pattern of a "welfare state" has as yet evolved nor is there a consensus on its definition or its determinants.[2] For our purposes, we refer to the welfare state as a society that has accepted legal responsibility to assure all its citizens a floor of income, nutrition, health care, education, housing and social care.[3] Although there are numerous theories purporting to explain the emergence of and similarities and differences among welfare states, we prefer to view these entitlements as a response to the need for a minimum measure of social and economic security because of changes brought about by modernization, that is, increasing urbanization, industrialization and the consequent division of labor, expansion of the economy, and the lessened capacity of the family and other informal social systems to deal with the problems of living in a more complex society.[4]

In this book we restrict our focus to social security or the income maintenance core of the welfare state. Social security is distinguished by its monetary character—in contrast to other service-based benefits such as health care, education and housing. These cash benefits address the risks most likely to occur in an industrial society where households depend primarily on income from wages, and where interruptions in earned income occur because of unemployment, old age, physical or mental handicap, work accidents, death of the breadwinner, short- or long-term illnesses, and similar contingencies.

Why another case study? From the many surveys seeking to explain national variations in the development of the welfare state and social security spending, it has become clear that "differences among rich nations do not yield to one or two single explanatory factors; . . . it is necessary to respect the uniqueness of each program in the light of its historical antecedents, social policy and economic and political constraints; detailed study of actual national practices is probably the best aid to further understanding." More specifically, "the role and function of income support can only be fully understood in the context of a particular society."[5] Most case studies, however, have been limited to the larger, highly industrialized nations, such as the United States, England, France, Germany or the Soviet Union, and there are very few case studies of small countries.[6] We believe that an analysis of the forty-year experience of Israel provides an instructive microcosm of key policy issues and trends in social security systems in modern societies and enables us to find answers to the following questions:

1. What role is played in initiating, supporting, or constraining social security policy by ideology, politics, economic development, and changing patterns of social life—such as those noted in demographic studies and public opinion polls?
2. What are the effects of different types of institutional structures and their bureaucratic character on the development and implementation of social policy?
3. What factors influence the cross-national, "societal" learning of small states?
4. Under what conditions can social protection reduce inequality and contribute to social integration in a society where socioeconomic cleavages overlap ethnic divisions?
5. What are the effects of an entitlement to a minimum income in a low-wage economy?
6. How do socialist and capitalist ideologies of work influence social policy?
7. In what ways does "party state corporatism" influence the development of a welfare state?

Welfare states have developed through a process of trial and error, as a response to their particular historical circumstances and their social, economic, and political patterns.[7] Israel shares with other welfare states the major objectives of achieving an acceptable level of social protection, equality and integration of the diverse elements in its population. These interrelated goals have generally been implicit if not explicit in the justification for most social legislation.

Social protection refers to various systems that protect the population against the major hazards of life in modern industrial societies, such as work accidents, physical and mental disabilities, illness, unemployment, death of the breadwinner, and old age. As a goal, *equality* seeks to reduce the extent of poverty and the social gap between the classes by redistributing resources from the wealthier population groups to the more disadvantaged and institutionalizing the benefits to the latter as one of the rights of citizenship and not as charity. In Israel there was, in addition, a strong ideological commitment to a socialist egalitarian society as part of the nation-building process. The third objective of *integration* was also particularly important in Israel because of the diversity and stratification among the more than eighty different immigrant groups in its population; hence the rationale for the melting pot philosophy of immigrant absorption as essential for national rebirth.[8] In retrospect, the feasibility of welfare states attaining all three objectives has been questioned; however, much can be learned from their effects in Israel on each other.

The Israeli social security system has undergone a fundamental change during the last three decades, one that has almost completely transformed Israeli society. In the early 1950s, the system consisted mainly of an extremely limited and mostly discretionary social assistance program. Within three decades, by the end of the 1970s, it had expanded to include a wide range of social insurance and income maintenance programs covering most of the causes of loss of income in a developing industrial society.

In the chapters that follow, we discuss how these changes came about in each of the major program areas for the *aged, children,* and *unemployed,* by considering five sets of questions:

1. What were the social policy issues, how did they arise and get on the national agenda?
2. What were the various sources of social policy change? What role was played by ideologies, political parties and other interest groups, and economic and social conditions?
3. What was the actual process of policymaking, that is, who initiated, supported, or opposed changes, and how were conflicts resolved?
4. What happened when these policies were implemented?
5. What can be learned from the Israeli experience? How is it similar to and different than the processes in other countries? What are the implications for social protection, the attainment of equality, and integration in other democratic welfare states?

The answers to these questions should be viewed in the context of a prior but broader query: How did the new, small, Jewish state in the Middle East succeed in developing a modern welfare state while also absorbing an unprecedented mass immigration that almost tripled its population in the first five years, developing a viable economy, and organizing a defense establishment capable of fighting five wars? One plausible explanation is that there is congruence between the requirements for nation building and the development of a welfare state. In this case, the Zionist ideology, with its socialist commitment to collective responsibility, together with the pre-state institutional structures which were transferred to the State of Israel, provided an appropriate social policy environment in which to strive for the goals of social protection, equality, and integration.[9]

But Zionist ideology is only one feature of of the Israeli landscape. Other relevant characteristics of the country are its size, population, economy, and sociopolitical structure.

Size

Israel is a small country in the Middle East, located on the historic crossroads between Asia and Africa and between the Mediterranean and the Red Sea. It borders Lebanon on the north, Jordan on the east, and Egypt on the southwest. The total area of Israel (which is about the size of New Jersey) is 13,000 square miles, half of which is desert. Israel can be crossed by car from the Mediterranean coast to the Jordan Valley in about an hour and a half, and from north to south (Rosh Hanikra near the Lebanon border to Eilat on the Gulf of Aqaba) in about seven hours—four of which are required to traverse the Negev Desert. Jerusalem and Tel Aviv, the two largest cities, are less than an hour apart by car, and about half of the nearly 5 million inhabitants in Israel live in the central part of the country in a series of urban and suburban clusters surrounding these two cities.

Population

By the end of 1988, Israel had a population of almost 4.5 million, about the same as Norway, of which 18.3 percent, or 818,000, was Arab. The Arab population was mainly Moslem but included 105,000 Christians and 78,000 Druze and others. These statistics exclude about 1.5 million Arabs in areas occupied since the 1967 War, but they do include the population of East Jerusalem. The Jewish population increased eightfold from 1948 until 1988; it doubled from 1948 to 1951 and doubled again by 1970. Almost two-thirds of the increase was due to immigration, of which 60 percent came from Moslem countries. The Jewish population of Israel increased from 650,000 in 1948 to 1,670,000 in 1953 to 2,031,000 in 1958 and to 3,575,000 in

1988.

The Arab population was 156,000 in 1949; as a result of a high birthrate and declining death rate, it reached 533,000 in 1976 and by 1988, including East Jerusalem, was about 818,000. The Arab population of Israel, which increased from 11 percent in 1949 to 18.3 percent in 1988, is also much younger.

The effect of immigration on Israeli demography has been dramatic. In 1948 only one-third of the entire population was born in Israel; in 1988 the Israeli-born population reached more than 62 percent. The population is still relatively young, though the birthrate has been falling in recent years. In 1988 about 46 percent of the Jewish population was younger than twenty-five, mainly because of the influx of young Asian and North African immigrants, who had a high birthrate and, consequently, large families. The proportion of older persons in the population has risen from 4 percent in 1948 to 8 percent in 1974 to about 9 percent in 1988. Life expectancy in 1988 had reached 73 years for men and 77 years for women.[10]

The Economy

The main feature of the Israeli economy since the establishment of the state in 1948 has been its rapid growth, at least until the mid-1970s. In the period between 1950 and 1965 the average annual rate of growth of the Gross National Product (GNP) was about 10 percent, and in spite of the increased population, the per capita GNP growth averaged 6.5 percent during the same period. Much of this growth was due to the flow of capital from foreign investment and aid, as well as improved productivity. From 1966 to 1973 there was only a slight slow down in these rates of growth, but since the mid-1970s the Israeli economy, like most others in the Western world, has grown at a much slower rate.[11]

Per capita income in Israel is lower than in Western European countries, but out of 118 countries that include the industrialized nations and the oil-rich countries, Israel was thirtieth, with a per capita income of $5,000 in 1982. This ranking put Israel near the top of the list of upper-middle-income countries, according to the World Bank. In 1987, 43 percent of the households had cars, 87 percent had washing machines, 80 percent had color televisions, 85 percent had phones, 10 percent had personal computers and dishwashers, and 20 percent had videocassette recorders.[12] The structure of the Israeli economy resembles that of developed nations: Agriculture accounts for about 5 percent of the GNP, industry 24 percent, construction 6 percent, and transportation, communication, and services account for the rest.

Since 1973, the slowed growth of the Israeli economy has been due to the general recession in the world economy as well as problems inherent in the structure of the economy and its overall political and mlitary situation. The economy's difficulties are reflected in rising defense expenditures, exceptional inflationary pressures, and an increasing deficit in the external balance of payments. Inflation increased from about 30 percent to 50 percent annually in the mid-1970s and to more than 400 percent in the early 1980s before it was possible to control it in 1984–1985. Defense expenditures have been a heavy burden on the Israeli economy through the years and they have been substantially more than in most other countries—from 20 percent to 30 percent of the total resources. Defense also takes human resources in the form of compulsory military conscription and annual periods of reserve service.

The 1988–1989 budget showed that 37 percent of governmental income was allocated for debt servicing, mainly as a result of past wars; 23 percent for defense, and 26 percent for all the social services.[13] Another notable feature of the economy is the influence of the state, which is involved in ownership of more than two hundred corporations, and the Histadrut (General Federation of Labor), which controls about 22 percent of the economy. The state depends extensively on foreign aid, partly from Jewish and other philanthropic institutions, and on loans and grants from the U.S. government.

It is somewhat paradoxical for Israel to be regarded simultaneously as a developing state and as a successful case of modernization. The country's most prominent features resemble those of a modern Western nation, even though strong traditional sectors and elements exist alongside them. Israel is highly urbanized; only about 4 percent of its population is engaged in agriculture. It has exceedingly high standards of medical care, literacy, unionization, scientific research, school enrollment, and economic and agricultural planning, to cite a few of the indicators of modernization. At the same time, more than one-fourth of its population, both Arab and Jewish, maintain traditional social patterns and orthodox religious ideologies that resist the national commitment to democracy, science, and technology.

From this perspective Israel can be viewed as being between a developed and a developing country—a Middle Eastern country with European cultural and political origins. Its reference groups are the advanced countries of the European Economic Community (EEC) and North America, and it has special ties with their Jewish communities.[14]

Political Structure

Israel is a multiparty state, but no party has ever received a majority in the national legislature, the Knesset. The largest party until 1977 was the Labor Party, which was aligned in a political bloc with some smaller labor parties. Together they prevailed in coalition governments from 1948 until 1977 when the Labor alignment lost its power for the first time.[15] The Likud, a center-right alignment, became the main political bloc in the Knesset and formed a coalition with several of the minor religious and other parties represented in the parliament. This situation changed somewhat after the 1984 elections when the two major political blocs, Labor and the Likud, gained parity in the Knesset and were forced into a power-sharing agreement in a government of National Unity.

The Knesset consists of 120 members elected by universal suffrage under a system of proportional representation for a four-year period. The cabinet, headed by the prime minister, is collectively responsible to the Knesset and continues in office for four years or until resignation or upon receiving a vote of no confidence. Ministers are usually but not necessarily members of the Knesset. The Israeli government generally has more than twenty different ministries responsible for specific functional areas. The titular head of the state is the president, who is elected by the Knesset for a five-year period and may be reelected for one additional term. The judiciary is independent and largely patterned on the legal system inherited from the British Mandate from 1921–1948.

There are three types of local authorities: municipalities, local councils, and regional councils, all of whom are partly financed by direct grants and long-term loans from the central government, which amount to about one-quarter of their revenue. The Ministry of the Interior is responsible for all matters concerning local government and has to approve local tax rates, annual budgets, and by-laws.

The outstanding feature of the Israeli power structure is the scope of concentrated influence in a few highly centralized, bureaucratic, and political institutions that can be described as "party state corporatism." Perhaps because Israel is a very small country and a consciously created state, there is a degree of authority wielded by the central government possibly unparalleled in any other nontotalitarian state. There is no aspect of life untouched by the state acting either unilaterally or in partnership with some other equally monolithic, bureaucratic, political institution.[16]

The state owns more than 90 percent of the land and its resources and is the largest employer of labor: more than half of the persons in the labor market are classified as working in the public sector. Through subsidies and quasi-public partnerships, the central government is the dominant influence together with the Histadrut in the economic and social life of the country. The major instruments of the state's power are the cabinet ministries, which are administered through hierarchical structures with policy decisions made centrally and with relatively little authority delegated to local or regional offices. Although quite similar to European ministries and the federal departments in the United States, the Israeli ministries are distinctive not only because of the great concentration of centralized power assigned to them, but also because of the extent to which they are politicized.

It is for this reason that Israel has been called a *parteienstaat*, a state organized on the basis of political parties with relatively little distinction between polity and society. Political parties in Israel—and this is particularly true of the once-dominant Labor Party—have an enormous domain: They are involved in newspaper publishing, economic enterprises, banks, insurance companies, agricultural settlements, housing developments, health and welfare institutions, sport clubs, community centers, and youth groups. Although 80 percent of the citizenry vote in elections, less than 10 percent of the population belongs to a political party; the per capita campaign expenditure rate in Israel is among the highest in the world. Because of the system of proportional representation, political parties have little accountability to voters, and successive efforts at electoral reform have not succeeded.[17]

The power of parties is evident in the widespread use of political criteria in bureaucratic decisionmaking regarding the allocation of resources, as well as in the more traditional areas of patronage, which have been refined and routinized. This latter systematic principle is known as the "key" whereby most positions in the government, the Histadrut, the Jewish Agency, and other public institutions are awarded on the basis of the percentage of votes obtained by the various parties in the Knesset elections. As a result, political parties not only control their own network of institutions but those included in the governing coalition also obtain considerable jurisdiction over the personnel policies and programs of the public bureaucracies.[18]

The Content and Structure of the Book

Our purpose, then, is to analyze the origins, processes, content, and consequences of social security policymaking in Israel. The intent is to provide a comprehensive understanding of the social choices made during the period from 1948 to 1990, that is, the types of social policies that evolved, how they were implemented, and the resultant changes in Israeli society.

Essentially a case study of Israel that can also serve as a microcosm of the key issues and trends in all social security systems in modern industrial societies, the analysis will also be viewed comparatively on a selective, cross-national basis where this is feasible. We begin in Chapter 2 with an overview of the five stages of the development of the welfare state in Israel. Chapters 3 and 4 describe the changing character of the social assistance program, which served as the first and only form of income support in the early, turbulent years of statehood. The discussion of the establishment of national insurance in Chapter 5 recounts the political and legislative struggle preceding the passage of the basic law adopted in 1953 and the further evolution of the system during the 1960s and 1970s.

The next three chapters analyze the development of the four major national insurance programs: for the elderly (Chapters 6 and 7), for children (Chapter 8), and for the unemployed (Chapter 9). Chapter 10 is devoted to a review of the social and economic impact of social security. The work concludes in Chapter 11 with a summary of the major trends and issues and some conclusions and generalizations about the social policy-making process in Israel and implications for the achievement of the main goals of the Israeli welfare state—social protection, equality and integration.

Notes

1. Useful accounts in English of the pre-state Jewish community in Palestine and the continuities in the new State can be found in S.N. Eisenstadt, *Israeli Society* (New York: Basic Books, 1967); Amitai Etzioni, "The Decline of Neo-Feudalism: The Case of Israel," in Ferel Heady and Sybil L. Stokes (eds.), *Papers in Comparative Public Administration* (Ann Arbor: University of Michigan Press, 1962), pp. 229–243; and Amos Elon, *The Israelis: Founders and Sons* (New York: Holt, Rinehart, and Winston, 1971), pp. 3–147.

2. On the absence of agreement on the definition of the welfare state, see Peter Flora and Arnold J. Heidenheimer (eds.), *The Development of Welfare States in Europe and America* (New Brunswick, NJ: Transaction Books, 1981), pp. 5–34.

3. This definition is similar to the one used in Harold L. Wilensky, *The Welfare State and Equality: Structural and Ideological Roots of Public Expenditures* (Berkeley: University of California Press, 1975), p. 1. See also Anthony King, "The Political Consequences of the Welfare State," in Shimon E. Spiro and Ephraim Yuchtman-Yaar (eds.), *Evaluating the Welfare State: Social and Political Perspectives* (New York: Academic Press, 1983), pp. 7–25.

4. This theory of the welfare state is developed in Arnold J. Heidenheimer, Hugh Heclo, and Carolyn Teich-Adams (eds.), *Comparative Social Policy: The Politics of Social Choice in Europe and America* (London: Macmillan Press, 1975). Critical assessments of this and other theories of the welfare state are found in Francis G. Castles (ed.), *The Comparative History of Public Policy* (Cambridge: Polity Press, 1989), pp. 1–15; and Joan Higgins, "Comparative Social Policy: The State of the Art," *Quarterly Journal of Social Affairs* 2:3 (1980), pp. 221–242.

5. Flora and Heidenheimer, op. cit., pp. 191–192.

6. See, for example, Gaston V. Rimlinger, *Welfare Policy and Industrialization in Europe, America, and Russia* (New York: John Wiley and Son, 1971); W.J. Mommsen (ed.), *The Emergence of the Welfare State in Britain and Germany 1850–1950* (London: Croom Helm, 1981); and Peter A. Kohler and Hans F. Zacher (eds.), *The Evolution of Social Insurance 1881–1981: Studies of Germany, France, Great Britain, Austria, and Switzerland* (London: Frances Pinter and New York: St. Martin's Press, 1982).

7. Douglas E. Ashford, *The Emergence of the Welfare States* (London: Basil Black-well, 1986).

8. Rivka Bar-Yosef, "Welfare and Integration in Israel," in S.N. Eisenstadt and Ora Ahimeir (eds.), *The Welfare State and Its Aftermath* (London: Croom Helm, 1985), pp. 247–261.

9. On the relationship between nation-building and the welfare state, see Baruch Kimmerling, *Zionism and Economy* (Cambridge, MA: Schenkman, 1983); and Dan Horowitz and Moshe Lissak, *The Origins of the Israeli Polity: Palestine Under the Mandate* (Chicago: University of Chicago Press, 1978), pp. 120–156.

10. These demographic statistics are found in the *Statistical Abstract of Israel 1989*, No. 40 (Jerusalem, 1990).

11. Yoram Ben-Porath (ed.), *The Economy of Israel: Maturing Through Crisis* (Cambridge: Harvard University Press, 1986). An earlier account is Nadav Halevi and Ruth Klinov-Malul, *The Economic Development of Israel* (New York: Praeger, 1968).

12. *Statistical Abstract of Israel*, op. cit., p. 298.

13. Yaakov Kop (ed.), *Israel's Social Services 1988–1989* (Jerusalem: Center for Social Policy Studies in Israel, 1989), p. 27.

14. Daniel J. Elazar, *Israel: Building a New Society* (Bloomington: Indiana University Press, 1986); and S.N. Eisenstadt, "The Israeli Political System and the Transformation of Israeli Society," in Ernest Krausz (ed.), *Politics and Society in Israel: Studies of Israeli Society*, Vol. 3 (New Brunswick, NJ: Transaction Books, 1985), pp. 415–427.

15. The term Labor Party refers to Mapai, the leading Labor party on the Israeli political scene untll the 1970s Since then it is known as Mifleget Avoda.

16. Peter Y. Medding, *The Founding of Israeli Democracy: Parties, Politics, and Government* (New York: Oxford University Press, 1990); Lev Grinberg, *Split Corporatism in Israel* (Albany: State University of New York Press, 1990). Earlier studies of the role of the state are: Benjamin Akzin and Yeheskel Dror, *Israel: High Pressure Planning* (Syracuse, NY: Syracuse University Press, 1966); Gerald E. Caiden, *Israel's Administrative Culture* (Berkeley: University of California, Institute of Governmental Studies, 1970); and Marvin Bernstein, *The Politics of Israel* (Princeton: Princeton University Press, 1957).

17. Daniel J. Elazar, "Israel's Compound Polity," in Krausz, op. cit., pp. 43–80; Asher Arian, *The Choosing People* (Cleveland: Case Western Reserve University Press, 1973). Also see references in note 14.

18. Don Peretz, *The Government and Politics of Israel* (Boulder, CO: Westview Press, 1979); Daniel Shimshoni, *Israeli Democracy: The Middle of the Journey* (New York: Free Press, 1982).

2

Emergence of the
Welfare State in Israel:
An Overview

Although the Jewish community in Palestine, known as the Yishuv, had a long pre-state history of collective responsibility, the process whereby the welfare state has evolved in the State of Israel was not a smooth one. As in other countries, every step in the inception of new social welfare and social security programs was accompanied by protracted political controversy. Yet the welfare state slowly emerged over a period of three decades as a consequence of the nation-building process, as a result of pressures for greater social protection in the face of mounting economic insecurity in a rapidly growing industrial society, and as a response to the shifting distribution of ethnic and social class power in a society based on mass immigration. Influenced at different times by the goals of social protection, equality, and integration, the welfare state in Israel moved through the following five phases:

1. Pre-State Origins (1920–1948)
2. Nation-Building (1948–1957)
3. Institutionalization and Formalization (1958–1967)
4. Expansion and Power Redistribution (1968–1977)
5. Uncertainty (1977–1990).

Pre-State Origins (1920–1948)

Ideological Roots

Two main sources influenced the structure of the Jewish state and its welfare institutions: the social and religio-cultural tradition of the Jewish people in their lands of dispersion and the development of political Zionism in the last two decades of the nineteenth century, which were preceded by earlier pioneering settlements in Palestine. The Jewish community that emerged first under Turkish rule—and after World War I during the rule of the British Mandatory government—was known as the Yishuv, the "state-on-the-way" or "the state within a state." Most social institutions in present-day Israel originated in the Yishuv and were subsequently transferred to the state.[1]

The early Jewish settlers, who came mainly from Eastern Europe, were strongly influenced by the ideology of Labor Zionism that rejected the possibility of a viable Jewish life outside of Palestine and stressed the values of pioneering and productivity, the dignity of labor, egalitarianism, mutual aid, and collective responsibility. These ideals were eminently suited to the tasks of nation-building and have much in common with the parallel development of other countries such as the United States, Canada, Australia, and New Zealand. Each of these "new societies" was founded by pioneers who migrated to new countries and underwent a frontier experience in which they attempted to create a new and modern social order unfettered by the class system and culture of their old societies.[2] The multiple goals of the Zionist movement, derived mainly from socialist ideas prevalent in Europe in the last quarter of the nineteenth century, sought not only the reestablishment of a modern Jewish state but one that would lead to a national cultural renaissance and the creation of a just society. As early as 1898, one of the leading ideologues of Labor Zionism, Nachman Syrkin, expressed the belief that:

> For a Jewish state to come to be, it must, from the very beginning avoid all the ills of modern life. To evoke the sympathetic interest of modern man, its guidelines must be justice, rational planning and social solidarity . . . the Jewish state can come about only if it is socialist; only by fusing with socialism can Zionism become the ideal of all Jewish people, of the proletariat, the middle class and the intelligentsia . . . the messianic hope which was always the greatest dream of exiled Jewry, will be transformed into political action.[3]

These values and goals of Labor Zionism were not conceived in utopian terms but were intended to be consistently implemented in the development of the institutions of the nation-building process known as "constructivism."

Mandate Palestine

When Britain accepted mandatory responsibility for Palestine following World War I, it assumed control over one of the most backward regions of the dissolved Ottoman Empire. Palestine was impoverished in every respect. It had a crippled economy with little industry or commerce, no natural resources, primitive communication, underdeveloped social services, and a tradition of unstable government. When the first census was taken in 1922, the Jewish population numbered only 84,000 out of less than 750,000.[4]

Article 2 of the League of Nations Mandate had entrusted Britain with the responsibility of promoting such conditions that would facilitate the establishment of the Jewish National Home. Contrary to the high expectations this aroused among many in the Jewish community, the Palestine administration showed little interest in intervening in the economic, political, and social life of the country. The only social legislation introduced by the Mandatory government consisted of the Workmen's Compensation Ordinance, which offered very limited coverage and protection for specific types of industrial injuries, and the Employment of Women Ordinance of 1945, which provided employed women with a modest maternity allowance for eight weeks and was paid by the employer.

In addition to the lack of initiative of the Mandatory government, the other major obstacle to the development of the country was the vast cultural-religious, social, and economic gulf between the Jewish and Arab populations. Horowitz and Lissak described Mandatory Palestine as a place where "two nations without a state existed side by side."[5] The reports of the Mandatory government during 1920–1925 are filled with references to the "troublesome" character of its administration because of "the existence side by side of two groups of working populations which each belonged to different cultural types."[6] Jews and Arabs each had a strong sense of separate identity, but both resented the British rule.

The Jewish community drew on a long tradition of community organization and with the assistance of Zionist organizations abroad, developed from the beginning of its modern settlement a large number of independent, voluntary, and quasi-nongovernmental organizations. These organizations were designed not only to meet the welfare needs of a pioneering, immigrant society but also to embody in a practical way the Zionist ideals of equality, mutual aid, and collective responsibility.

Subsequently, three sets of separate and often competing social service systems were developed in the Yishuv, which substituted for and supplemented the meager social legislation of the Mandatory government: the Va'ad Leumi and the Histadrut, which became the two major social welfare structures for the Yishuv, and a wide range of voluntary charitable organizations. At the beginning most of these organizations were orthodox religious charities whose adherents had lived in the Holy Land for generations and who depended almost completely on contributions from abroad. Later, other voluntary organizations began to operate, principally those established by women's and other Zionist groups in the country and abroad.

The Va'ad Leumi—the National Council of the Jewish Community in Palestine—was established as the official elected body that represented the Jewish community.[7] It operated on a budget raised by voluntary taxation, and its jurisdiction over internal disputes, labor problems, and a range of social services was recognized in 1927 by the Mandatory government. The most important service in the field of social security was the social assistance program, which began in 1932 when a Social Welfare Department was established. It grew very rapidly and by 1947 the department maintained a network of local social service bureaus, which were responsible for providing financial aid and family and child care for the entire Jewish population. Because of the absence of any social security provisions in Palestine, these social service bureaus were the primary resource for all forms of financial need. The Social Welfare Department of the Va'ad Leumi received some support from the Mandatory government from 1939 on, but there was always a severe shortage of funds and only meager financial assistance could ever be offered.

In 1920 the General Federation of Jewish Labor—more commonly known as the Histadrut—was founded. More than a conventional trade union, it had three functional branches: an entrepreneurial economy whose aim was to build a modern economic structure in agriculture, industry, and housing; a trade union for all employees; and social services known as a mutual aid system, which included health care, old-age security, unemployment assistance, death benefits for widows and orphans, discounts for day-care centers, and other educational and vocational training services—to which all members had certain rights because of an income-linked membership fee.

The most important of the services established by the Histadrut for its members was health care. The first voluntary health insurance fund was founded before World War I in 1912 by the Union of Agricultural Workers. It started with only 150 members but it eventually became the sick fund of the Histadrut, known as the Kupat Holim, and by 1922 it already had a membership of 10,000, including dependents. By 1930 the membership had grown to more than 34,000—nearly 20 percent of the total Jewish population—and in 1947 it grew to 304,000, including dependents, and covered about 47 percent of the Jewish population.

Kupat Holim provided its members with full medical care through a network of local and regional health clinics, hospitals, and other facilities, which were built all over the country. Membership in Kupat Holim followed automatically from membership in the Histadrut—workers first joined the Histadrut and then, as one of the benefits, obtained coverage through Kupat Holim. Thus Kupat Holim became one of the largest and most important social insurance institutions of the Histadrut and the dominant factor in the provision of health care in the country. At the same time there were a number of smaller, voluntary sick funds established during the Mandate period by other political or public nonprofit groups that provided medical care to their members.

It is significant that these social insurance and mutual aid institutions of the Histadrut were not regarded as "welfare," which would have contradicted the prevailing Labor Zionist ideology. Rather, the prototype of what later became the social security system was considered to be part of the pioneering activities aimed at building the new Jewish workers' socialist society. The Labor Zionists thought that welfare was an unacceptable way to deal with social problems because they assumed that the future socialist society would not contain any social problems that would require the intervention of welfare institutions.[8]

These three systems of welfare (Va'ad Leumi, Histadrut, and voluntary) differed in their ideologies, target populations, and administrative-organizational structures. As separate, quasi-voluntary infrastructures with a very broad scope within the Jewish community, they were at the same time highly particularistic, that is, restricted to their members or adherents. They were, however, alike in their lack of political authority and inadequacy of resources to cope effectively with the precarious nature of life under the British Mandate.[9]

In the aftermath of World War II, Palestine was also influenced by the flourishing ideas on the postwar reconstruction of Europe and, in particular, by the Beveridge Report and its guiding principle of social insurance as part of a comprehensive social policy. In December 1945, the Histadrut submitted a memorandum to the Mandatory government in which it pointed out the need to introduce a comprehensive system of social insurance in the near future. Surprisingly, and for the first time, the Mandatory government did not reject the proposal to introduce a social insurance program and stated publicly that such legislation might be contemplated seriously.[10]

In summing up the Yishuv, one can understand the pride of the Jewish community in the wide range of social welfare institutions it developed, although there was also widespread awareness of their shortcomings. Yet, in the context of the political and economic conditions of the Mandate regime and the wide gap between the Jewish and Arab populations, the contribution of these Yishuv institutions to the welfare of the Jewish population was considerable. However, the arrangements that were essential under the Mandate regime were later to become a primary obstacle to the development of a national social security system in Israel.

The First Decade (1948–1957): Nation-Building

The struggle for the welfare state in Israel started with the establishment of statehood in 1948. It was preceded by a civil war between Jews and Arabs, which broke out soon after the partition plan was adopted by the UN General Assembly. The fighting increased during the last stages of the British withdrawal and intensified when six Arab armies invaded the newly declared State of Israel. There was an extensive and unplanned "exchange of populations" as many Arabs left the areas which had been won by Israel or allocated to it under the 1949 cease-fire lines, which became the de facto borders of the new state. The Arab population that left Israel was replaced by more than 1 million Jews, which included a disproportionate number of elderly and disabled persons, most of whom were forced to leave Moslem countries as a result of the Arab defeat. By 1952, the Arab population in Israel was dwarfed by that of the Jews, whose numbers had doubled in four years. Although the new immigrants were given citizenship at once, it was another matter for the fledgling state to be able to provide any measure of security beyond day-to-day survival.

With the establishment of the state, the few social welfare services of the Mandate government and those of the Va'ad Leumi were merged into a newly created Ministry of Social Welfare—the Saad. The Histadrut network of social insurance and health care services continued, however, to operate as an independent and separate system. The political leaders who shaped the thinking of the Histadrut and the labor movement at the time were strongly opposed to giving up the social service system, which was considered to be one of its major achievements.[11] Ironically, the existence of a network of social security and health care services, which operated under the auspices of the most powerful organized political force in the country, became the major institutional constraint on the future development of these services in Israel. Their evolution was marked by a continuous struggle between the Histadrut and the state: on the one hand, the Histadrut wanted to maintain its separate service system; but on the other hand, there were increased political and bureaucratic pressures to integrate the existing separate systems into a unified national system.

At the same time there were also strong voices within the labor movement who argued that the new Jewish state was morally obligated to establish what the Yishuv had demanded for years from the Mandatory government—a comprehensive system of social security. Its proponents believed that despite the very difficult, unstable economic conditions and the continuous threat to national security, the time was right to establish the foundations of a future welfare state that, by providing social protection, would contribute to the integration of the society and the building of a nation.

The essential elements of these aspirations were articulated in a social insurance plan for the State of Israel prepared by the Social Research Institute of the Histadrut and published in June 1948,[12] one month after independence was declared. At that critical point in the very middle of the War of Independence, the government had no time to deal with social security issues, even though circumstances of the mass immigration forced it to confront daily the problems of unemployment, social welfare, and social security. Because there were also pressures within the labor movement for the government to adopt a policy on social insurance, the Provisional government appointed an interministerial committee in January 1949 to study and prepare plans for a comprehensive social insurance program in Israel. The committee was headed by Itzhak Kanev, from the Histadrut Social Research Institute and author of the earlier social insurance plan. Early in 1950, the Kanev committee submitted its report, which proposed the introduction in stages of a comprehensive system of social insurance. These recommendations constituted an Israeli version of the Beveridge Report, which largely influenced its contents.[13]

For the next three years, 1948–1951—which were marked by economic upheavals, rampant inflation, severe austerity and rationing as part of the initial effort to absorb the newcomer population—the struggle for the implementation of the Kanev plan took place. Leaders within the government and in most financial circles questioned whether, under the prevailing economic conditions, it was possible or even desirable to establish wide-ranging social security programs.[14] By the end of 1953, proponents of the various conservative political interests overcame their doubts and made a modest beginning with the passage of the first National Insurance Act.[15]

Thus the basic foundations were laid for the welfare state in Israel. This legislation also established the National Insurance Institute as a semiautonomous state agency that could serve as the organizational and administrative base for the future development of the core of the country's social security system. The controversies around these first small but significant steps were not easily resolved, but the ability to forge a fragile consensus among the various competing interests helped pave the way for the steps to come.

In retrospect, the very fact that Israel could even consider, during these turbulent years, and ultimately adopt a rudimentary social security program was in itself no small achievement. One must bear in mind the enormous problems then facing the new state. It was still in the process of asserting its legal and moral authority and was confronted on all sides with a constant threat to its national security. It had to wrestle with the difficult task of transferring governmental functions from powerful pre-state institutional interests that were reluctant to give up their power. At the same time, it had to provide for the initial absorption of the hundreds of thousands of impoverished immigrants from Arab countries and European survivors of the Holocaust. The ability to lay the foundations of the welfare state in the midst of this chaos and uncertainty was indeed noteworthy.

The Second Decade (1958–1967): Institutionalization and Formalization

One of the main factors that strongly influenced the evolution of the Israeli welfare state since the end of the first decade was the change in the country's ideological climate. The close of the 1950s marked the end of an era. The ideological commitment that was the driving force behind the Israeli labor movement's initial struggle for social insurance legislation exhausted itself toward the end of the first decade. This was also the beginning of "the end of ideology."[16] Until then the Israeli labor movement strove to change the existing order and to transform society according to its vision of socialist Zionism. Without the influence of this ideology no national insurance program could possibly have been adopted in 1953.

From then on, the labor movement lost its momentum and it did not produce any more proposals to change the social structure of Israeli society. The additions and changes to the initial social security core of the welfare state, which were made throughout the second decade—the 1960s— were almost all the products of the new bureaucracy of professional civil servants. Although the new bureaucracy asserted its power, the older "Kanev guard" continued to express its views; but it not only lacked ideological fervor, it also had little to offer in terms of positive answers to the changing needs of Israeli society, particularly in the area of social security.

After the turbulent first decade, most of the years in this second stage were marked by relative peace, some reduction of tension on the borders, exceptionally rapid economic growth of about 10 percent per annum, and an increase in national prosperity. The improved political and economic situation provided opportunities for planned social change. In a piecemeal way and without much ideological zeal, the welfare state expanded its activities to provide better protection to the population and to facilitate the process of integration of the large immigrant population groups into the mainstream of Israeli society. In other words, the welfare state in Israel gradually became institutionalized.

The main logic for the further development of the welfare state was provided by the process of industrialization and modernization. In the face of rapid economic growth and improved living conditions, broader areas of social need were recognized as proper fields of government intervention, and new social programs were established to deal with them. The organizational and administrative machinery of the state was the main carrier of these incremental reforms. The process could thus be seen as a continuation of nation-building without the ideological commitment of the earlier phase.

The social policy debates and controversies in this stage, although of a different nature, were no less fierce than before. The struggles, however, were mainly among "technipols" within the large state bureaucracies on issues of who should do what;[17] among various political, professional, and economic interest groups, and on the organizational, administrative, and financial aspects of the policies and programs under discussion. The slow, piecemeal nature of the programs adopted and the benefits they provided constituted the base for the limited consensus they obtained.

In more concrete terms, the period until the immediate aftermath of the Six Day War was characterized by increasing consolidation and formalization in both the national insurance and social assistance programs. Levels of assistance were gradually increased in the latter, and specially favored groups were transferred from the residual social assistance program to national insurance coverage. Other small but important changes were made in all the insurance schemes. The relaxation, for example, of the full-retirement requirement as an eligibility condition for old-age pensions enabled large numbers of elderly people to partially retire and receive their old-age national insurance pension at the same time.[18]

The main field in which important additions were made to the national insurance program during this period was in children's allowances. In 1959 the large families' insurance scheme was introduced providing for the payment of children's allowances for the fourth and each additional child. In 1965 the employed persons' children's insurance scheme was added, covering the first three children of employee families. By the end of this period, with the exception of the first three children of nonemployees, all children in Israel were covered by this program. The role of the new children's allowance schemes was actually threefold: to supplement the income of all employee families; to attempt to bridge the income gap between small and large families; and also to narrow the gap between the settled and the new immigrant population, which consisted mainly of large families.

In the field of social assistance, the Social Welfare Services Act was passed in 1958. It established, for the first time, a legal basis for the operation of the local welfare bureaus and for the granting of financial aid to the needy. In practice, the new law included no change of policy toward the poor, nor any improvement in the assistance provided to them, because it continued to be based on the principles of local responsibility, means testing, and relatives' liability. But the steps taken to put the law into practice in the early 1960s resulted in increasing pressures to raise the assistance levels and led eventually to the improvement of the threshold of social protection to the most vulnerable population groups.

The Third Decade (1968–1977): Expansion in Response to Shifts in the Distribution of Power

The third stage, which lasted from the aftermath of the Six Day War in 1967 until the ascent of the Likud right-wing coalition to power in 1977, was a period of intensive social policy initiatives. As a result, Israel became by the end of this stage a welfare state similar to those among the more industrialized nations. This process can best be understood in the context of the shift in the distribution of power between social classes and ethnic groups, a struggle that dominated the Israeli scene throughout the period.

The major factors behind the frequently feverish political activities during this stage were the discovery, or rediscovery, of poverty among large groups of the population;[19] the growing recognition of increasing inequality in the distribution of income and opportunities among various social groups, as manifested in the "social gap" between the more established elements of the population of European origin and the newer immigrant groups from the Arab countries; the increased communal tension among these ethnic groups, which was dramatized by the appearance of an Israeli Black Panthers movement in Jerusalem; and the efforts of other socially underprivileged groups to assert their rights and to improve their position within Israeli society.

Although many of these events were a delayed reaction to the widely publicized War on Poverty in the United States during the 1960s, they were sufficiently rooted in the distinctive conditions of Israeli society to be perceived as a serious threat to social stability and to the established political order. Together, they stirred the government to action on some of the existing social problems and led to the appointment of two major committees in the early 1970s: the Committee on Income Distribution and Social Inequality, headed by David Horowitz, then governor of the Bank of Israel; and the prime minister's Commission for Children and Youth in Distress, headed by Golda Meir herself, and coordinated by Dr. Israel Katz, director of the National Insurance Institute. The reports of these committees became critical political events and eventually crystallized government thinking and actions. Thus it was the growing fear of major social upheavals based on long-standing ethnic cleavages that forced the government to introduce reforms and expand the welfare state.

Most social welfare reforms were introduced in the period of relative economic prosperity that lasted until the Yom Kippur war in 1973. The high cost of the war, the 1973 oil crisis, and the economic stagnation that followed seriously limited the country's capacity to further expand the welfare state. For example, defense spending, which accounted for 19.6 percent of the government budget in 1965–1966, more than doubled to 49.3 percent in 1973–1974 after the Yom Kippur War. Yet the welfare state programs remained mostly intact throughout the period between 1973 and 1977, even though their growth rate began to slow in 1975.

The most significant reforms introduced during this stage in the social security system were the establishment of the Unemployment Insurance scheme, which came into effect in 1973; the General Disability Insurance program, which began in 1974; the amalgamation of the existing children's allowances in 1975 into one program that covered all children in the country, and a substantial increase in the level of these allowances; and the gradual relaxation of the insurance principle in most national insurance schemes. In addition, a guaranteed minimum income was established for all citizens in the early 1970s by combining the existing national insurance benefits, children's allowances, and an income-conditioned supplementary benefits system.[20]

These reforms were not limited to the social security system. Important changes also occurred in other areas of the welfare state, such as the promotion of school integration projects, an enormous expansion of higher education, and the introduction of a whole range of new or enlarged programs in the fields of housing, health, and personal social care services.

Underlying these reforms was the recognition by the political leadership that as a result of demographic changes, a major shift in the power relationship between the various ethnic segments of the population was overdue. It was assumed that broadening and improving welfare programs would serve as a stabilizing factor and as an effective response to social and political tensions by helping integrate the non-European communities into the mainstream of Israeli society.

In summary, by the end of this stage the social security core of the Israeli welfare state had been greatly expanded and it became the principal means of promoting the goals of social protection, equality, and integration. The progressive extension of the system resulted in coverage of the entire population against most risks of loss of income, and by strengthening personal security it contributed to improving the quality of life for the individual Israeli citizen. The comprehensive social security system also brought about a modicum of redistribution of incomes among the population and helped narrow income differentials and reduce the incidence of poverty. Finally, during this take-off period the universal provision of a minimum level of income and its institutionalization as an entitlement assisted in the social integration of the most underprivileged groups in Israeli society.

The Fourth Decade (1978–1990): Uncertainty and Slowed Growth

The fourth and most recent stage, from 1978 to 1990, was again marked by a sharp swing in the pendulum that brought an abrupt halt to the rapid growth of the welfare state that had taken place in the previous decade. Perhaps the most important factor that influenced this change was the sharp decline in the ideological support for the welfare state among the ruling political groups and also among large segments of the general population. This trend also reflected the radical political and social changes that had occurred in Israeli society during the first forty years of statehood. Israel moved from being dominated by a strong Socialist-Zionist, collectivistic, and egalitarian ideology, to being governed by a conservative and populist coalition committed to free enterprise and individualism and opposed to government intervention. The sources of these changes in attitudes toward the welfare state can be found in the following social and political factors.

First, the basic sense of solidarity that provided moral and political support for the welfare state was weakened. With the rapid increase in national prosperity during the 1960s and 1970s, well-to-do population groups emerged that adopted a political philosophy of unrestrained free enterprise and actively opposed redistributive welfare policies. This group gained the upper hand in Israeli politics in the 1980s and were the chief supporters of the welfare backlash and demands to curtail the welfare state.

Second, there was a drastic realignment of Israel's major political parties. In 1977 the long and uninterrupted rule of the Israeli Labor parties came to an end, and the right-wing Likud coalition gained power and altered the political center of gravity in Israel. One of the Likud coalition's primary objectives was to arrest the trend toward universalistic social policies of the Israeli welfare state.

Third, the Israeli Labor Party itself was transformed. Instead of being a party that represented the interests of the country's working population, in the 1980s it became a party that drew the majority of its electoral support from the new middle classes and the managerial groups in Israeli society, while the country's workers largely transferred their support to the Likud right-wing bloc.[21] This process brought about a major shift in the Labor Party policies toward the welfare state and made it almost indistinguishable from the antiwelfare policies of the right-wing parties.

Fourth, the "social gap" persisted among former immigrants from Arab countries. Although they composed more than half of the Jewish population in the 1980s and had in the last two decades made enormous social, economic, and political progress, a disproportionate number still remained in the lower income strata. Their dissatisfaction with their persistently low social and economic status brought them, paradoxically, to vote for the various right-wing parties that openly opposed the welfare state and the redistributive policies from which these groups have the most to gain.

In addition to these factors, there was a climate of opinion about the "crisis of the welfare state" during the 1970s and early 1980s on the international scene, which had an effect in Israel.[22] Although no political party overtly identified itself with the antiwelfare state politics of Ronald Reagan or Margaret Thatcher, beliefs about retrenchment, privatization, and the free market filtered into the thinking and actions of Israeli politicians and opinion-makers across the ideological spectrum. As in the 1960s, when Israeli social policies were greatly influenced by the U.S. War on Poverty, so in the 1980s they were affected by Reaganomics and Thatcherism. The effects in small countries of cross-national "societal learning" from great powers, like the United States and Britain, is quite evident in the shift of attitudes toward the welfare state in Israel in the 1980s.

Underlying these developments was also the continuous crisis of the Israeli economy. The stagnation that began in the mid-1970s continued through the 1980s. The inept management of the economy by the Likud government of the early 1980s produced galloping inflation, which reached an unprecedented annual rate of 400 percent in 1984 until it was tamed in 1985 by the National Unity coalition government. At the same time, Israel continued to maintain a very large military establishment and faced additional costs from the 1983–1983 war in Lebanon. Under the circumstances of a prolonged economic crisis, the growth of military expenditures—which preempted a third of the government budget—became a powerful limitation on continuing support for the welfare state.

As a result, the allocations for many programs in education, health care, and personal social services were substantially reduced; user charges were introduced or increased; the use of income testing for eligibility became preferred policy; and the rhetoric of planned, further cutbacks became a common strategy in policy debates.

In spite of these developments, the core of the Israeli welfare state, its social security system, remained intact. Strong opposition by the public and in the Knesset to the attempts to cut national insurance benefits were successful. Although the Treasury was able to reduce the rate of increase in social security spending, total expenditures were not reduced. Even more significantly, culminating almost a decade of effort, the Income Support Benefits Act was passed in 1980, which brought about a transformation of the country's outdated social assistance system.[23] The new law, which came into effect in 1982, considerably improved the last-resort safety net of minimum provisions for the most needy population groups and actually strengthened their rights to these benefits. The resilience of the Israeli public social security system in the face of adversity proved to be quite remarkable.

The Social Security System at the End of the 1980s

After an evolutionary process of about four decades, the Israeli social security system in the 1980s reached a high level of maturity: It covered the entire population against most major risks of loss of income in an industrialized society; and it assured the right to a minimum level of income in times of need and hardship to every person in Israel.[24]

The most salient characteristics of the system are: (1) its normative institutional base; (2) its mixture of universalistic and selectivist principles; and (3) a blend of egalitarian and status-preserving components. The combination and close interrelationship of these characteristics reflect both the complexity of the system and its differential impact on the well-being of various population groups.

The *normative* institutional elements of the system mark its transformation from being a privilege, initially based on governmental discretion, to the institutionalization of entitlements as legally binding norms that can be claimed by everyone who qualifies. This process began with passage of the first National Insurance Act in 1953 and was finally completed with the implementation of the Income Support Benefits Act in 1982.

The *universalistic* elements of the system are reflected in the fact that every national insurance scheme and statutory benefits program has, in the course of time, extended its coverage to the whole population-at-risk in the area of its concern. Thus, for example, old-age and survivors insurance and maternity insurance schemes eventually covered the entire population. Work-injury insurance at first covered employed persons only, but after a short period of time, it was extended to the self-employed. Unemployment benefits covered all employees. Children's allowances and disability benefits followed a similar path from partial to universal coverage.

Selectivist elements operate in three ways. First, there is the residual income support benefits program, which is specifically designed to provide a minimum income to the most needy population group. Benefits in this relatively small and minor program are income-conditioned and means-tested.

Second, there are the supplementary benefit programs which provide additional income to old age, survivors, and other recipients of national insurance benefits to bring up their income to the level of the guaranteed national minimum when they have no other income or have very small additional income. These benefits are also income-conditioned and provided on the basis of a test of income. This extensive program plays a major role in assuring a minimum level of living, chiefly to the country's aged population.

Third, there is the children's allowances program, which is universal in principle, and its benefits are not income-conditioned. In practice, the program plays a highly selective role in supplementing the incomes of families with children and particularly of large families among the low-income population. The children's allowance program is of major importance, both in terms of the population it covers and in the size of its benefit payments.

The *egalitarian* features of the system are reflected in its benefit structure. Most of the major national insurance programs, such as those for old age, survivors, and disability, provide low flat-rate benefits to the recipient population; the benefits vary only with family size. The contributions paid by the insured population are, however, connected to wage and income. The equalizing effect is achieved by everyone contributing according to his ability and receiving benefits, if not according to needs, at least at an equal minimum level. The flat-rate benefits are set as a percentage of the national average wage and thus explicitly favor low-income population groups.

The system also has some *status-preserving* elements. The work injury, maternity, and to some degree, the unemployment insurance programs all intend to safeguard the customary level of living of its target population. The benefits of these programs are therefore connected to wage and income and are designed to maintain the relative position of the recipient population while it receives benefits. Thus, the effect of this part of the system is to leave intact the existing pattern of income distribution.

The problems of the system are typical. Its most acute problem is that the national insurance schemes that provide long-term benefits, such as those for old age, survivors, and disability, are inadequate. These schemes have the limited aim of providing minimum level, flat-rate benefits. Unfortunately, these schemes have not succeeded in achieving even these limited aims. The income-conditioned supplementary benefits, which were introduced in the 1960s, have improved the economic circumstances of the needy, by raising their incomes to the guaranteed minimum income level; but these supplementary benefits have not mitigated the inherent inadequacy of these programs.

Finally, with the gradual expansion of its scope, the Israeli social security system has also assumed considerable economic significance. Contributions collected, for example, to finance the national insurance programs have risen from 2 percent of the GNP in 1955 to 4.6 percent in 1975 to 5.7 percent in 1986. Total benefits paid by the National Insurance Institute, contributory and noncontributory (including statutory and other benefits not included in the national insurance schemes), have risen from 2.1 percent of the GNP in 1965 to 6.5 percent in 1975 and to about 8.5 percent in

1986.[25] This growth in benefits during those years does not always reflect a real increase. About 1 percent of the increase can be accounted for by the substitution of national insurance cash benefits for certain income tax allowances that were canceled. Compared, however, to the cost of social security in other advanced industrialized countries, the outlay for Israel's social security system has remained relatively modest.

Notes

1. Dan Horowitz and Moshe Lissak, "Authority Without Sovereignty: The Case of the National Center of the Jewish Community in Palestine," in Ernest Krausz (ed.), *Politics and Society in Israel: Studies of Israeli Society*, Vol. 3 (New Brunswick, NJ: Transaction Books, 1985), pp. 19–42. Other useful accounts in English of the prestate Jewish community in Palestine and the continuities in the new State of Israel are: S.N. Eisenstadt, *Israeli Society* (New York: Basic Books, 1967), pp. 2–68; Amitai Etzioni, "The Decline of Neo-Feudalism: The Case of Israel," in Ferel Heady and Sybill Stokes (eds.), *Papers in Comparative Public Administration* (Ann Arbor: University of Michigan Press, 1962), pp. 229–243; Amos Elon, *The Israelis: Founders and Sons* (New York: Holt, Rinehart, Winston, 1971), pp. 3–147.

2. Daniel J. Elazar, "Israel's Compound Polity," in Krausz, op. cit., pp. 43–80.

3. Nachman Syrkin, "The Jewish Problem and the Socialist Jewish State," in Arthur Herzberg (ed.), *The Zionist Idea: A Historical Analysis and Reader* (New York: Doubleday and Herzl Press, 1959), p. 348.

4. Albert M. Hyamson, *Palestine Under the Mandate* (London: Methuen, 1950), pp. 37–38; Palestine Government, Department of Statistics, *Vital Statistics Tables 1922–1945* (Jerusalem, 1947).

5. Dan Horowitz and Moshe Lissak, *The Origins of the Israeli Polity: Palestine Under the Mandate* (Chicago: University of Chicago Press, 1978), p. 11.

6. Palestine, *Report of the High Commissioner on the Administration of Palestine 1920–1925*, Colonial No. 15 (London: HMSO, 1925), pp. 2–24.

7. It was established under the Religious Communities Ordinance of 1926. In addition to the religious authorities, it consisted of a lay legislative and administrative system that ranged from local councils in all Jewish communities, through an elected assembly, to a general council.

8. On the structure and role of the Histadrut, see Eisenstadt, op. cit., pp. 24–68; Michael Shalev, *Labor and the Political Economy in Israel* (New York: Oxford University Press, 1992); Margaret C. Plunkett, "The Histadrut: The General Federation of Jewish Labor in Israel," *Industrial and Labor Relations Rev.* 11:2 (1958), pp. 155–182; J. Joseph Loewenberg, "Histadrut: Myth and Reality," in Michael Curtis and Mordecai Shertoff (eds.), *Israel: Social Structure and Change* (New Brunswick, NJ: Transaction Books, 1973), pp. 249–256; Israel Kolatt, "The Concept of the Histadrut: Experience and Change 1920–1948," in Isaiah Avrech and Dan Giladi (eds.), *Labor and Society in Israel: A Selection of Studies* (Tel Aviv: Tel Aviv University and the Histadrut, 1973), pp. 204–227.

9. Joseph Neipris, *Social Welfare and Social Services in Israel: Policies, Programs, and Issues in the Late Seventies* (Jerusalem: Hebrew University, Paul Baerwald School of Social Work, 1978), pp. 3–13.

10. Memorandum submitted to the director of Department of Labor of the Palestine government, 31 December 1945 (in the files of the Jewish Agency Political Department, General Zionist Archives, Jerusalem); Palestine, Department of Labor, *Annual Report for 1945*, No. 10 of 1946, p. 20.

11. The most fervent opposition came from the Mapam left-wing Labor party. See, for example, Z. Shapira, "The Histadrut and the Institutions of the State," *Al-Hamishmar*, 1 July 1948; G. Benari, "Let Us Not Dismantle the Histadrut," *Al-Hamishmar*, 21 July 1948; and H. Robin's statement of the Mapam position at the Histadrut Council held in December 1948, Minutes of 7 December 1948, p. 134 (Hebrew).

12. I. Kanevsky, "A Social Insurance Plan for the State of Israel," *Khikrei Avodah* (Labor Studies) 2:1–2 (June 1948) (Hebrew). Kanevsky later shortened his name to Kanev.

13. *A Social Insurance Plan for Israel*, Report of the Interministerial Committee for Social Insurance Planning (Tel Aviv: Ministry of Labor and Social Insurance, 1950) (Hebrew).

14. Don Patinkin, *The Israeli Economy: The First Decade* (Jerusalem: Falk Project for Economic Research in Israel, 1960).

15. *Divrei Haknesset* (Parliamentary Records), Vol. 15, November 17, 1953. (Hebrew).

16. Daniel Bell, *The End of Ideology*, rev. ed. (New York: Free Press, 1965). Also see: Horowitz and Lissak, op. cit., pp. 120–156; and Baruch Kimmerling, "Change and Continuity in Zionist Territorial Orientations and Politics," in Krausz, op. cit., pp. 176–195.

17. "Technipol" refers to governmental staff members whose technical expertise is augmented by their potential for exerting political influence.

18. Giora Lotan (Lubinsky), *National Insurance in Israel* (Jerusalem: National Insurance Institute, 1969).

19. R. Roter and N. Shamai, "Patterns of Poverty in Israel," *Bitachon Sotziali* (Social Security), No. 1 (1971) (Hebrew).

20. Abraham Doron, Nira Shamai, and Yossi Tamir, *Income Maintenance from a Family Policy Perspective: Description and Analysis of Programs in Israel* (Jerusalem: Hebrew University, Paul Baerwald School of Social Work, and National Insurance Institute, 1981).

21. Yael Yishai, "Israel's Right-Wing Jewish Proletariat," in Krausz, op. cit., pp. 233–244.

22. See, for example, Ramesh Mishra, *The Welfare State in Crisis* (Brighton: Wheatsheaf Books, 1984); Organization for Economic Cooperation and Development, *The Welfare State in Crisis: An Account of the Conference on Social Policy in the 1980s* (Paris: OECD, 1981); S.N. Eisenstadt and O. Ahimeir (eds.), *The Welfare State and Its Aftermath* (London: Croom Helm, 1985).

23. A. Doron and U. Yanay, "Income Support Benefits: A Change in Social Policy and Realities of Implementation," *Bitachon Sotziali* (Social Security), No. 31 (February 1988) (Hebrew).

24. L. Achdut and G. Yaniv, (eds.) *Annual Survey 1987* (Jerusalem: National Insurance Institute, Bureau of Research and Planning, 1988) (Hebrew).

25. Ibid.

3

From Social Assistance to Income Support

We begin with the evolution of the social assistance (SA) program partly because, as Vera Shlakman noted, the "study of the residual may be a good way of putting the whole into focus."[1] The value of SA in illuminating the larger system of social security is based on its conception as a historical, residual set of functions generally described as the safety net. As a set of means-tested benefits, SA is regarded as the last-resort form of public income support in cash, kind, and/or services. Those who slip through the meshes of the existing network of social insurance programs and other forms of income support become dependent on SA for their basic subsistence, which is provided at a level that society regards as the minimum necessary for survival. Inevitably, SA requires a definition and determination of need, based on considerable discretionary staff judgment rather than an unequivocal right, and it is regarded, therefore, much less favorably than first-line entitlements.

In most countries SA has confronted the same dilemmas and has undergone the same process of contraction: from being an inclusive income support program for all to a program serving the residual only. Gradually, over the years, major population groups such as the aged, disabled, or unemployed were removed from SA and offered the protection of various forms of social insurance and other first-line entitlement programs. The rationale for such transfers is rooted in values such as social obligation, gratitude, sympathy, or particularly in Israel, ideology. But aside from these social values, the reason many people were transferred from SA to other programs was because it became politically unacceptable to leave large population groups dependent on less-desirable, minimum-level, means-tested income support.

Introduction

In Israel the SA program is a good starting point, not only because of the insight it provides into the role of sociocultural, political, and economic variables on the policymaking process but also because among the social security programs at the core of the welfare state, it is the one that has changed the most. The Israeli SA system has undergone a radical transformation in the last thirty years: In the 1950s it was the most important income support program in the country and provided relief to tens of thousands of impoverished immigrants from dozens of countries. Almost every immigrant family that arrived in Israel during the first decade of statehood at one time or another applied for and received some form of financial assistance. The comprehensive social security system that subsequently developed was at that time nonexistent, and SA was the only source of support for those without sufficient income.[2]

In those years SA had to cope with enormous and unprecedented problems for which it was not prepared, neither in terms of adequate resources nor in a coherent set of policies to guide its administration. Consequently, SA functioned in a haphazard and inconsistent manner, without clear rules of eligibility or uniform level of benefit provision, with wide discretionary power vested in the frontline social workers, and with great variations between and within the local welfare offices.[3]

The change in the SA system reflects the changes that have taken place in Israeli society and in the nature of its welfare state. The establishment of a comprehensive national insurance program, the adoption of a broad variety of statutory allowances, and the expansion of work-related occupational welfare schemes have gradually limited the role of SA and relegated it to serve only as a last resort or safety net for those not covered by any of the newly established programs. From being the main instrument of support for almost the entire population, it has become a residual program designed for a relatively small number of persons.

In addition to changes in its social role, its mode of operation has also been drastically altered. Instead of being a nationally supported, locally operated, highly discretionary and social-work oriented program, it has become the direct responsibility of the national government, with the right to assistance that was established in the 1980 Income Support Benefits Law. The granting of financial assistance has been separated from social work services; discretion has been limited to a minimum; and the program has been transferred to the National Insurance Institute, which is responsible for the country's entire national insurance system and other social security programs.[4] In this way, in about thirty years Israel recapitulated the history of the transformation of the English Poor Laws from parish relief to national responsibility, a process that took more than three hundred years.

The evolution of SA into a national entitlement program has been characterized by both incremental change and continuity, as seen in the persistence of traditionalist values along with equally strong trends in Israeli society toward modernization. In retrospect, many factors were involved in the transformation of SA; of those, the most significant was the interaction among ideology, program, and organizational-administrative elements. In addition, the process was affected by critical events, processes, and key persons; by societal learning; and, of course, by the political economy of Israel. Together these factors can help account for both the changing and the enduring character of SA in Israel during a time in which it moved from being responsible for the basic maintenance of almost the entire new immigrant population to serving as a safety net for less than 5 percent of the families, which in recent years, have included a growing number of the working poor.

Two main processes facilitated the reform of the SA program: First was the adoption of two pieces of legislation by the Knesset in 1958 and in 1980, each of which significantly changed the legal basis of the SA program.[5] Second, from the beginning of the 1960s and throughout the 1970s, continuous organized efforts were made, both in and outside the government, to improve the program by raising the level of benefits, reducing inequalities, and improving access to the system.[6]

These processes were aided by the gradual expansion of the social insurance program as additional risks and disadvantaged groups were slowly added to the evolving national insurance system and removed from the assistance rolls. The process was constrained mainly by ideological factors; the economy, particularly the prevalence of low wages; and negative attitudes of the public and its political leadership as well as the low status and weak power of the Ministry of Social Welfare.

In this chapter and the next we summarize chronologically by decade the major events and processes in the evolution of social assistance in Israel from 1948 to 1987. (See Tables 3.1 and 3.2.) In this chapter we describe the first three decades, with the next chapter devoted to the period between 1977 and 1987. The historical account is followed by an analysis of four key program characteristics and organizational-administrative policy issues: (1) the means test, levels of assistance, and a low-wage economy; (2) relatives' liability; (3) fiscal and administrative relationships between local and national government; and (4) the separation of social assistance from casework, and the transfer of social assistance to the National Insurance Institute.

The chapters conclude with an examination of the factors that can provide a plausible explanation of the radical transformation of social assistance in about thirty years of statehood.

TABLE 3.1 Chronological Summary of Major Events and Processes in the Evolution of Social Assistance in Israel

Year	Summary of Events and Processes
1931	The Social Welfare Department of the Va'ad Leumi is established in the Yishuv on the principle of combining financial assistance with social casework.
1948	Newly established Ministry of Social Welfare takes over Va'ad Leumi social welfare structure, functions, staff, and policies.
1952	UN reports by T.S. Simey and Dorothy Kahn are critical of principles and procedures of social assistance based on local responsibility, means test, relatives' liability and inadequate aid.
1958	Existing practices are formalized as the first Social Welfare Services Law is adopted by the Knesset. Philip Klein's report strongly condemns the philosophy behind the operations of social assistance and sparks public debate.
1963	Minister of Social Welfare appoints a public committee to determine minimum subsistence levels, which submits its report in 1966.
1969	The Black Panther movement emerges and directs public attention to the persistence of poverty among Oriental Jews and to the "social gap."
1972	Report of the Prime Minister's Committee on Children and Youth in Distress recommends improvements in social assistance and other programs for the poor.
1977	The Ministry of Social Welfare is absorbed into a combined Ministry of Labor and Social Affairs.
1980	Passage of the Income Support Benefits Law provides a minimum subsistence income as a right to all citizens.
1982	Implementation of the Income Support Benefits Law by the National Insurance Institute: transfer of assistance payments from local welfare bureaus to the National Insurance Institute and final separation of social casework from social assistance.

TABLE 3.2 Summary of Program Changes in Social Assistance, 1948-1980

Original Program	*Changed Program*
Mass public relief	Safety net for income support for less than 5 percent of the population
Public charity	Income support as a right
Local responsibility	National responsibility
Extensive staff discretion in determining need and levels of assistance	Statutory determination of minimum income required for subsistence
Extensive relatives' liability	Relatives' liability limited to nuclear family
Variability in administration among and within localities.	Uniform national administration
Inadequate levels of assistance	Assistance level at a national minimum based on percentage of average monthly wage
Singling out and stigmatizing persons who need assistance	Inclusion of the poor in the national social security system
Financial assistance linked to social work	Functional and organizational separation between financial assistance and social work
Mostly national funding and local service delivery	Funded nationally and administered by the National Insurance Institute

The First Decade of Statehood: 1948–1957

As noted in the previous chapter, there was considerable continuity in the character of the institutional frameworks established at the beginning of statehood in 1948. Along with other governmental functions, social assistance was transferred from the local Va'ad Leumi welfare bureaus, together with the very limited welfare functions of the Mandatory government to the new Ministry of Social Welfare (Saad) of the State of Israel.

This process was not without considerable controversy. From the very beginning, leaders of the Labor Party, who carried over their earlier opposition to the social work programs of the Va'ad Leumi in the Yishuv, objected to the establishment of the Saad as an independent ministry on the grounds that it represented a continuation of the past system of charity and that it conflicted with the new socialist goals of the state.[7] Some agreed that a limited welfare service might be needed for marginal groups, but this could be handled by a small subunit in the Ministry of the Interior. Although the opponents of the Saad failed to prevent its establishment, they were successful in relegating it to one of the small religious parties, first to the Agudat Israel and later to the National Religious Party (NRP). This arrangement set a precedent for the next thirty years whereby in each successive coalition the social welfare portfolio was left in the hands of the NRP, and as a result, the Ministry of Social Welfare had a very low status and relatively little power.

Although a new name and structure were given to the government's responsibility for social assistance, the ministry and its programs continued to carry the poor image attached to its predecessor organization in the Yishuv. Equally important for policy was the fact that the original social work and administrative staff of the Va'ad Leumi moved almost in toto to become the top officials of the Saad. In addition to financial assistance, temporary or regular, for those unable to support themselves, the range of services that were developed included: supplementary grants for exceptional needs; personal social care services for families and children; child care and other forms of institutional care; and special categorical services for the blind, the mentally retarded, and the aged. In these ways, the social assistance program was designed to provide basic maintenance for all those who were not able to support themselves through work.

These service programs were administered by local welfare bureaus, a significant number of which had previously been established by the Va'ad Leumi and continued to operate on the basis of means testing and relatives' liability, which provided only subminimal financial assistance.

These policies were implemented through a highly decentralized, fragile organizational structure with insufficient staff, funds, and facilities. This fragile structure had to bear the brunt of a public relief system totally swamped by the unprecedented mass immigration of almost 1 million Jews from Europe and North Africa, which resulted in a threefold increase of the population within a few years.

The influx of such a large, impoverished immigration resulted in a rapid growth in the number of welfare bureaus, which increased to 180 within a few short years. Yet, three assistance programs developed, as in the Yishuv. The Jewish Agency took responsibility for at least the first six months and/or occasionally the first year for new immigrants, many of whom were housed in tents, huts, and other temporary shelters, abandoned houses on the outskirts of towns and cities, or in new development towns "planted" throughout the country as part of a population dispersal plan. The Saad functioned as a residual program for everyone else, particularly the large number of immigrants who were still not part of the working population.

A third assistance program began in 1950. Malben, a special relief agency established in Israel by the American Joint Distribution Committee (JDC), relieved the government of responsibility for many of the aged, chronically ill, and handicapped new immigrants who required some form of long-term physical and vocational rehabilitation or institutional care.

Throughout the 1950s the local welfare offices functioned under continuous conditions of crisis because of the insufficient resources allocated for their overwhelming tasks. There were few national policy guidelines for the overworked local staff, which reflected in part the reluctance to give a higher priority to the social welfare function of the government. There was no legislative framework for the administration of social assistance, nor was there any clear-cut division of authority between the national and the local government. Although the national government provided the bulk of the funds for financial assistance and the social care services provided by the local welfare bureaus, there was no formula, nor were there any recognized standards to guide the annual allocation; consequently, all aspects of this process were bargained for and negotiated. By 1955–1956, however, a sliding-scale formula came into use by the national government that subsidized from 40 percent to 100 percent of the local authority's welfare budget.

This state of affairs was criticized in the first of a series of reports by UN experts that began in 1952–1953. Even though they recognized the limitations of the prevailing austerity during those early years, they were still critical of the absence of sufficient rules, guidelines, and appropriate political and financial support, which resulted in totally inadequate assistance to many thousands of poor families. These reports by T.S. Simey and Dorothy Kahn had very little influence at the time, but they helped lay the groundwork for the Klein Report six years later, which did have a significant impact.[8] On the whole, apart from these two reports and some local expressions of dissatisfaction, there was surprisingly little pressure for change, and the Welfare Ministry did not alter in any essential manner the underlying philosophy and operating principles of the welfare bureaus until the mid-1960s. As an astute observer summed it up: "These services had already become so institutionalized that they contained bureaucratic structures and had a memory bank of precedents which restricted modification or innovation in the new political entity and rapidly changing society."[9]

During this first decade of statehood, the evolution of a more permanent and comprehensive social policy toward the population in need began with passage of the first legislation in 1953, which established the National Insurance program. The program started to pay benefits in 1955 to survivors and later, in 1957, to the elderly. The development of national insurance was subsequently to have a profound effect on social assistance and the whole system of income support.

The Second Decade: 1958–1967

The major processes of structural change in social assistance were set in motion by two events in 1958: passage of the first piece of welfare legislation, the Social Welfare Services Act, which gave a legal framework to the administration of financial assistance and social work; and the eventual publication of the Klein Report, which put social assistance on the governmental agenda and initiated a series of policy changes to improve its major deficiencies.

The initiative to enact the 1958 Welfare Services Act came during the early 1950s mainly from officials of the Ministry of Social Welfare and not from any of the political parties, which showed little interest in the operation of the welfare programs.[10] The purpose of these officials was not to introduce any major changes into the existing welfare system; rather, they sought the necessary legal and administrative justification to maintain the existing system but in a more efficient and less costly manner. Consequently, they proposed to formalize the principle of local responsibility; to enable the ministry and local welfare bureaus to enforce relatives' liability; to establish in law the principle that assistance is given chiefly as a loan, which the recipient would be required to return upon improvement of financial circumstances; and to provide the system with the necessary legal backing to undertake broad inquiries regarding the resources of applicants.[11]

The original bill, which consisted of only eight short clauses, was first tabled in the Knesset in June 1956, where it received a very cool reception.[12] It had been vetoed earlier by Israel Rokach, then minister of the Interior, a former mayor of Tel Aviv, who strongly opposed the principle of local authority responsibility for the social assistance program.[13] The bill was strongly criticized later by other members of the Knesset because of its sparse content, although there seemed to be general agreement on the intent of the measure to prevent overuse or misuse of the program by shifting the costs to relatives and by strengthening the powers of inquiry and enforcement. Under the proposed bill the local authorities were required only "to maintain a welfare bureau for providing social care to the needy." No mention was made of providing financial assistance or the needy person's right to assistance. In the committee stage, and under pressure from practically all of the Knesset members in the committee, the bill was rewritten to include the duty of the local welfare bureaus to provide assistance to the needy; it was finally approved in 1958.

With ten of the thirteen sections of the Welfare Services Act concerned with the responsibilities of the applicants and their relatives to the welfare bureau, the Ministry of Welfare officials basically achieved their objective of formalizing the existing system without changing its original character in any essential way. They established for the first time a legal framework for the country's social assistance program, but because it did not significantly change prevailing policies and practices—it did not establish the right to assistance or the criteria for eligibility—the bill had practically no impact on the needy population for many years. In sociological terms, the particularistic system of the traditional charity was continued on the level of state bureaucracy and reinforced by the case-study method of the professional social worker.

One of the reasons social assistance had been difficult to provide in Israel is that "unlike the charity in the traditional Jewish community, public assistance was not an integral part of a total social conception; it did not assume a common value system or express norms of mutuality between givers and receivers."[14] The 1958 act did, however, provide the reference point, the legal base for changes to come.

The Klein Report

In retrospect perhaps the initial impetus for policy change came from the controversial UN Technical Assistance Program Klein Report in 1958, which put the subject of social assistance on the national agenda for the first time, and whose recommendations served to stimulate a process of incremental modifications in social policy that eventually transformed the entire structure and function of social assistance. Philip Klein, a distinguished U.S. social work educator and researcher, based the report on his observations and studies after living in the country for over three years and his familiarity with the reports of his two UN predecessors. Klein's approach was broad and perceptive in its scope and characterized by a candor not usually found in such reports. His recommendations were based on an analysis of five main problems: the political culture of Israel; the attitudes of the long-time residents of the country to the immigrant population; the prevalent attitudes toward the needy; the perception and function of public assistance; and the problems of organization and administration in the Ministry of Social Welfare.

Klein was unsparing in his exposure of the intolerance and lack of public sympathy for the "nonproductive" sectors of the population, of the arrogant superiority on the part of the old-timers and pioneers toward the "primitive" new immigrants from Moslem countries. He exposed the fallacious, popular stereotypes of the needy as "naturally lazy and unbalanced" that were used to justify the abysmally low level of assistance, and he concluded that Israel's welfare policy constituted a steady regression toward the standards of forgotten periods.

Although Klein acknowledged the inferior political position of the Saad in the competition for government funds, he charged that the ministry itself was responsible for many of the deficiencies in organization and administration. Klein proposed many far-reaching changes to meet the economic needs of clients, which included linking assistance to the cost-of-living index. Essentially, Klein identified the major issues of access, adequacy, and administration, which subsequently became the ongoing objectives of efforts for change both outside and within the Ministry of Social Welfare.

Numerous attempts were made by the ministry and the government to persuade Klein to modify his report and to blunt his criticism and recommendations. Although these efforts failed, they succeeded in preventing its publication as an official UN document. Eventually some of the findings were leaked to the press, which stimulated public discussion in the Knesset and other government circles and forced a reexamination of social policy. Although members of all political parties in the Knesset knew about the extremely low level of assistance payments during the second half of the 1950s, their recognition of this problem was heightened by the unofficial publication of the Klein Report and was reflected in the parliamentary debates of the time. For example, during the annual budget debate of 1958–1959 Rachel Tzabari (Labor) stated plainly that "the assistance rates are hunger rates. It is difficult to understand why the Ministry of Welfare did not take any steps to raise the pitiful rates."[15]

There were also, however, Knesset members who were plainly not pleased with the Klein Report. Sara Kafri (Labor) said that in her view Klein "does not know reality; he does not recognize the mentality of the population. He approaches our problems with American standards, having in mind possibilities that exist there without taking into account the human material that lives here."[16] Devorah Netzer (Labor) who was also a strong defender of the government, sarcastically asked Klein when he appeared before the Knesset Public Services Committee, "if the situation is so bad why aren't there people dying of starvation?" Klein's reply was that "they are dying but only slowly."[17]

Beginning in early 1960s and continuing to the latter part of the 1970s there were two processes at work: a continual struggle to raise the levels of assistance;[18] and at the same time, new contingencies and population groups were being removed from the SA program and provided protection under the evolving social insurance system. During these years, much of the leadership to improve the legal and administrative status of the SA program and its subsistence levels came from a new group of senior officials in the Ministry of Welfare, many with considerable legal, political, and administrative skills, who became the department heads in the ministry, gradually replacing the retiring cadre of social workers from the Va'ad Leumi in 1948.

The Shrinking of Social Assistance

During the 1960s, in a manner somewhat similar to that which occurred in other countries, four major groups were eventually removed from social assistance.

The first large population group that was removed from social assistance was the *aged*. In April 1957 the National Insurance Institute began to pay old-age pensions to the insured elderly who had reached the age of sixty-five (women) and seventy (men). Because these pensions were then two or three times higher than the prevailing social assistance rates, the majority of the elderly were no longer dependent on social assistance. Several large groups of the elderly, however, were still not covered by National Insurance old-age pensions. These included those who were sixty-seven years old in 1953 when the National Insurance Act was passed and new immigrants who upon arrival in Israel were already sixty years old. It took another twelve years, until 1969, before these two groups were finally covered by noncontributory old-age pension schemes operated by the National Insurance Institute.

The struggle to remove *low-income families with children* from the assistance program continued until the mid-1970s. The first children's allowances program began to pay benefits to families with four or more children in 1959, and in the 1960s an additional program for the first three children of employed families was established. Only in 1975, however, was a comprehensive reform of the children's allowances program implemented, which made the allowances universal, increased the benefit amount substantially, and finally removed low-income families with children from the assistance program.

The third group to be removed from the assistance program was the unemployed. *Unemployment insurance* came into effect only in 1973; until then the unemployed were supported mostly by relief work programs with direct assistance provided only as a last resort when no relief work was available.

The last large group removed from social assistance and covered by the National Insurance was the *disabled*. When the General Disability Insurance Program came into effect in 1974 it originally included only persons who recently became disabled, but later coverage was extended to those who were already disabled at the time when the law was passed. The entire process of removal from SA was completed by the end of the 1970s. Thus, the social assistance program eventually changed from a catchall system for the poor to a safety net for those who fell through the mesh of national insurance and other benefit programs.

Raising the Assistance Levels

Raising the benefit levels of social assistance was a more formidable task than the gradual transfer of certain groups to the national insurance program. Although the below-subsistence level of the assistance rates had been substantiated by the Klein Report and the testimony of social workers was not contested, the Treasury still refused to acknowledge this as a problem. The resistance continued despite the Wadi Salib riots in 1959 in Haifa, when for the first time there was an outbreak of open protest by impoverished Oriental Jews who expressed their frustration at having to support large families with insufficient income.[19]

At that time in the late 1950s the social assistance rates for a single person were only about 5 percent of the average national wage and it was not until the mid-1970s that they rose to 15 percent. This situation was aggravated by the generally low level of wages prevailing in the Israeli economy during the 1960s and the less-than-subsistence wages in the work relief programs. Yet the belief that a higher level of assistance would affect the incentive of new immigrants to work and therefore interfere with their absorption into Israeli society was repeatedly stressed by a succession of ministers of Labor. As a result, the principle of "less eligibility," which originated in nineteenth-century England prevailed; no assistance was granted even when the income from full-time work fell below the current relief rates.

Another factor limiting any significant improvement was the suspicion of the major coalition partners in the government that the Saad would not use additional funds to improve its services to the needy, but rather to promote the religio-political interests of the National Religious Party. At least this appears to be a rationalization of the Labor Party for not appropriating additional funds to the Ministry of Welfare. This mistrust contributed to the reluctance of the ministry's officials to press for larger allocations based on their perception of the disadvantaged, competitive position of their ministry vis-à-vis the Treasury.

Then, too, the prevailing conditions of the local administration of assistance were disorganized and uncertain. There was no authoritative standard, legal or administrative, that could set the level of support for the needy in the 180 different welfare offices. The rates that were set by the ministry from time to time were not always adhered to by the local welfare bureaus because they lacked the funds, disagreed with the policy, or permitted the social workers to distribute aid according to their professional discretion and not necessarily in accord with instructions from the ministry which, in any case, lacked sufficient authority and capacity to monitor and enforce its policies.

Finally, significant change in the system was inhibited by lack of public awareness of the situation and by belief in the efficacy and inevitability of the process of immigrant absorption and in the cultural backwardness of many of the persons who received assistance.

By late 1962, Minister of Social Welfare Joseph Burg decided that a more substantial effort should be made to improve the administration of social assistance. The first question that had to be resolved was: What was the amount needed for a minimum existence? Accordingly, a public committee of nineteen professionals was appointed on January 10, 1963, and headed by Israel Katz, newly designated director of the Paul Baerwald School of Social Work of the Hebrew University, and later slated to head the National Insurance Institute and the Ministry of Labor and Social Affairs. For three years the committee debated various ways of calculating the amount of support needed to survive in Israeli society. However, the standards for food and other basic needs that the committee ultimately recommended—over the opposition of the Treasury representative—would have meant that the support rates would have to be doubled. Because he believed that it would not be politically feasible to obtain this increased support, Burg discharged the committee in 1967 to avoid the embarrassment of accepting recommendations which would then serve as an unwanted source of pressure. Instead, he appointed two of his officials who were on the committee to submit a report to him on the work of the committee so that at least the ministry had some documentation if it might later try to raise the level of support to the needy.[20] Thus, even though the committee process from 1963 to 1966 did not produce any change in policy, it provided both a philosophical justification and a factual basis for the gradual increase in rates that occurred in later years.

The Third Decade: 1967–1977

The period following the Six Day War in 1967 was one of the most dramatic eras in the country's turbulent history and it ushered in a series of changes that affected every aspect of Israeli society. Among the significant social developments was a greater consciousness and public awareness of the persistence of poverty in an increasingly affluent society. This also led to a heightened awareness of what was described as the "social gap," that is, the greater proportion of low-income families among former immigrants from North Africa and other Arab countries, who constituted nearly half of the population by 1970 but were more than 70 percent of the recipients of social assistance. (See Table 3.3.) Immigrants from these countries were known as Eidot Hamizrach.

As awareness of the plight of the Eidot Hamizrach increased, extensive mass media coverage was given to the charges of discrimination and the demands of the Black Panthers, a group of young political activists mainly from the Musrara neighborhood in Jerusalem. They vociferously, and for the first time, openly articulated the deep resentment, alienation, and occasional open hostility among the Eidot Hamizrach toward the Ashkenazi establishment, which they held responsible for discrimination and the vast differences in their income, social mobility, and political power.[21]

This grass-roots challenge in the form of confrontation politics and the controversy it engendered about the social gap indirectly served to bring about significant improvements in the social assistance programs. While the Black Panthers directed attention to the persistent social inequalities in income, status, and power after twenty years of statehood, Prime Minister Golda Meir responded on another level by appointing in 1971 the Prime Minister's Committee for Children and Youth in Distress, and again Israel Katz was chosen as the coordinator.

The work of this committee and its report—buttressed by the findings of the Horowitz Committee on Income Inequalities—turned out to be a critical step for social assistance during the 1970s as it recommended minimum standards and the strengthening of the children's allowance program.[22] The committee involved more than two hundred people who made hundreds of recommendations that affected ten different social service areas. The broad scope and extensive participation in the committee's work succeeded in directing public attention to the existence of poverty among large sections of the Israeli population and in generating sufficient support for changes in social policy, which the government evidently could not ignore. Despite the Yom Kippur War that broke out soon after the report was released in 1973, and despite the economic crisis that

TABLE 3.3   Recipients of Social Assistance, by Head of Family's Place of Birth and as a Percentage of the Total Jewish Population

	Israel	Asia	Africa	Europe/America	Total
1964–1966	3.2	28.5	42.3	26.0	100.0
1965–1966	3.5	27.7	42.2	26.6	100.0
1968–1969	3.6	26.6	44.5	25.3	100.0
1969–1970	9.4	27.5	44.3	18.8	100.0
1971–1972	8.7	28.5	43.5	19.1	100.0
1974–1975	8.1	29.6	42.6	19.7	100.0
1975–1976	8.7	30.0	42.4	18.9	100.0

Source: Calculated from Ministry of Social Welfare, Division of Research, Statistical Publications for the various years.

followed and made it increasingly difficult to support an expansionary social welfare policy, many significant steps were taken to expand and improve the educational, social security, and social welfare services in Israel.

It was widely believed that because Oriental Jews constituted such a large proportion of those receiving social assistance, these improvements would also contribute to the reduction of poverty and ethnic tensions in the society. It was also hoped that these steps would be perceived as official recognition by the government that injustice and inequality could not be tolerated in Israeli society.

Subsequently, the recommendations that were related to raising the support rates were put into practice in a relatively short time. The committee rejected its predecessors' preoccupation with the minimum food basket on the grounds that a rise in living standards had made it obsolete. Instead, it adopted the principle that the minimum income of a family should reflect the condition of other families in the economy. Hence, it was recommended that a minimum income level for a family of two children in 1973 be set at approximately 40 percent of the average wage in the economy.[23]

Although the raises were very gradual, their incremental value doubled—as a percentage of the average wages in the economy—from the beginning to the end of the 1970s. What had seemed impossible in the middle of the 1960s with regard to the first set of recommendations from the ministry's committee to determine the needs of the poor had become a reality in the middle of the 1970s. Indeed, the public assistance support rates at this time reached the level of the rates that the committee itself had recommended. Two decades after the Klein Report, the effective support rates rose by 300 percent relative to average wages.

It should be noted, however, that despite these increases, the level of assistance rates was still too low to ensure an adequate standard of living during the 1960s and early 1970s. It was found that they still fell below the poverty line by about 20 percent.[24] This was due mainly to the low wages in some of the labor-intensive parts of the economy, such as agriculture, the service industries, and parts of the textile industry. A rise in the rates of public assistance payments invariably brought them into conflict with the wage system in these sectors. Attempts to raise the rates beyond this point did not succeed because of the unacceptably narrow income gap that would have been created between the working population and the social assistance beneficiaries, with the latter in a more advantageous position.

In addition to the existence of a low-wage economy, social policy was also influenced by public attitudes. A survey conducted in 1970 by the Ministry of Welfare found that 37 percent of a representative sample of the population believed that assistance payments encouraged people not to work. What was significant was that this opinion was nearly twice as common among the higher income groups as it was among those in the lower income range. This is in sharp contrast to findings in other countries where the more affluent groups usually hold more liberal attitudes toward extending public assistance. In Israel, it seemed that the newly acquired affluence and status of comparable groups had not yet liberated them from negative attitudes toward the poor, and this had a strong influence on the formation of social policy.

During the 1970s, in addition to the influence of the Prime Minister's Committee for Children and Youth in Distress in improving the income maintenance programs, there were two other significant developments: some early experiments in local welfare bureaus in which the administration of financial assistance was separated from the provision of social casework, and the consolidation of the ministries of Labor and Social Welfare by the Begin government in 1977.

Separation

The combination of financial aid with personal social services began to be considered problematic in the late 1960s, even though the policy had been in effect since the inception of social assistance before the establishment of the state.[25] It was increasingly recognized by both professional and governmental circles that not all applicants for financial aid required social care, and in any case this function was not one for which social workers possessed special expertise. Indeed, over the years social work ideology, particularly in the United States, tended to denigrate the granting of material relief by social workers and ascribed much greater professional prestige and status to the more clinical and intangible forms of social work practice that involved counseling and various forms of casework.[26] During the 1950s when most of the staff time was being devoted to the administration of public relief, few Israeli social workers had completed their professional education. However, as the number of graduates of university schools of social work increased, there was growing frustration and resentment at the fact that about 40 percent of their time was devoted to the determination of eligibility for financial assistance for about 20 percent of their caseload. As a result of various pressures, including those from social work staff, the Ministry of Social Welfare began in the early 1970s to experiment with training eligibility clerks in a few local welfare bureaus to handle financial assistance requests.[27]

At the same time, there was growing support in certain governmental circles for a single national authority to disperse all forms of financial assistance. In the early 1970s, Minister of Labor Joseph Almogi introduced a proposal to establish a national center for social benefit payments. About the same time, Israel Katz, who was head of the National Insurance

Institute (NII), invited a British expert, Olive Stevenson, to explore the possibility of integrating social assistance into a scheme similar to the Supplementary Benefits in the United Kingdom, an idea that had been previously considered by the public committees he chaired in 1966 and 1972. Stevenson's report in 1971 was followed by two public commissions in 1975, which also endorsed the idea of separating social assistance from the personal social services and integrating the former into the national insurance system.[28]

By 1975 a high degree of agreement was reached on the validity of the separation principle in both professional and governmental circles, so that there seemed to be sufficient justification for the NII in 1975 to commission a detailed plan for this new approach to social assistance.[29] After being tested in two towns, a legislative proposal was circulated in spring 1978 that subsequently was embodied in the Income Support Benefits Law of 1980, which will be considered in the next chapter.

The Creation of the Ministry of Labor and Social Affairs

In the wake of the electoral victory of the Likud parties in 1977, important changes took place in the organizational structure and administrative leadership in the ministries of Labor and Social Welfare that significantly affected the social assistance program.

The creation in 1977 of a combined Ministry of Labor and Social Affairs by the first government of Menachem Begin was actually the outcome of a prolonged debate on the structure of the Israeli government. The political changes produced by the 1977 elections, which ended the more than thirty years of domination by the Labor Party, and the ascent to power of new, right-wing political forces made it possible to begin to consider restructuring the government and implementing some of the changes that had been advocated since the early 1970s.[30] The proposals to streamline the governmental structure and make it more efficient by reducing the number of ministries had their sources in the Prime Minister's Committee on Children and Youth, which was appointed by the Meir government in 1971, and in the Hausner Committee, which was appointed by the Rabin government in 1974.[31] Among these proposals, which were strongly influenced by the British example of the establishment of the Department of Health and Social Security, was the creation of a new super-ministry of labor, welfare, and health. Because of the opposition of the National Religious Party, a coalition partner for more than thirty years that would have lost much of the power it gained through its control of the Social Welfare Ministry, it was not possible to implement this recommendation before the 1977 political change.[32]

The issue was again reopened with the ascent to power of the Likud bloc after the 1977 summer elections. The first government formed by Begin was committed to the introduction of broad changes into many policy areas. Its major coalition partner—Dash, the new Democratic Movement for Change—was particularly interested in reorganizing the governmental structure. Because the influence of the National Religious Party was greatly reduced in this new government, it was no longer able to prevent changes as in the past. Under these new political circumstances, the Begin government decided to set up a new super-ministry to include the former ministries of Labor and Welfare and to appoint Israel Katz to represent Dash as the first minister of Labor and Social Affairs.[33] This institutional change and the advent to power of personalities like Katz strongly influenced the future course of social assistance.

The Essential Features of the Assistance Program in the Late 1970s

Before proceeding to the analysis of the major structural changes in SA that took place in the next decade (1977–1988), we shall review the essential features of this program as they developed during the preceding thirty years.

The distinctive character of social assistance that persisted through the 1970s was the result of two interacting sets of constraints inherent in the four operating principles of the program and those stemming from the interorganizational funding and administrative relations between the national and local government. Although the operating principles of the SA program were portrayed in modern social work terms, they were basically a combination of slightly modified, old Poor Law principles carried over from the pre-state experience in the Yishuv. Despite the rapid social and economic changes in Israeli society, its SA program continued to rely on means testing with no right to assistance, on relatives' liability, on the concept of less eligibility, and on local responsibility—each of which will be briefly reviewed.

The Right to Assistance and the Means Test

Until the 1980s there was no explicit right to assistance in Israel. To the extent that it existed, the right was indirect and stemmed from the obligation of the local authorities to maintain a welfare bureau and to provide relief to the needy. The right to assistance depended on what the definition of need was, but because need was never clearly defined in the Welfare Services Act of 1958 or in the subsequent regulations, eligibility for assistance was influenced by the decisions of the social workers with regard to the actual or potential resources available to the applicant. Local welfare bureau staffs had broad powers of investigation and access to information to help them determine eligibility; these powers, by their intrusiveness, often violated civil rights. In addition, bureau staffs were considerably inconsistent and inequitable in the administration of SA.[34]

Relatives' Responsibility

As part of the eligibility conditions for social assistance, the principle of relatives' responsiblity was applied in Israel much longer than in most other countries. It reflected the ongoing strain in Israeli society between the forces of traditionalism and modernism, and there were enormous variations in the application of the rules of relatives' responsibility among different communities and even among different social workers in the same bureau.[35] The long list of liable relatives did not change much, and Israel obligated all of its citizens to be bound, first, by their respective religious laws governing the personal status of Jews, Muslims, and Christians; and second, by the Family Law Amendment (Maintenance) Act of 1959. The administrative regulations of this legislation, which were adopted in 1963 by the Saad, stated unequivocally that only after all liable relatives had exhausted their ability to assist its family members could the granting of social assistance be considered. Despite the variations between and within local bureaus in enforcing this policy, it was not modified in any significant way until the 1970s. Together, the means test and relatives' responsibility contributed to the persistent stigma that was attached to this form of assistance.

Eligibility and the Assistance Rates

Until the 1960s the assistance rates were neither clearly defined nor uniform, nor did they insure even minimal subsistence. Beginning in the mid-1960s the rates were gradually increased and by the end of the 1970s they reached a level of 40 percent of the average national wage for a family of four. In practice, the actual assistance rates were somewhat higher because they usually included increments and certain benefits-in-kind. In comparison to those of the previous decades, the increased rates of the late 1970s represented a notable improvement, but they were still too low to insure an adequate standard of living for the indigent population.

The assistance payments also had the usual shortcomings of means-tested benefits. The effective rate of taxation on any income that a recipient could obtain from work was so high that it created a work disincentive. In effect, the system bound the recipient population to a minimum subsistence level of income, which became a maximum and a poverty trap from which it was difficult to escape. Any small earnings, when combined with the assistance grant, could not exceed the income tax threshold, and as a result, the actual tax rate was very high and came close to 100 percent.

Interorganizational Relationships Between Local and National Government

Although local administration of SA is part of both the Jewish community and the Anglo-Saxon tradition as a responsibility to be shared with family, relatives, and neighbors, it was an anomaly for Israel. A façade of local responsibility and administration was created in a small, highly centralized state with a strong ideological rejection of welfare by the dominant political power structure. Because of the small tax base of local governments, they had to be heavily subsidized by the national government to be able to perform their welfare function. The existence of central fiscal and administrative authority in the Saad, without direct responsibility for the program provided a convenient way for the national government to avoid full social and fiscal responsibility and enabled it to participate in financing those programs it chose without actually being responsible for them and without tying its hands in any significant way.

In addition, the highly politicized and unstable local administrations were part of a dual system of authority that produced numerous conflicts. With more than 180 local bureaus, each of which was dependent on the whim and political complexion of its municipal council, the welfare offices were frequently caught in the middle of three-way power struggles among themselves, the ministry, and the local authorities that were expected to implement national policies. It is not surprising that the local authorities had difficulty in employing qualified social workers who were willing to live in the small immigrant towns, located far away from the urban centers, and be subject to the uncertainty, stigma, and often physical abuse and violence frequently directed against them.

Another constraint of the Saad was its low status and prestige as an organization, which stemmed from its minority political status. The ministry had been in the hands of the National Religious Party almost from its inception until 1977 and its marginal place in the governing coalition was only grudgingly accepted. The relative lack of political power of the ministry put it in a weak bargaining position with the Treasury and it was frequently charged that the ministry did not even request a budget sufficient for the social assistance system. At the same time the dominant political groups were reluctant to improve welfare programs because this would inevitably strengthen a minority party.

Contrasting with the traditional public charity approach of SA were two other trends that reflected opposing tendencies toward modernization and greater efficiency, rationalization, and equity. One was the inauguration of an appeals system in 1965 and an ombudsman in 1971, and the other ultimately involved the voluntary participation of most of the welfare bureaus when the ministry computerized all welfare payments in the late 1960s.

Notes

1. Vera Shlakman, "The Safety-Net Function in Public Assistance: A Cross-National Exploration," *Social Service Review* 46:2 (June 1972), p. 207.

2. Abraham Doron and Ralph M. Kramer, "Ideology, Program, and Organizational Factors in Public Assistance: The Case of Israel," *Journal of Social Policy* 5:2 (April 1976), pp. 131–149.

3. Abraham Doron, "Public Assistance in Israel: Issues of Policy and Administration," *Journal of Social Policy* 7:4 (October 1978), pp. 441–460.

4. Abraham Doron and Uri Yanay, "Income Support Benefits: A Change in Social Policy and Realities of Implementation," *Bitachon Sotziali* (Social Security), No. 31 (February 1988) (Hebrew).

5. The Welfare Services Act of 1958 and the Income Support Benefits Act of 1980.

6. The outcome of these efforts can be found in the adoption of most of the recommendations found in Abraham Doron and Tzippi Suesskind, *Income Support Benefits—A Program Proposal* (Jerusalem: National Insurance Institute, Division of Research and Planning, 1978).

7. Joseph Neipris, *Social Welfare and Social Services in Israel: Policies, Programs and Current Issues* (Jerusalem: Hebrew University, Paul Baerwald School of Social Work, 1981), pp. 26–27.

8. T.S. Simey, *The Coordination of Social Services in Israel*, Report of Expert Appointed by the Technical Assistance Administration of the United Nations, 1952 (ST/TAA/K/Israel/2); Dorothy C. Kahn, *Organization and Operation of Welfare Services in Israel*, Report of Expert Assigned from the Secretariat of the United Nations, 1953 (ST/TAA/K/Israel/2); and Philip Klein, *Proposals on Program and Administration of Social Welfare in Israel*, Prepared for the Government of Israel under the United Nations Program of Technical Assistance (New York: Report No. TAO/ISR/29, January 1961).

9. Neipris, op. cit., p. 13.

10. Ministry of Social Welfare, *Proposals for the Social Welfare Law—1950*, Ministry of Social Welfare File No. 5121/11.

11. These purposes of the proposed legislation were spelled out clearly in a memorandum prepared by the legal adviser of the ministry in 1953; see *Proposals for the Social Welfare Law—1953*, June 14, 1953, Ministry of Social Welfare File No. 5121/11.

12. *Divrei Haknesset* (Parliamentary Records), Vol. 23, June 12, 1956, pp. 1995–2009, and June 18, 1956, pp. 2028–2036 (Hebrew).

13. Letter of the legal adviser of the Ministry of Interior to the legal adviser of the Ministry of Social Welfare, July 15, 1953, Ministry of Social Welfare File No. 5121/11.

14. Rivka Bar-Yosef, "Welfare and Integration in Israel" in S.N. Eisenstadt and Ora Ahimeir (eds.), *The Welfare State and Its Aftermath* (London: Croom Helm, 1985), p. 256.

15. *Divrei Haknesset* (Parliamentary Records), Vol. 24, March 17, 1958, pp. 1338–1358 (Hebrew).

16. Ibid., Vol. 26, March 31, 1959, p. 1764.

17. Quoted by Moshe Sneh. Ibid., February 9, 1959, p. 1034.

18. See the 1963 public statement of the Association of Social Workers on *Families in Distress in Israel*; and Ministry of Social Welfare, *Report on the Work of the Committee to Determine Minimum Subsistence Levels*, submitted to the minister of Social Welfare by E. Milo and A. Blum (Jerusalem: February 1967) (Hebrew).

19. Government Press Office, *Excerpts from the Report of the Wadi Salib Inquiry Committee Presented to the Government on 17 August 1959* (Jerusalem: August 1959).

20. *Report on the Work of the Committee to Determine Minimum Subsistence Levels*, op. cit.

21. Menahem Hofnung, "Public Protest and the Public Budgeting Process: The Influence of the Black Panthers on Allocations for Social Welfare" (M.A. thesis, Hebrew University, November 1982) (Hebrew).

22. Prime Minister's Committee for Children and Youth in Distress, *Report Submitted to the Prime Minister* (Jerusalem: June 1973) (Hebrew); and Horowitz Committee, *Report of the Committee on Income Distribution and Social Inequality* (Tel Aviv: 1971).

23. Prime Minister's Committee For Children and Youth in Distress, Annex 1, *Report of Team on Income Maintenance* (Jerusalem: October 1972) (Hebrew).

24. R. Roter and N. Shamai, "Patterns of Poverty in Israel," *Bitachon Sotziali* (Social Security), No. 1 (1971) (Hebrew).

25. These principles were already established in the 1930s by the Social Service Department of the General Council (Va'ad Leumi) of the Jewish community in Palestine. In a circular published in 1939, "Principles and Foundation of Social Work in the Jewish Community," it stated, "In modern social work, extending material help is not its only function. At its basis is the social investigation which results in diagnosis and a determination of ways of treating the client with the goal of making him productive and useful to himself and society." The same principle was espoused by professional social work educators in the United States, although most of the Va'ad Leumi social workers had emigrated from Germany in the 1930s.

26. Eveline M. Burns, "What's Wrong with Public Welfare," *Social Service Review* 36:2 (1962).

27. Emanuel Straus (ed.), *Organization and Administration in the Social Welfare Bureaus* (Jerusalem: Ministry of Social Welfare, Division of Social Welfare Bureaus and Community, April 1976) (Hebrew).

28. Olive Stevenson, *Report to Dr. Israel Katz, Director General of the National Insurance Institute of Israel* (Jerusalem: 1971). See also *Recommendations of Committees on the Organization of the Local Welfare Services* (Jerusalem: Ministry of Social Welfare, Division of Research and Planning, December 1975) (Hebrew).

29. A. Doron and T. Suesskind, op. cit.

30. The significance of this election is analyzed in Asher Arian (ed.), *The Elections in Israel—1977* (Jerusalem: Academic Press, 1980).

31. Prime Minister's Committee for Children and Youth in Distress, *Summary of Recommendations: Recommendations for Structural Improvements and Changes in the System of Welfare and Public Services* (Jerusalem: Szold National Institute for Research

in the Behavioral Sciences, July 1973); First Recommendations of the Ministerial Committee (Hausner Committee) on the Reorganization of Government Ministries, Efficiency, and Savings, cited in Moshe Shani, "The Hausner Committee: An Initial Evaluation," *Netivei Irgun Veminhal*, December 1975 (Hebrew).

32. See, for example, Aharon Geva, "Welfare and the Coalitionary Reality," *Davar*, October 7, 1975 (Hebrew).

33. Prime Minister Begin announced the establishment of the new ministry and the appointment of Israel Katz to head it at the Knesset on October 24, 1977.

34. Dan Shnit, "The Right to Public Assistance in Israel" (Doctor of Law thesis, Hebrew University, December 1974) (Hebrew).

35. Abraham Doron and Rami Rosenthal, "Relatives' Responsibility in the Israeli Welfare System," *Publication Series in Social Welfare and Social Work* No. 5 (Jerusalem: Hebrew University, Paul Baerwald School of Social Work, 1971) (Hebrew).

4

The Transition to National Responsibility: 1977–1987

In the previous chapter we concluded with an analysis of some of the social assistance programs that were developed during the early 1970s. Together, these developments ultimately brought about the most substantial reorganization of the structure and function of social assistance since its inception. A detailed policy proposal commissioned by the National Insurance Institute (NII) in 1975 included the recommendation to transfer the entire social assistance program to the NII and thus achieve two major policy objectives: the separation of financial assistance from social work, and the establishment of the NII as the national authority to disburse all forms of cash benefits.[1] Immediate efforts were made to implement these proposals; their prospects were strengthened, however, with the consolidation of the Labor and Social Welfare ministries by the new Likud coalition government in 1977, and the appointment of Israel Katz to head the new ministry.

There were still two major obstacles to reforming social assistance: the continued opposition of the Treasury to what it viewed as the spiraling costs of a flood of undeserving claimants, and the political philosophy of the Likud coalition, which was committed to economic individualism, a free market, and a more limited role for government.[2] The political opposition was gradually overcome by the effective lobbying of the NII leadership, particularly the ability of Katz to persuade both the Treasury and Prime Minister Begin that the proposed income support benefits program would actually be a significant social and political asset to the government. The new Likud government had practically no social legislation on its agenda, even though it was elected on a platform of promises to improve the living conditions of the population as a whole and particularly of underprivileged groups.[3] The proposed income support benefits scheme, which will be described in this chapter, was thus reluctantly accepted by the Begin government as a way of fulfilling its electoral promises, and it was subsequently the only important piece of social legislation passed by the first Likud administration.

The Income Support Benefits Bill was finally tabled in the Knesset in October 1979. Although there was little opposition to the bill, it was not received with any enthusiasm. Many members of the Knesset argued that adopting minimum income support legislation before enacting a minimum-wage law was putting the cart before the horse. It was claimed that the proposed law would weaken the position of low-wage earners and reduce their incentives to work. The government, however, was determined to pass the bill, and it was approved with a few minor changes and without opposition in November 1980.

Final passage of the Income Support Benefits Law made the new scheme an accomplished fact, and the transfer of assistance payments to the National Insurance Institute was implemented with a minimum of difficulty, even though there was initial resistance to the transfer by some local welfare officials and social workers who feared loss of their clientele.[4]

The Essential Features of the New Scheme

The new Income Support Benefits Law brought about the final transformation of the old social assistance program from a public charitable institution to an integral part of the country's social security system. In addition to the functional and organizational changes already mentioned, five features of the new scheme marked the end of the traditional approach to the needy population.

1. The Right to Income Support. One of the most important features of the new scheme was that it established a legal right to benefits. Prior to 1980 there were serious doubts whether a needy person possesed any legal right to assistance at all. To the extent that such a right existed, it was only an indirect one; that is, although local governments were assigned the duty to provide assistance to the poor, the individual person in need had no legal entitlement.[5] The new legislation clearly states that "every resident of Israel of the age of 18 and over shall be entitled to benefit ..." provided that the resident meets the required conditions prescribed by the law.[6]

The establishment of the legal right to income support benefits has further significant consequences in three main areas: (a) raising the social status of the recipient population; (b) limiting the discretionary powers of the authorities administering the scheme; and (c) providing the right to review and appeal within the judiciary system.

(a) The changed conditions that entitled the needy to income support and directed all payments to come from the NII practically ended the segregation of the needy population from other groups receiving social security benefits. Because all residents in Israel receive at one time or another some social security benefit, the needy population in this respect was put on an equal footing with the population as a whole. Thus, the Income Support Benefits Law removed some of the stigma attached to the needy and raised their social status.

(b) The new law and regulations spelled out for the first time the eligibility criteria for benefits. In place of the discretionary powers of the local welfare bureau staff, the NII and its claim officers were left with very little discretion whether to grant or deny a benefit.

(c) In its review and appeal procedures, the new law provided the needy population the right of access to the country's courts for grievances against the NII. Under the old social assistance program, the only recourse in the case of a dispute was to an appeals committee, whose decision was final. Experience showed that the composition and structure of these appeals committees were totally inadequate to protect the needy population against the actions of the local welfare bureaus, and studies carried out in the 1960s and 1970s documented these deficiencies.[7] Although efforts were made to remedy some of the gross inequities, little change took place.

In the new legislation, a person who is dissatisfied with a decision by the NII regarding an income support claim is able to apply to the special labor courts which have jurisdiction over the operation of all other national insurance programs. The final outcome of an appeal is determined by judicial precedents, which regulate the day-to-day operation of the scheme.

2. *National Responsibility.* The new scheme also put an end to the long-cherished principle of local responsibility, which was one of the chief operating principles of the old assistance program. In place of the formal responsibility of the local government authorities "to extend relief to indigent persons," the national government accepted full and direct responsibility for the operation of the new scheme. Paragraph 25 of the Income Support Benefits Law states unequivocally that the benefits will be paid from the state Treasury and that these will be provided by the NII. The significance of this change is that the national government, by gaining direct control of the operation of the new scheme, is in a position to correct the inequities and inadequacies of local responsibility and the inequalities created by more than 180 autonomous local welfare bureaus.

3. *The Level of Assistance.* The assistance rates set in the new law were basically at the same level as those in effect in the old assistance program in 1980. The important change was that for the first time the assistance rates were written into the law itself. Under the old program the assistance rates were set from time to time by the Ministry of Social Affairs with the approval of the Treasury. The rates were published in the form of administrative circulars of the ministry for local welfare bureaus, but no attempt was made to make these rates public. Moreover, the rates could be changed

at any time without prior notice or public discussion because virtually all power was concentrated in the hands of a few officials of the Ministry of Social Affairs and the Treasury.

All this was radically changed in the 1980 Income Support Benefit Law; the rates became an integral part of the new law itself and any change could be made only by an act of the Knesset. The changeover from administrative discretion to parliamentary rule has strengthened the political and procedural safeguards to keep the assistance rates at a publicly acceptable level. The assistance rates set by the law are on two levels: a regular rate, and an increased rate designed for persons who have to maintain themselves on the regular benefit for longer periods of time. The two assistance rates are both determined by the national average wage, which makes them sensitive to changes in the level of living of the country as a whole; thus, the population in need has a better chance to share in the increasing national prosperity. The actual rates are shown in Table 4.1.

4. The Requirement to Work. One of the important features of the new law is the work requirement. Every person who claims benefits is required to do the utmost to earn a living from work. Registration with the local office of the state employment service is required to prove that the effort has been made. Only persons for whom no suitable job can be found by the employment service are eligible for the income support benefits. There are, however, several categories of persons who are not required to work or prove their readiness to work as a condition for receiving the benefit, such as the following:

Mothers of Young Children. Included in this category are mothers who have one child under the age of five, or a number of children, the youngest under the age of ten. This rule applies to single as well to

TABLE 4.1   Income Support Benefit Rates by Family Composition

Family Composition	*Regular Rate*[a]	*Long Term Rate*[b]
	As a Percentage of National Average Wage	
Single person	20	25
Couple	30	37.5
Couple with one child	35	42.5
Couple with two children	40	47.5

[a]Given to claimants of working age who are receiving the benefit for a period of less than twenty-four months.

[b]Given to all who received the benefit at the regular rate for twenty-four months.

Source: 1980 Income Support Act, Paragraph 5 and Supplement.

married women, but the requirement to work falls on both spouses in the case of a married couple, and the women are excluded from this requirement only if they have young children.

Widows. Widows are not required to work if they have children up to the age of eighteen living with them.

Elderly. Men who are sixty-five or older and women who are sixty or older are not required to work nor are persons who devote most of their time to care for their sick spouse or child who is in need of constant attention.

The major change in the new law affects mothers with children. Under the old program, social workers invested considerable effort to "rehabilitate" these mothers, that is, to find jobs for them or to help them secure training for work. In addition, it was necessary to place their very young children in day-care centers or nursery schools the cost of which was in many cases much higher than what the mothers could earn by working. In this instance, the new scheme reflects a more pragmatic and less ideological approach.

5. *Incentives to Work.* At the same time, the new scheme includes a series of ostensibly liberal incentives to work among the recipients of income support in the form of "disregards" of income from work. The disregards consist of two components: a credit for expenses incurred by going out to work (commuting, meals, and so on) and disregards for a certain percentage of income obtained from work, that is, a marginal tax rate lower than 100 percent. The credit for work expenses set by the law is at the rate of 13 percent of the average wage, and the work disregard is at the rate of 40 percent of the income after deducting the credit for work expenses, which results in a marginal tax rate of 60 percent.

In practice, however, these disregards do not have much meaning because of the imposition of an income ceiling that effectively cancels their value. The ceiling not only serves as a disincentive to work but actually makes it difficult for many income support recipients to change their circumstances and move out from their disadvantaged circumstances.[8] Without the income ceiling, the growing number of low-wage earners seeking and receiving supplementation to their wages in the years from 1984 to 1985 would have been much larger.

Initial Experience of Implementing the Law

The Income Support Benefits Law was implemented in 1982 and a follow-up study from 1983 to 1984 in three different types of communities with a sample of 467 families showed, on the whole, a number of very positive outcomes from the transfer of responsibility to the NII.[9] The change made it possible for those in financial need to move out of the welfare system. In addition, more than 20 percent of these former clients of the welfare bureaus obtained regular national insurance benefits from the NII, which they were entitled to but had not previously received. The payments they received from the NII became more regularized, with no shame or stigma attached and with automatic, built-in adjustments to changes in the average national wage.

Almost three-fourths of the recipients of the income support benefits received more uniform assistance payments, and about 10 percent obtained higher benefits than they were receiving from the local welfare bureaus. These higher benefits were not the result of any change in the official rates; rather, they resulted from a stricter adherence to eligibility rules by the NII staff in contrast to the much greater use of discretion in the local welfare bureaus.

Another change occurred in the composition of the recipient population. Among the families transferred to the NII, 33.6 percent had four or more children. The percentage of these families among the new claimants of income support benefits dropped to only 7.5 percent and apparently was the result of improvements in the existing children's allowances for large families. There was also a slight reduction in the number of families receiving personal-care social services from about 1 out of 2 to 4 out of 10, which suggests that about 40 percent of the welfare bureaus' clients did not need, or at least receive, such services either before or after the transfer of responsibilities to the NII. Generally, the transfer process itself seems to have been quite satisfactory from the standpoint of the population in need as well as that of the social workers who were freed from the burden of having to deal with the financial problems of their clients; presumably they could then devote most of their time and professional skills to the delivery of personal social care.

The Scope of the Income Support Benefits Program

With the completion of the transfer of assistance payments to the NII, the average monthly number of recipients of the new income support benefits in 1982 was 9,914, 17 percent less than the equivalent number in 1981, the last year of the old social assistance scheme was in operation. The reduction in the size of the recipient population could be attributed to NII's eligibility review of all cases receiving benefits, the absorption of some former assistance recipients into contributory national insurance programs, and the relatively satisfactory situation in the labor market.[11] This situation, however, changed rapidly after 1983.

In 1983 the average monthly number of income support benefits recipients was 11,004, an increase of about 12 percent from the previous year; in 1984 the number was 14,328, an increase of 30 percent compared to 1983;

and since 1985 the number accelerated even more rapidly. In April 1985 the number of recipients was 17,070, and in December of that year it reached 31,780 recipients. The average monthly number in 1985 was 24,564 recipients, an increase of 71 percent compared to 1984. (See Tables 4.2. and 4.3.)

This enormous and unexpected increase in the number of income support recipients was partly related to the growth of unemployment in the Israeli economy, but it was chiefly a result of the rapid erosion of the minimum-wage levels based on national wage agreements. This erosion reached its peak toward the end of 1985 when the *minimum wage level dropped to only 28.65 percent of the average wage* (compared to 34.2 percent in 1984 and about 35 to 39 percent in 1983).[12] Another factor was the considerable publicity in the press and other media of the right of low-wage earners to receive supplementation to their low wages, and as a result, there was a *threefold increase in the number of persons claiming benefits from the program.*

The Level of Assistance and Low Wages

In Israel, as in other countries, there has always been a close relationship between low wages and the levels of social assistance. This relationship has been even more significant in Israel because of the persistence throughout the years of low wages in large sectors of the Israeli economy.

TABLE 4.2   Recipients of Income Support Benefits from the NII Monthly Average, 1982–1988

Year	No. of Recipient Family Units	% of Change from Previous Year	% of Recipient Family Units Receiving Full Assistance Rates		% of Low-Wage Earners	% of Income Support Benefits from Total NII Expenditure
			Regular	Long-Term		
1982	9,914	-17	49.4	0.2	9	1.1
1983	11,004	+12	59.8	4.4	12	1.3
1984	14,328	+30	48.6	18.4	13	1.9
1985	24,564	+71	36.9	15.9	33	3.0
1986	31,492	+28	31.8	17.4	32	3.3
1987	26,653	-15	27.0	27.0	28	2.8
1988 (March)	24,065	-9	23.0	19.0	22	2.5

Sources: National Insurance Institute, *Quarterly Statistics*, No. 1 (April-June 1989), p. 75; National Insurance Institute, Bureau of Research and Planning, *Annual Survey 1988* (Jerusalem, October 1989), pp. 7 and 137.

TABLE 4.3 Recipients of Income Support Benefits and Payments, 1982–1987

Year	Number of Recipient Family Units	Index 1982 Base	Payments at 1985 Prices in Thousands of New Shekels	Index 1982 Base
1982	9,914	100	23,866	100
1983	11,004	110	26,913	112
1984	14,328	144	42,072	176
1985	24,564	247	72,339	303
1986	31,492	317	89,340	374
1987	26,653	268	78,780	330

Source: National Insurance Institute, Quarterly Statistics, No. 1 (April-June 1989), pp. 14 and 75.

The fear that higher assistance rates would inevitably clash with low pay and produce disincentives to work always played a major role in the decisions regarding assistance rates. These considerations were even more complicated by the fact that most of the workers in the low-wage paying jobs were new immigrants of Oriental origin, as were at least two-thirds of the assistance recipients. Consequently, it was feared that high assistance rates would interfere with the absorption of these immigrant groups into the modern Israeli society.

The implicit policy of the social assistance program until the late 1960s was not to supplement low wages; in fact, the existing policy was a "wage stop," as it is known in the British national assistance and later supplementary benefits program.[13] The principle of the wage stop, which is a modern version of the nineteenth-century concept of "less eligibility," is that people should not be better off receiving social assistance than they would be if working full time in their normal occupations.[14] In practice, therefore, no assistance was to be granted in cases where the income a person obtained in full-time work fell below the current assistance rates. The wage-stop policy had, however, very little practical meaning until the late 1960s because the extremely low assistance rates throughout this period made it impractical for people to seek supplementation of their low wages. In virtually all cases, income from full-time work exceeded the existing very low assistance levels. Within the loosely administered and highly discretionary system of the period, this type of income did not rule out the possibility that in some cases, supplementary assistance payments to low-wage earners were made on an individual and temporary basis.

Additionally, the explicit governmental policy at that time was to supplement low wages via special schemes that operated outside the social assistance program. These schemes had no specific legislative basis because they were established and operated under ad hoc agreements with the Histadrut and the Employers Association. Throughout the 1960s and early 1970s, these schemes were identified by different names, such as Bread Grants, Low-Wage Allowances, Low-Wage Subsidies, and so on, and they were considered part of the government's selective incomes policies. All of them were implemented by the employers who, on the basis of some combined test of income and family size, added the supplements to the pay packet of their low wage workers. The employers were later reimbursed by the government through the National Insurance Institute. Only in the 1970s when a series of studies showed the inefficiency of these schemes, did the government finally decide to replace them with children's allowances.[15] The children's allowances programs were in operation since 1959, but they were not very effective in supplementing low wages. Only in 1975, as part of the comprehensive reform of the existing programs, were children's allowances able to serve this purpose.[16] Since then, all supplementation of low incomes to families with more than two children, whether they have insufficient income wages or low assistance payments, were made by means of children's allowances.

With the gradual increase in the assistance rates in the 1970s and the liberalization of the entire assistance program, the Ministry of Social Welfare quietly abandoned its wage-stop policy. The specific eligibility rules established in the administrative instructions of this period, which included the assessment of resources of people requesting financial help and the various disregards of their income, made it possible to supplement low wages. This policy, like many others, was not announced officially, but it became operative in practice on a small scale. The same policy, with some modifications, was later written into the Income Support Benefits Law and became an integral part of the new program.

Conclusion: Explaining the Changes in Social Assistance Policy

The interaction between the following structural and historical factors can help account for the transformation of social assistance from 1948 to 1980: the economy, ideologies, the political system, program and administration, and a series of critical events, persons, and processes.

The Economy

The state of the economy and the nature of the labor market shaped the assistance program from its inception. Because of disruption from the 1948 War of Independence, which came soon after the strains of World War II, the underdeveloped Israeli economy was obviously unable to absorb the hundreds of thousands of impoverished and unskilled immigrants who arrived following the establishment of the state. In the absence of jobs, industrial development, or capital for development of industry or agricultural settlement, the social assistance system—including work relief—served as a replacement or substitute for wage income for many years.

It was only during the periods of accelerated economic growth that there was readiness to consider modest increases in the below-subsistence levels of social assistance. At the same time, because the Israeli economy has always been characterized by a large number of workers earning substandard wages and without the benefit of a minimum-wage law, it was feared that any greater increase in the level of social assistance would adversely affect the incentive to work. Hence, when the poverty line for social assistance eligibility was finally agreed upon in the early 1970s, it was set at 40 percent of the average national wage for a family of four, and it was gradually brought into effect throughout the decade.[17]

The low-wage economy continued to operate as a brake on adequate standards of assistance by setting a very low ceiling on an acceptable level of benefits. This constraint persisted even after the passage of the Income Support Benefits Law of 1980 when about one-third of the recipients were eligible because of low wages. By the end of the 1980s, the condition of the economy encouraged the development of social assistance both as a residual program for a small number of persons who were not active in the labor market and as a wage supplement program for those earning marginal incomes because of substandard wages.

Ideologies

The four ideological elements that follow were part of the context within which the social assistance program developed.

1. *Labor Zionism* was a distinctive blend of socialism and Jewish nationalism based on pioneering, productive work, collective responsibility, and egalitarianism.[18] Emphasizing the values of agriculture and rural settlements, this "religion of work" denigrated the "nonproductive" elements in the population and perceived them invidiously. Consequently, the legitimacy and the necessity of social assistance was continually challenged by the dominant political decisionmakers, who were usually unsympathetic, if not strongly opposed, to improvements in the levels of assistance. This, in turn, reinforced negative public attitudes toward those who were not self-supporting and also discouraged the development of any organizations of the poor.

2. *Traditional Jewish attitudes toward charity and poverty* were often invoked, but they conflicted with the ideology of work and the prevalence of strong, petit bourgeois, middle-class values that also encouraged the stigmatization of those who were dependent on the state for their sustenance.

3. *The professional ideology of social work* as a cause and as a function had

both constraining and facilitating effects. As a cause, many social workers—as participants in their national professional organization—performed an important advocacy and leadership role in pressing for policy and program changes that would benefit their needy clientele. In their day-to-day professional capacity, however, the overemphasis of social workers on individual, intrapsychic factors deflected attention from the structural sources of poverty in the society. The tendency of many social workers to psychologize problems, which was partly why they opposed separating casework from financial assistance, together with ethnic and social class differences, contributed to an uneasy relationship with clients and helped perpetuate this residual system.

4. *A conservative, right-wing political ideology* was espoused by a rising number of persons who stressed individualistic values, self-reliance, and less government responsibility and intervention. This conservative ideology was espoused by the more upwardly mobile groups who had advanced on the social and economic ladder and expected that others would be able to do likewise. As members of the first generation recently out of disadvantaged backgrounds, they sought to distance themselves from their former social class. Rather than identify with those who remained lagging behind, they regarded the latter as a threat to their newly acquired status and opposed increased governmental expenditures for the support of low-income groups.

Political System

The dynamics of the corporatist, democratic-centralist, coalition politics of Israel generally operated against the improvement of social assistance.[19] We have already referred to the ideology of the dominant Labor Party in which there was no legitimate place for a social welfare function; consequently, the welfare portfolio was relegated for thirty years to a weak, minority religious party. The Ministry of Social Welfare was thus disadvantaged politically in the annual struggle over the budget, and social assistance levels continued to be less than adequate in meeting the needs of its clientele. In 1977 the ministry further lost its independence and visibility by being combined with the Ministry of Labor and being given a subordinate role.

It is ironic, however, that the most significant change in the social assistance program occurred shortly thereafter because of the changed political constellation. Begin's government was persuaded to support the adoption of the Income Support Benefits Law in 1980 because up to that time the Likud bloc had no other piece of social legislation that it could claim as benefiting one of its major constituencies—low-income persons within the Eidot Hamizrach.

Program and Administration

There was continuity in the operating principles of social assistance from the pre-state period, with little change until the mid-1960s. The program was marked by inadequate levels of support and great variability in administration that resulted in inequities, stigma, and inefficiency. It was a residual program, intended to function as a last-resort safety net and it became an entitlement only after its legal basis became firmly established in the Income Support Benefits Law.

Until 1977, the administration of social assistance was an anomaly in a highly centralized system: The program was run by a national ministry that had weak authority and power, was responsible for funding local welfare bureaus with a paucity of resources and a lack of accountability, and for many years was without a legal framework or policy guidelines. Continual strain and interorganizational conflict plagued the Ministry of Social Welfare, which lacked leadership, responsibility, and political power. In addition, local bureaus lacked incentive to change or innovate because they depended on centralized instructions and national funds.[20]

Critical Events, Processes, and Persons

The preceding factors are essentially "structural," that is, inherent in the system, but they do not fully account for the timing of the changes and the process by which they actually occurred. To supplement this more or less deterministic account, we should add a discussion of critical—and at times fortuitous—events, processes, and persons or groups that played key roles in facilitating changes in the system. Among the most important of these were governmental committee reports. Their findings and recommendations in 1958, 1966, and 1971 served to get the subject of social assistance on the national agenda and to keep it there by providing a series of facts and specific recommendations that became part of the public debate in the Knesset and in the media.[21] Essentially, these reports helped convert a social *condition* into a social *problem*, that is, a situation about which something had to be done.[22]

Related to this was the transfer of social work education in Israel to the universities, especially the establishment of the Paul Baerwald School of Social Work at the Hebrew University in 1958. These new, university-based professional schools produced new knowledge, and they served as a continuing source of policy and research data. They also provided independent, critical assessments of social policy during the 1960s and 1970s as well as specific policy recommendations, which formed the basis of various demonstration projects and, ultimately, legislation.

Three other events can be noted chronologically: the 1958 Social Services Act; the 1977 transfer of the Ministry of Social Welfare to the Ministry of Labor, and the appointment of Israel Katz as its head; and finally, the 1980 Income Benefits Support Law. In addition, the Black Panthers movement in the late 1960s directed public attention to the unsolved problems of poverty and lack of social mobility among the Eidot Hamizrach, whose difficulties are embodied in the term "social gap."

Other less dramatic processes occurred inside the government. In the Ministry of Social Welfare, younger administrators gradually replaced the social workers who had beeen inherited from the Va'ad Leumi; this changed the composition of the upper echelon of the ministry. There were also key persons who exerted considerable influence on the processes of policy change by performing critical functions at the right time. The list would certainly include Philip Klein, author of the UN report in 1958; and Israel Katz in his various capacities as director of the Baerwald School of Social Work, Director of the National Insurance Institute, and as Minister of Labor and Social Affairs in the Likud government from 1977 to 1980.

In the next and succeeding chapters, we leave the subject of social assistance and focus on the evolution of the major social insurance programs in Israel. We begin with the adoption of the basic national insurance law of 1953.

Notes

1. Abraham Doron and Tzippi Suesskind, *Income Support Benefits, A Program Proposal* (Jerusalem: National Insurance Institute, Bureau of Research and Planning, 1979).

2. Shlomo Maoz, "Ehrlich, Gafny Oppose Minimum Income Bill," *The Jerusalem Post*, 13 June 1978; "The Finance Minister Is Against Assuring a Minimum Income to 180,000 Citizens," *Davar*, 13 June 1978 (Hebrew); Uri Laor, *Comments and Objections to the National Insurance Institute Law Proposal on Minimum Income Assurance* (the Treasury, Bureau of Budget Memorandum, August 1978) (Hebrew).

3. Yoram Aridor, a senior Likud politician, made it clear that the proposed legislation was actually promised in the Likud election platform. See "Aridor: The Income Support Law Will Cost Less Than a 100 Million IL," *Davar*, 21 June 1978 (Hebrew).

4. Abraham Doron and Uri Yanay, *The Implementation of the Income Support Benefits Law—A Research Report* (Jerusalem: Hebrew University, Paul Baerwald School of Social Work, 1985) (Hebrew).

5. Dan Shnit, "The Right to Public Assistance in Israel" (Doctor of Law thesis, Hebrew University, December 1974) (Hebrew).

6. Paragraph 2 of the 1980 Income Support Benefits Law (Eligibility Conditions) *National Insurance Law* (Jerusalem: National Insurance Institute, 1987) (Hebrew).

7. Abraham Doron, "The Appeal Board in the Jerusalem Welfare Service", in I. Zamir, *Administrative Tribunals in Israel*, Part A (Hebrew University, Faculty of Law, December 1971) (Hebrew); Dan Shnit, op. cit.

8. Ernie S. Lightman, "Earning Disregards in Canada, Britain, and Israel," *Bitachon Sotziali* (Social Security), No. 35 (June 1990) (Hebrew).

9. Abraham Doron and Uri Yanay, "Income Support Benefits: A Change in Social Policy and Realities of Implementation," *Bitachon Sotziali* (Social Security), No. 31 (February 1988) (Hebrew).

10. Uri Yanay and Abraham Doron,"The Effect of the Income Support Benefits Act on the Clientele Previously Served by the Local Welfare Bureaus," *Society and Welfare* 7:4 (June 1987) (Hebrew).

11. Leah Achdut and Tzippi Suesskind, "Income Support Benefits Law: Description of the Population Claiming Income Support Benefits Since the Law Came into Effect in January 1982," Background Memorandum (Jerusalem: National Insurance Institute, June 1982) (Hebrew).

12. Shmuel Greenspan, "Wage Developments in the 1980s—Policy and Application," *Economy and Labor* 4 (February 1987) (Hebrew).

13. Tony Lynes, *The Penguin Guide to Supplementary Benefits* (Harmondsworth, England: Penguin Books, 1974).

14. See, for example, Michael E. Rose, *The English Poor Law 1780–1930* (Newton Abbot: David and Charles, Ltd., 1971), pp. 73–74.

15. Abraham Doron, "Supplementary Cash Grants: A Case Study in Selective Income Maintenance Services," *Journal of Social Policy*, 1:3 (July 1972); Abraham Doron and Raphael Roter, *Low Wage Earners and Low Wage Subsidies* (Jerusalem: Hebrew University, Paul Baerwald School of Social Work, and National Insurance Institute, 1978).

16. Raphael Roter and Nira Shamai, "The Reform of Taxation and Transfer Payments in Israel, July 1975," *Bitachon Sotziali* (Social Security), Nos. 12–13 (March 1977) (Hebrew).

17. Prime Minister's Committee for Children and Youth in Distress, *Report of Income Support Team* (Jerusalem, October 1972) (Hebrew).

18. Reuben Schindler, "The Pioneering Ideology and the Roots of Social Welfare in the Pre-State Period of Israel," *Journal of Jewish Communal Service* 52:4 (Winter 1976), pp. 384–392.

19. Yonatan Reshef, "Political Exchange in Israel: Histadrut-State Relations," *Industrial Relations* 25:3 (1986), pp. 303–319.

20. Ralph M. Kramer and Abraham Doron, "Ideology, Programme and Organizational Factors in Public Assistance: The Case of Israel," *Journal of Social Policy*, 5:2 (April 1976), pp. 131–149.

21. Philip Klein, *Proposals on Program and Administration of Social Welfare in Israel*, Prepared for the Government of Israel under the United Nations Program of Technical Assistance (New York: Report No. TAO/ISR/29, January 1961); and Prime Minister's Committee for Children and Youth in Distress, *Report Submitted to the Prime Minister* (Jerusalem: June 1973) (Hebrew).

22. On the relationships between a social condition and a social problem, see Robert K. Merton, "The Sociology of Social Problems," in Robert K. Merton and Robert Nisbet (eds.), *Contemporary Social Problems* Fourth Edition (New York: Harcourt Brace Jovanovich, 1976), pp. 3–44.

5

Social Insurance:
Establishing the Core
of the Welfare State

The cornerstone of the social insurance program in Israel was laid in the first half of the 1950s at the same time that the foundations of the new state and its institutions were being established. In a comparative historical perspective, the establishment of the program reflects the early nature of Israel's social policy. First, it shows the acceptance by Israel, at the beginning of its national existence, of the welfare state's role of providing social protection to its citizens. Second, it illustrates the process of the adoption of an income maintenance system based on the principle of entitlement as a right of citizenship rather than a system of relief for only the poor. Third, it expresses the universalistic and egalitarian aspirations of the program as conceived at the time by its major protagonists.

The process of legitimation of governmentally administered social security systems began in Bismarck's Germany toward the end of the last century with his establishment of the first state-controlled social insurance schemes.[1] The British adopted similar measures during the first decade of the present century.[2] Most industrial nations, including the United States, established rudimentary forms of social insurance in the period between the two world wars, but none was capable of providing adequate protection against the loss of income resulting from the economic depression and political upheavals of the 1920s and 1930s.[3] Only in the aftermath of World War II and as an integral part of the postwar settlement, did a radical transformation of social security occur in all industrialized countries that made it a major instrument of governmental social policy to maintain and improve the level and even the quality of living of the population.[4]

The transformation of social security and its emergence as the core of the postwar welfare state reflected the willingness of the new political regimes that came into power in the immediate postwar period to assume major responsibility for the welfare of the population as a whole. The acceptance of this enlarged responsibility can be understood in the context of the particular circumstances of the period, such as the following:

1. The still-fresh memory of the widespread suffering and economic hardship of the population during the depression of the 1930s, and the inability of governments to cope with such distress.
2. The strong sense of social solidarity in Europe that developed during World War II under conditions of resistance to the Nazi occupation, which affected most of the population.
3. The changes that were taking place at the same time in mainstream economic theory, and the new, intellectual justification that Keynesian concepts gave to governmental intervention and the management of national economies, which included the rationale for the development of social security systems.
4. The administrative experience that governments gained during the war that encouraged the belief that governmental intervention could correct the failures of market economies to deal with social problems.
5. Last but not least, the Cold War and the need for democratic governments to gain the support of their citizens, especially the working classes, against the perceived threat of Soviet expansion.[5]

Although Israel, because of its location and status under the British Mandate, was not directly affected by most of these trends, the circumstances of the period nevertheless influenced the founders of its social security system. On one level, these developments in Europe and North America provided a modern, intellectual rationale for the adoption of a social security program as the nucleus of the welfare state that Israel sought to become.

The economic and social protection aspects were, however, no less important than the contribution that social security could make to the nation-building process. It did this by helping establish the legitimacy of the new state, which was struggling to assert its own authority to supercede the power of the older, quasi-public institutions that had developed in the Yishuv as the state-on-the-way. Nevertheless, the battle for social insurance—ostensibly a major objective for the labor movement—became highly controversial and was the source of conflict between the government and the Histadrut and between the two major Labor parties over *who* should be insured, for *what* risks, and at what level. Even more significant, however, was the dispute over who should administer and control the social security system.

As in many other countries, the development of social insurance—its scope, content, and pace of growth—has been shaped in large part by the organizational interests of the labor movement and its political and economic institutions. This influence has varied in different national settings; for example, the Scandinavian experience contrasted with that of the United States and England.[6] In Israel, the role of the Histadrut changed over time as it moved from its original role as predecessor to opposition in the early stages and shifted between competition and support in the later phases.

Three major topics are discussed in this chapter: (1) the political process that led to passage of the basic National Insurance Law of 1953, (2) the administrative organization of the National Insurance Institute, and (3) the subsequent development of social insurance programs until the late 1980s. As an aid in following the legislative process in the early, formative years of the State of Israel, which culminated in the establishment of national insurance, Table 5.1 provides a summary of the principal events.

Background

The social insurance program of Israel was established within the first five turbulent years of independence. Even before the cease-fire agreements with the Arab states in 1949, the new provisional government had already appointed an inter-ministerial committee to prepare the plans for a social insurance program in Israel.[7] This decision was in response to the harsh

TABLE 5.1 National Insurance Programs in Effect by 1980

Program	Date Program Began	Payment of Benefits
Old-Age	April 1, 1954	April 1, 1957
Survivors	April 1, 1954	April 1, 1955
Work injuries (employees)	April 1, 1954	April 1, 1954
Work injuries (self-employed)	July 1, 1957	July 1, 1957
Maternity	April 1, 1954	April 1, 1954
Large families allowances	Sept. 1, 1959	Sept. 1, 1959
Employees' children's allowances	Sept. 1, 1965	Sept. 1, 1965
replaced by children's allowances	July 1, 1975	July 1, 1975
Unemployment	April 1, 1970	Jan. 1, 1973
Disability	April 1, 1970	April 1, 1974
Reserve service equalization fund	July 1, 1952	July 1, 1952
replaced by reserve service insurance	Oct. 1, 1977	Oct. 1, 1977
Accident injury	April 1, 1981	April 1, 1981
Rights of volunteers	Jan. 1, 1976	Jan. 1, 1976
Employees in cases of bankruptcy	April 1, 1975	April 1, 1975
Long term care	April 1, 1980	April 1, 1988

realities of the times and the urgent need to address the economic problems of the population. It also reflected the continuity of the ideological commitment of the labor movement to some form of social security in the newly established Jewish state.

The development of Israel's social insurance program was influenced by the social policy origins of the program, the particular circumstances that existed at the time when its basic pattern was molded, and the institutions originally designed to implement it. Accordingly, the account that follows will describe in some detail the factors that shaped the distinctive features of the social insurance system as it evolved in Israel.

The prototype for the Israeli social insurance system was largely based on the voluntary mutual aid institutions of the Histadrut that developed during the period of the British Mandate. These were, in turn, influenced by the workers' voluntary mutual help associations established in Europe during the second half of the nineteenth century, such as the Friendly Societies in England; the pattern of socialist thinking at the turn of the century; and the trade union movement before World War I.[8] As noted in Chapter 3, the special contribution of these Histadrut institutions was the concept of a social right to benefits, which contributed to social solidarity. This concept was in contrast to the traditional, religio-charitable character of the other help-providing institutions at the time.

During the Mandate period, the Histadrut established a variety of social insurance and mutual aid institutions, the largest and most important of which was the health insurance fund—Kupat Holim—which was founded in 1912. Modeled after European counterparts, the other funds were designed to provide very modest benefits to the unemployed, the disabled, the aged, widows, and others. Except for the Kupat Holim, the scope of these institutions was exceedingly limited because of the meager resources at their disposal. The other limitation of all these institutions was their voluntary character and their inclusion of only Histadrut members.[9]

Like other colonial authorities, the British Mandatory government did little to develop social insurance programs for the population during its thirty years in Palestine. There were, of course, objective factors that can explain the Mandate government's inaction, such as the underdeveloped economy of Palestine, the fact that most of the population consisted of rural Arabs unacquainted with modern concepts of social security, and the persistent tensions and conflicts between the Arab and Jewish communities.[10] Although this environment was not conducive to the development of modern social services, the Mandatory government did take several preliminary steps to establish the foundations of social security. In 1927, the first legislation for workers' compensation was passed. Even though the law, based on British legislation that originated in 1897, was regarded as obsolete from the start, it still established the legal foundation for the payment of monetary and other types of compensation to victims of work accidents. This ordinance was modified several times during the 1940s and was completely revised in 1947 shortly before the departure of the British.

Another initiative of the Mandatory government was income protection for working women during pregnancy and childbirth. The Employment of Women Ordinance of 1945 assured certain categories of working women leave with pay for eight weeks after childbirth, which was paid by the employer. This order later became the basis of part of the maternity insurance scheme adopted by the State of Israel.

The First Social Insurance Plans

With the British Mandate nearing its end in 1947, the Jewish community in Palestine—the Yishuv—began the formal organization of the governing institutions of the future state. The months that preceded the Declaration of Independence on May 14, 1948, were filled with feverish political and military activity. The country was engaged in a full-scale civil war between Jews and Arabs. On the international scene, the Arabs tried to reverse the UN resolution partitioning Palestine into two independent states. Although the Jewish community moved ahead with its preparations to establish the necessary governing institutions for statehood, under the circumstances, little attention could be given to any plans for social legislation.

Nevertheless, during these hectic months the first plan for a social insurance program was prepared by the Social Research Institute of the Histadrut, headed by I. Kanev.[11] Although the planning had no official backing from the organized Jewish community, the persons who constituted the planning committee were mostly intellectuals who held high positions in either the Histadrut or the Jewish community, and they were soon to occupy dominant posts in the subsequent Knesset, National Insurance Institute, and other governmental agencies. The plan was published in June 1948, at the height of the War of Independence. The provisional government of Israel was too preoccupied with the urgent problems of the war for the plan to have had any impact, but the report is significant because it expressed the social policy aims of the Jewish state that was emerging. These included most of the demands for social legislation that had previously been proposed to the Mandatory government. In spite of the fact that it produced no immediate results, the plan proved to be the lever that induced action soon afterward.

What characterized this first program, published in June 1948, was its comprehensive and universal substantive content in its coverage of most of the risks to health and loss of income. Its universality was evidenced by inclusion of the entire population in a national health service and all salaried workers in the other insurance programs. It proposed administration by a single central, national institution that would be autonomous and solely responsible for the entire program, which was to be phased-in over a period from five to ten years.

All the main features of this program were strongly influenced by the Beveridge Report, which was published during World War II and was then being adopted and put into action by the post-war Labor government in Britain.[12] In this way, Kanev and his colleagues aspired to make the newly established Jewish state a full-fledged social democratic welfare state from the beginning. The model of the Beveridge Plan was apparent in all of its details, such as the universal health service designed along the same lines as the British National Health Service and the centralization of the entire social security program under one roof within the framework of a unified national system. All in all, from its earliest inception, the development of social security in Israel was a classic example of the role of cross-national "societal learning" on social policy.[13]

The early years after the establishment of the state were, however, not conducive to the realization of such broad social goals. The war with six Arab countries, the prolonged and acute economic crisis, the mass immigration and problems of its absorption—all of these were formidable obstacles to adopting a comprehensive social insurance program. But the main difficulty turned out to be political: a power struggle between the Histadrut and the state, and internal controversies within the labor movement and its major parties. On the one hand, the Histadrut and the workers' unions could be expected to be the primary supporters of a broad-based social insurance program. On the other, the leaders of the Histadrut began to fear for the future of their institutions, which they had developed over the years with so much difficulty. They were afraid that transferring these functions to the state would remove the vital core of Histadrut membership and bring about the weakening of its power.

A sharp dispute over these issues broke out between the two major Labor parties during this period—Mapai and Mapam—when the latter also included the Achdut Avoda Party. Mapam was violently opposed to any attempt to transfer any of the voluntary social insurance institutions and programs of the Histadrut to the government, and it strongly castigated Mapai for any tendencies in this direction. Mapam's position was clearly expressed by one of its leaders, Chanan Rubin, in his remarks to the council of the Histadrut that met in December 1948: "We shall not agree to it—however it may happen, whether it will be called 'social insurance' or any other name—that Kupat Holim should be dismantled and no longer be the property of the workers. We shall not permit that in the name of 'social insurance,' other mutual aid institutions of the Histadrut should be dissolved."[14]

In addition to the dispute between the two Labor parties, opposition developed within Mapai itself to the transfer to the state of certain aspects of Histadrut social insurance. The programs of national insurance that were subsequently developed were primarily in those areas that did not clash directly with the special interests of the Histadrut social insurance programs, such as old-age pensions and health insurance. This close relationship of the Histadrut with the Mapai Party essentially determined the specific patterns of development and the special character of national insurance in Israel during the first years of the state, and it continued to be the primary influence for the next thirty years.[15]

The dispute over the proposed program centered on three major questions: Was it realistic to assume that the state would be able to carry out such a comprehensive social security program within the short period of five years? Should the population as a whole be included or only the wage earners? Finally, should the program be carried out chiefly within the framework of the Histadrut or the national government?[16] Although these questions were the subject of continuing controversy in all future discussions of social security, at this early stage it was evidently still possible for the government to avoid taking a specific stand and to rely on vague or equivocal principles.

Between June and December 1948 the foundations were laid for the administrative structure of government. Each new ministry was entrusted with specific functions and immediately confronted with the difficult problems of unemployment, health, and social welfare; and they all soon started to develop their own plans for dealing with them. In November 1948, the minister of Social Welfare, Rabbi I.M. Levin, announced that the government intended to introduce social insurance programs and that his ministry had already begun negotiations with the other social ministries.[17] Similar programs were also being planned in the other ministries, and there was no doubt that all these plans conflicted with the idea of a national system of social insurance.

Kanev saw the danger in planning a national social insurance program that might become dispersed among the various ministries and other bodies, with each pursuing its own narrow interests and going its own way. Kanev and his supporters therefore began to convince the government, and especially the leading force within it—the Mapai Party—to adopt a clear policy toward national social insurance planning. The demands put forward were for the appointment of a state commission empowered with the task of preparing a coordinated plan for social security.[18] As a result of these pressures, on January 20, 1949, the provisional government appointed an interministerial committee for planning a social insurance program in Israel, and Kanev himself was appointed to head it.

The appointment—and the task—of this governmental committee were significantly different from the circumstances that surrounded the preparation of the first Kanev social insurance plan. This time it was an official action of the government and included the four major ministries that were directly concerned with the income maintenance needs of the population: the ministries of Labor, Social Welfare, Health, and the Treasury. These four ministries also represented the major political partners of the government coalition as well as the special interests of its various members.

The committee, which also became known as the Kanev committee, worked intensively on its report throughout 1949. The circumstances under which it prepared its proposals included the harsh social and economic realities of severe austerity and a major economic crisis that placed formidable limitations on the ability of the state to implement a comprehensive social insurance program. Various interest groups, such as the physicians who appeared before the committee, also exerted considerable pressure on it.

At the same time, the Histadrut conducted its own deliberations, and there were serious divisions within its ranks on the subject. The sharp differences of opinion between the two Labor parties, Mapai and Mapam, continued with regard to the respective roles of the Histadrut and the state in general and with respect to social insurance. In addition, the right-wing political parties initiated their own efforts to prevent the Histadrut from controlling the program that the committee would eventually recommend.[19]

In spite of these many pressures, Kanev steered the committee's activity in the direction of his previous program, which he saw as an Israeli version of the Beveridge Plan. He considered his comprehensive program a practical expression of the aspirations of the Jewish Yishuv in the field of social security, a program that was seen as an inseparable part of nation-building. Eventually, Kanev succeeded to a great extent in convincing the committee to adopt most of his ideas.[20]

The Kanev committee completed its work a year later and submitted its report at the beginning of 1950. It recommended a comprehensive social insurance program to be implemented in stages over a period of several years. Essentially, it was similar to Kanev's first proposal because it was still comprehensive and universal, although it included some important changes in the health field. The committee's recommendations no longer spoke of a health service for the entire population, but only for wage earners. This change, of course, meant maintaining the Kupat Holim of the Histadrut as an independent body and clearly reflected the powerful pressures on the committee in this matter. But evidently Kanev was willing to compromise on this issue of coverage mainly because of his loyalty to Kupat Holim.

In the other areas of social insurance, the program remained both comprehensive and universal. Within the committee, however, there was substantial opposition to the inclusion of a proposal for unemployment insurance; although it was ultimately recommended, this program was postponed until a future date. Actually it did not become part of the national insurance program for twenty years—not until 1973. The remainder of the recommendations were basically unchanged concerning those forms of insurance already included in the previous proposal.

The Kanev committee took a significant position regarding the type of administrative organization for the social insurance system it recommended. The committee identified four possible ways in which the system could be organized and it analyzed the advantages and disadvantages of each: (1) direct administration by the government alone; (2) administration by various groups of the insured population and their organizations; (3) administration by a single autonomous institution of the insured population without the participation of the government; and (4) administration by a single institution common to both the insured and the government.[21]

Although the committee did not take a clear position regarding any one of these types, Kanev preferred the third model, which was featured prominently in the report. This third model expressed not only the desire to preserve the autonomy of the social insurance system but also the suspicions and doubts that had historical roots in the labor movement. In all of the plans for the organization of social security institutions proposed by the international labor movement and the Socialist Internationals, there was always a clear demand for autonomous administration by the insured and preservation of their independence from the employers and the state. This stemmed from both the traditional antagonism of the state toward the claims of the organized labor movement and the lack of confidence within it regarding the intentions of the state. There were other practical reasons to favor an autonomous administration: for example, to prevent the government or the employers from using the money accumulated in the social insurance funds; more positively, to create employment and training opportunities for members of the labor movement and workers' organizations; and, of course, to preserve and increase trade union membership by strengthening the independent social security programs of the workers.[22]

The Preparation of the First Social Insurance Legislation

Soon after publication of the Kanev Report, the government charged the Ministry of Labor with the task of preparing legislative proposals for the implementation of the various social insurance programs. It took, however, almost two years of complicated political maneuvering until the first national insurance bill was actually brought to the Knesset in December 1951. During this period the broad scope of the Kanev committee's recommendations was gradually diluted to accommodate the much more limited goals of the government. From the original Kanev plan to include health, sickness, disability, maternity, and old-age and survivors insurance, the government settled for old-age and survivors, maternity, and work injury insurance schemes only.

The first casualty was unemployment insurance, which even in the Kanev committee, received only lukewarm support. The most powerful interest groups in Israel were opposed to cash benefits: the Histadrut, the ruling Mapai Party, the right-wing parties, and the government all favored relief work through manual labor as the most appropriate and least costly way of facilitating integration of the unemployed new immigrants into Israeli society.[23]

The second important casualty in the process was health care insurance. In the evolution of the welfare state in practically all industrial societies, the organized medical profession has constituted the most significant privately based resistance to the introduction of public health care provisions.[24] In the Israeli case, the government proposals for health care insurance included the provision that it should be carried out through the Kupat Holim, the existing sick fund system. The physicians feared that the proposed compulsory health insurance scheme would leave many of them without employment and adversely affect their private practices. A minor coalition partner, the Progressive Party—which was supported by a considerable segment of the medical profession—adopted the physicians' views, and members of that party were able to veto the various proposals that included health care in the new national insurance program.

The failure to include health care insurance in the original national insurance plans resulted not only from the necessity of yielding to the physicians' political power, but also because of the opposition within the Histadrut and the labor movement as a whole. For example, several Mapai ministers within the cabinet expressed the view that a compulsory national health insurance scheme, even if implemented through Kupat Holim, would still eventually undermine its autonomous position. At this early stage, then, health care insurance was therefore ruled out as a feasible political possibility.

The inclusion of the industrial injuries insurance scheme in the proposed legislation was fortuitous. This plan was actually excluded from an earlier version of the legislative proposal and its later inclusion immediately aroused the opposition of the private insurance companies that had been insuring employers under the existing Workmen's Compensation legislation. The insurance companies' lobby, supported by the banking interests, strongly opposed the "nationalization" of this field of private insurance. Despite the insurance companies' lobbying efforts, the government did not back down and continued to stand behind its original proposal. In the prevailing mood of austerity of the early 1950s and the lack of confidence in the capacity of the state to finance broad social programs, no serious consideration was given to include other social insurance programs such as sickness, disability, or children's allowances, which were relegated from the start to some indefinite time in the future.

In addition to the conflict between the state and the Histadrut over the responsibility for the country's social security system, there was another dispute between the state and organized religion over some of the fundamental values in modern social legislation. Although the political parties representing organized religion in the government did not have a particular point of view about the proposed social insurance legislation, it was assumed that they would generally support its positive social goals. Their sole objection was, however, of another order. The bill included in its definition of a wife, "a woman publicly known to be the wife, and living with the man in question." The Ministry of Social Welfare, which was controlled by a religious party, considered this definition a serious breach of Jewish religious law and of public morals and, characteristically, strongly opposed adoption of the legislation.

The introduction of the National Insurance Bill in the Knesset in February 1952 coincided with another important event—the beginning of the government's new economic policy "to curb inflation, encourage the flow of investment capital, and increase productivity.[25] This new policy left little room for additional public expenditures on a new social insurance program, and Minister of Labor Golda Meir, in presenting the bill, made it clear that national insurance "will be, at least in its first few years an instrument for the accumulation of capital ... and this will be its contribution in combating inflation."[26] She also stressed, however, that the bill was only the first phase of a comprehensive program that would eventually also include health, disability, and unemployment insurance schemes.

During the first reading all parties declared themselves in favor of the bill and almost all participants in the debate advocated broader measures than the government was proposing. The government defended its position and argued that the economic situation did not permit broadening of the program at this stage. Eventually, the bill passed its first legislative stage without opposition, as "no party wanted to be the first to oppose the beginning of Israel's Beveridge Scheme."[27] From the floor of the Knesset the bill was sent to a special subcommittee of the Parliamentary Labor Committee to deal exclusively with it. The bill remained with this subcommittee for more than a year and a half, until November 1953—when it received its final reading.

The bill undoubtedly required considerable time for preparation in the subcommittee stage, but the long delay was mainly due to the hesitant and equivocal attitude of the government which could not decide whether to pass the bill or not. The bill was left to rest in subcommittee where some of the major issues were again contested among the opposing parties. The most controversial issue raised in the subcommittee concerned industrial injuries insurance. The private insurance companies tried again to prevent the "nationalization" of a part of their business.[28] Their position was strengthened at the end of 1952 when the General Zionist Party, which primarily represented business interests, joined the government. Although the government in principle supported the inclusion of the industrial injuries insurance scheme, it did not want to alienate the private insurance companies. The settlement of the issue was thus left to negotiations between the insurance companies, the Knesset subcommittee, and the Ministry of Labor.

The negotiations with the insurance companies went on under pressure to find a solution that would somehow simultaneously satisfy them and also keep intact the framework of the proposed scheme. When the scheme was almost at the point of being abandoned, the insurance companies were offered the right to compete with the government's industrial insurance scheme, but they rejected the offer. Because they rejected it, their arguments against "nationalization" were less convincing and the industrial injuries insurance scheme managed to survive.

Another disputed issue was the question of coverage of persons older than sixty. The bill proposed to extend the coverage in old-age and survivors insurance to all residents from the age of eighteen to those reaching sixty on the day the law would go into effect, or on the day they first became residents of the country. After lengthy negotiations, a compromise was reached under which coverage was extended to all persons, both male and female, who on the day of the adoption of the law had not attained the age of sixty-seven. The compromise reflected the desire to include as many of the elderly living in the country as possible. It contained, however, an element of discrimination against new immigrants who arrived after adoption of the law; coverage remained limited if a new immigrant had reached sixty (for a man) or fifty-five (for a woman) by the day of becoming a resident.

The decision to fix the age limit at sixty-seven was obviously an arbitrary one, and it excluded the entire elderly population for whom there was no income support provision other than social assistance. The problem was acute for those who came to the country in their youth and as pioneers contributed to the building of the Jewish state, but who were not included in the legislation. The inadequacy of the new arrangement was evident, but it persisted for almost two decades. Nevertheless, the original decision to extend coverage until the age of sixty-seven was in itself an important achievement.

The perennial issue of whether old-age pensions should be a flat or wage-related rate (and thus provide a higher percentage of previous income) was also hotly contested in the subcommittee. Surprisingly, the representatives of Labor and the Histadrut supported the flat-rate minimum level of pensions proposed in the bill, although the representatives of the manufacturers and the right-wing parties demanded wage-related pensions of up to two-thirds of wages and salaries.[29]

These arguments did not mean that Labor became converted to the liberal creed of Beveridge or that the Israeli industrialists decided to embrace state intervention. Instead, each side was alert to promote its own interests. The Histadrut was anxious to protect its pension funds, which were a source of power over its membership and also over significant financial resources. The manufacturers' association thought that the transfer of the entire old-age pension system to the state-controlled national insurance program would kill two birds with one stone: It would limit the power of the Histadrut, and it would make possible a reduction in the pension costs to the employers. Finally, the government's flat-rate pension proposal carried the day. Although economic circumstances of the time probably did not allow for any other choice, the decision laid the foundations of the country's future two-tier unintegrated pension system in which the government ultimately plays only a subordinate role.

The bill was finally returned to the Knesset for its third and final reading and was passed on November 17, 1953. Before it was passed, Minister of the Treasury Levi Eshkol had to be persuaded of its financial advantages in addition to its benefits to the population. The endorsement of the Treasury was finally obtained because of the promise of the accumulation of large reserves that would support the fiscal policies of the government and also serve as a lever for the economic development of the country.

On the Knesset floor the bill was adopted with no opposing votes, but some left-wing parties—Mapam, Communist, and Siat-Hasmol (Left Socialist)—abstained and declared that they could not support the bill because it did not include unemployment insurance.[30] After the vote was taken Golda Meir stated, "Everything which has been created in this country is the work of those who did not shun modest beginnings. I am sure that important additions will be made to the law shortly, for it is only the first step. . . . The foundation was laid today for legislation that symbolizes the values for which this country stands."[31] Thus, after a long struggle the first national insurance program became law.

The establishment of the National Insurance program clearly reflected the choice made by Israel to abandon the social assistance principle of need and the means test as a basis for its future social security system. Although the government would continue to rely heavily on social assistance for many years, it was assumed, as in the United Kingdom and the United States, that its importance would decline as successive population groups would be removed and transferred to social insurance where the right to social security benefits was rooted in an entirely different set of legal and program principles.

The major differences between social insurance and social assistance were described earlier in Chapters 3 and 4: Social insurance implies the absence of the principle of need and shuns the use of a degrading means test that demarcates the social classes of recipients; social insurance is based on the use of insurance metaphors whereby benefits are earned rights presumably based on past contributions and hence no stigma is attached to receiving them. In addition, there is more predictability and security attached to social insurance, not only because it is an entitlement of citizenship available to all on the basis of open, uniform rules rather than at the discretion of bureaucratic or professional staff but also because it includes the right to appeal adverse administrative decisions.

The Social Organization of the National Insurance System

As noted earlier, four different administrative structures were considered by the Kanev committee, but ultimately an autonomous, highly centralized state agency was created especially for this purpose—the National Insurance Institute. The institute, which has a relatively high degree of independence, is subject to supervision by the minister of Labor and Social Affairs, who carries parliamentary responsibility for it.[32] In more recent years the NII has accepted additional income maintenance functions, such as paying the new income support benefits, as described in Chapter 4, but its principal role has been to implement the national insurance programs.

The director of the NII and its board have broad authority over the program, and they carry major responsibility for its daily operation.[33] The composition of the board has changed throughout the years, but generally members of the board are the director of the NII, the deputy director and the assistant directors. They are all officials appointed by the minister of Labor and Social Affairs after consultation with the NII Public Council. This structure concentrates a great deal of power in a small group of senior officials, whose attitudes and values have immense influence on the functioning of the entire social security system. In particular, the position of the NII director has acquired significant political power in shaping the country's social security policy.[34]

Another body supervising the NII's operation is its Public Council, which is composed of more than fifty members who are appointed by the minister of Labor and Social Affairs. The council members represent various organized interest groups such as trade unions, the employers association, the self-employed, women's organizations, and so on. Under the law, the council is the supreme authority of the NII, but in practice it is an advisory body that serves as an important channel of communication and a mediating link with the various interest groups. In this capacity, it too exerts considerable influence on NII activities.[35]

The first director of the NII was Giora Lotan, one of the few well-known authorities on social insurance in the country, who had headed some of the social welfare programs of the Va'ad Leumi in the 1940s. Lotan had drafted the original social insurance legislation, which he skillfully steered through the government bureaucracy and Knesset during a three-year period. He had also worked closely with Minister of Labor Golda Meir, who had full confidence in him, so he was the natural choice to head the newly established NII.

In the beginning, the major concern of the NII was to ensure an effective and efficient management of the program as a whole. During its first years of operation the NII was quite successful in creating a relatively competent administrative apparatus, but with an underlying conservative philosophy emphasizing the accepted insurance basis of the program. The public was thus constantly reminded that its contributions were similar to paying premiums to a private insurance company. Only at the beginning of the 1960s, when its power was already well-consolidated and there was a revival of public interest in national insurance, did a change in NII policy occur. It gradually shed some of its cautious conservatism and eventually became an advocate of overdue changes in the various schemes. Indeed, the institute's top bureaucracy, at this point, actually became an instigator of social policy change.[36]

More radical changes in the NII attitudes took place in the late 1960s and early 1970s with the retirement of Lotan and his replacement by Israel Katz as the new director general. Katz, a well-known social activist and champion of the disadvantaged, was at that time director of the Paul Baerwald School of Social Work of the Hebrew University. Under his leadership the NII became more sensitive to the need for social change and it was often in the forefront of demands for changes in social policies.

This change in approach was closely connected with the growing awareness at the time of the social and economic deprivation among large population groups, mainly of Oriental origin, and a desire to use the national insurance system as a means of ameliorating that deprivation. Among the major changes subsequently introduced were the relaxation—or even the abandonment—of the insurance principle, which had a crucial influence on the societal role and public image of the NII. This advocacy role of the NII has been sustained despite the increased politicization and more frequent changes in its top leadership during the 1980s. In this task the NII has encountered increased opposition from the Treasury.

As in most modern states, the Treasury in Israel has decisive powers in setting the priorities for allocating national resources. The relative autonomy of the NII, and its location outside the government ministries, enabled it over the years to maintain a high degree of independence vis-à-vis the Treasury. In recent years, however, the Treasury has acted to curtail NII autonomy and to assert its own control over the public expenditure of transfer payments in order to have them conform with current economic and fiscal policies. This has created a conflict with the NII seeing itself responsible for the welfare of the insured population while the Treasury seeks to protect the current fiscal requirements of the state.

The frequent, open political contests between two groups of technipols in the Treasury and the NII inevitably had a damaging effect on the national consensus concerning the role of the country's social security system. In order to maintain its organizational integrity, the NII has had to devote much of its energy to safeguarding its unique position in Israeli society and its greatly expanded role in assuring the social security of the Israeli population as a whole.

The Evolution of National Insurance: 1954–1980

The initial national insurance program that began to operate in 1954 included only old-age and survivors, work injuries, and maternity insurance. Coverage was extended over the next thirty years to include children's allowances, unemployment, general disability, and a range of other small national insurance schemes. The *old-age and survivors* insurance program started to pay its first pensions to survivors in 1955 and to the elderly in 1957. It thus relieved these relatively large population groups from dependence on social assistance payments for their livelihood. The struggle to extend the national insurance program and to assure an adequate income to *families with children* continued till the mid-1970s. The first national insurance children's allowances scheme was established in 1959 and covered only large families with four or more children younger than eighteen. In 1965 an additional children's allowances program was introduced covering the first three children of wage and salary earners. Only the comprehensive reform of the children's allowances, adopted in 1975, made the program universal by extending its coverage to all children in Israel.[37]

The most difficult objective was to extend national insurance protection to the *unemployed*. During most of the 1950s and 1960s, when Israel suffered from very high rates of unemployment, the only help available to the unemployed was the social assistance program described in Chapter 4, and a variety of work relief projects operated by the government. Only after a prolonged debate was unemployment insurance added to the national insurance program in 1973.

The *disabled* were the last large population group to which national insurance protection was finally extended. Until their inclusion in 1974 the disabled composed nearly half of all those receiving social assistance payments. With the addition of the disability insurance scheme, the national insurance program covered practically all major risks of loss of income in contemporary industrial society. It thus marks the completion of the comprehensive program originally envisaged by the Kanev Committee and initiated in the first national insurance legislation of 1953.

Notes

1. Peter A. Kohler and Hans F. Zacher (eds.), *The Evolution of Social Insurance 1881–1981: Studies of Germany, France, Great Britain, Austria, and Switzerland* (London: Frances Pinter and New York: St. Martin's Press, 1982); W.J. Mommsen (ed.), *The Emergence of the Welfare State in Britain and Germany 1850–1950* (London: Croom Helm, 1981).

2. Bentley B. Gilbert, *The Evolution of National Insurance in Great Britain: The Origins of the Welfare State* (London: Michael Joseph, 1966).

3. Peter Flora and Arnold J. Heidenheimer (eds.), *The Development of Welfare States in Europe and America* (New Brunswick, NJ: Transaction Books, 1981); Theda Skocpol and John Ikenberg, "The Political Formation of the American Welfare State, Social and Political Perspectives," *Comparative Social Research* 6 (1983), pp. 87–148.

4. Peter Flora (ed.), *Growth to Limits: The Western European Welfare States Since World War II* (New York: Walter de Gruyter; Vols. 1 and 2, 1986, Vols. 3 and 4, 1987); Harold L. Wilensky, *The Welfare State and Equality: Structural and Ideological Roots of Public Expenditures* (Berkeley: University of California Press, 1975).

5. Norman Johnson, *The Welfare State in Transition: The Theory and Practice of Welfare Pluralism* (Brighton, England: Wheatsheaf Books, 1987), pp. 18–19; T.H. Marshall, "The Welfare State: A Sociological Interpretation," *European Journal of Sociology*, 11:2 (1961), pp. 284–300; T.H. Marshall, *Social Policy* (London: Hutchinson University Library, 1965), pp. 75–89; Pat Thane, *The Foundations of the Welfare State* (London: Longman, 1982), p. 282.

6. On the role of trade unions in the development of social insurance, see Hugh Heclo, *Modern Social Politics in Britain and Sweden: From Relief to Income Maintenance* (New Haven: Yale University Press, 1974), pp. 263–265, 268.

7. *A Social Insurance Plan for Israel*, Report of the Interministerial Committee for Social Insurance Planning (Ministry of Labor and Social Insurance, 1950) (Hebrew).

8. Bentley Gilbert, op. cit.

9. I. Kanevsky, *Social Insurance in Eretz Israel: Its Achievement and Problems* (Tel Aviv: Briut Haoved, 1942) (Hebrew).

10. See, for example, Government of Palestine, Department of Commerce and Industry, *Report on the Economic and Commercial Situation of Palestine to 31 March*

1921 (Jerusalem, 1922), p. 8; Palestine, *Report of the High Commissioner on the Administration of Palestine 1920–1925*, Colonial No. 15 (London: HMSO, 1925), pp. 22–24; Great Britain, *Report by His Britannic Majesty's Government to the Council of the League of Nations on the Administration of Palestine and Transjordan for the Year 1927*, Colonial No. 31 (London: HMSO, 1928), p. 105.

11. I. Kanevsky, "A Social Insurance Plan for the State of Israel," *Khikrei Avodah* (Labor Studies) 2:1–2 (June 1948) (Hebrew).

12. Sir William Beveridge, *Social Insurance and Allied Services* (Beveridge Report) (London: HMSO, Cmd. 6404, November 1942).

13. On societal learning, see Hugh Heclo, op. cit., pp. 284–322; and also Stein Kuhnle, "The Growth of Social Insurance Programs in Scandinavia: Outside Influences and Internal Forces," in Flora and Heidenheimer, op. cit., pp. 125–150.

14. Minutes of Histadrut council meeting No. 62, Moetzet Hahistadrut Hasameh-Bet, 7 December 1948, p. 134 (Hebrew).

15. On the relationships between the Histadrut and Mapai, see Peter Medding, *Mapai in Israel* (Cambridge: Cambridge University Press, 1972).

16. Social Research Institute, Proceedings of General Meeting on 13 and 27 January 1948, *Khikrei Avodah* (Labor Studies) 2:1–2 (June 1948) (Hebrew).

17. *Palestine Post*, 19 November 1948.

18. "Toward the Coordination of Planning," *Khikrei Avodah* (Labor Studies) 2:3–4 (December 1948), p. 154 (Hebrew).

19. *Divrei Haknesset* (Parliamentary Records), First Knesset, twelfth meeting, 10 March 1949, p. 126, and ninth meeting, 9 March 1949, p. 75 (Hebrew).

20. *A Social Insurance Plan for Israel*, op. cit. See also I. Kanev, *Society in Israel and Social Planning* (Tel Aviv: Am Oved, 1962), Chapter 18 (Hebrew).

21. Kanev, op. cit., pp. 34–38.

22. Goran Therborn, "Classes and States: Welfare State Developments, 1881–1981," *Studies in Political Economy: A Socialist Review* 14 (Spring 1984), pp. 7–41.

23. See, for example, "Who Pays the Bill?" *The Israel Economist* 6:2 (February 1950), p. 30.

24. Douglas E. Ashford, *The Emergence of the Welfare States* (London: Basil Blackwell, 1986), p. 166.

25. *Divrei Haknesset* (Parliamentary Records), Vol. 10, 1952 (Hebrew).

26. Ibid., p. 1213.

27. *Jerusalem Post*, February 18, 1952.

28. Giora Lotan, *National Insurance in Israel* (Jerusalem: National Insurance Institute, 1969), p. 21.

29. *Divrei Haknesset* (Parliamentary Records), Vol. 15, February 17, 1953, p. 163 (Hebrew).

30. Ibid., November 17, 1953, p. 178.

31. *Jerusalem Post*, November 19, 1953.

32. Lotan, op. cit., pp. 69–72.

33. Ibid., 75–76.

34. Abraham Doron, "National Insurance in Israel—Patterns of Structure and Change," *State, Government, and International Relations* 13 (Winter 1979) (Hebrew).

35. Ibid., p. 71; Lotan, op. cit., pp. 73–75.

36. Abraham Doron, "National Insurance in Israel—Patterns of Evolution and Change," in Brij Mohan (ed.), *Towards Comparative Social Welfare* (Cambridge, MA: Schenkman Books, 1985), pp. 123–124.

37. Rafael Roter and Nira Shamai, "The Reform of Taxation and Transfer Payments in Israel, July 1975," *Bitachon Sotziali* (Social Security), Nos. 12–13 (March 1977) (Hebrew).

6

Pensions for the Elderly Population

In the previous chapters we have examined in considerable detail the origins of the national insurance (NI) system. We concluded Chapter 5 with a brief overview of its subsequent development in the last two decades whereby the scope of insured risks was enlarged and diversified, and the level of benefits was improved. The chapters that follow are devoted to the process of policy development and a critical analysis of the three major social security programs affecting the elderly, children, and the unemployed.

In this and the next chapter, which are concerned with income provisions for the elderly, we shall devote somewhat more attention to structure, substantive character, and the comparative evaluation of effectiveness than to the historical development of policymaking. In contrast to other national insurance schemes—such as children allowances, unemployment insurance, and the earlier program of social assistance—there was much less political opposition to the old-age insurance program. Even though there was controversy, consensus was more easily attained because the proposed program appeared to pose little threat to the existing Histadrut-affiliated and other occupational pension schemes.

Introduction

Toward the end of the 1950s, the major political parties of the time, particularly the Labor Party, took a position that was not challenged by other parties on the left or the right until the 1970s; namely, that the welfare state was established when the national insurance program came into existence in 1954. Although it was widely acknowledged that the core programs needed to be expanded and improved, social security policy did not have a high priority except around election times when the major political parties would take a position on an outstanding social security policy issue. For example, it was within the National Insurance Institute that all three major initiatives for change as well as most other improvements in the old-age insurance program originated: the modification of the retirement requirement, the introduction of the selective social supplement, and the raising of the level of flat-rate pensions and making the level wage-related.[1]

This was not a new development because the pressures for change since the late 1950s in the established national insurance program came chiefly from the service bureaucracies. The top officials of the NII, mostly apolitical civil servants who led the struggle for the changes in the old-age insurance program, were invariably opposed by their counterparts in the Treasury, while the politicians, labor unions, and the general public played only a minor part in these struggles. The low political salience of the issue and the lack of a wider interest in social policy, as well as the absence of a lobby for the aged, reflected the general public acceptance of governmental responsibility for basic social and economic security. The election of the new political regime of the Likud in the late 1970s brought with it a change in this consensus and eventually resulted in a different approach to social policy.

In this chapter we focus mainly on the first of the two-tiered system for income provision for the elderly in Israel, which consists of a universal, egalitarian component of flat-rate pensions. (The second tier, which consists of a more particularistic, status-preserving element based in the occupational system, is the subject of Chapter 7.) After a brief description of the character of the aged population in Israel and the five policy choices in this field, we identify the income goals of the programs that have been developed, and analyze the changes in policies regarding eligiblity and adequacy of the universal flat-rate pension. This analysis addresses the problem of defining retirement to determine eligibility and discusses critical issues in the struggle for a more adequate level of benefits, such as linkage to the average national wage and the establishment of a supplemental benefit system. As part of an evaluation of the income provision system, we conclude this chapter with a binational comparison of old-age pensions.

The Aged Population

As in most industrialized countries, the aged population in Israel has been steadily increasing. By the end of 1985, persons who were sixty-five and older constituted 8.8 percent of the Israeli population as compared with 6.0 percent in 1965. Among the Jewish population in 1988, the elderly constituted 10.0 percent of the total, again as compared with 6.3 percent three decades earlier.[2] This increase was mainly due to a longer average life span, which resulted from improved conditions of nutrition, hygiene, medical care, housing, and so on. Life expectancy in Israel in 1988 was among the highest in the world; at birth it was 73.5 years for males and 77.0 years for females. At the age of sixty-five the average life expectancy for both males and females was 15.1 years.[3] Though the proportion of the aged population in Israel was still relatively small compared to other countries such as Sweden and Britain, it is expected to increase in the future.

Not only the size but the special character of the aged population must also be considered. The elderly, like most of the Israeli population, are recent newcomers to the country. The social and political upheavals that led to their emigration to Israel and the relatively short period of time the elderly spent in the country meant that few were able to make adequate provisions for their old age. Their dependence on governmental provision for their maintenance was therefore much greater than in countries with a more stable demographic pattern.

The Policy Choices Available

Because old age and retirement inevitably disrupt the regular flow of income to most people, a major concern of all contemporary industrialized societies is how to assure a continuous flow of income to the growing elderly population. To prevent a steep decline in the postretirement standard of living of the elderly, industrialized countries have developed the following forms of income provisions during the last half of the twentieth century:

1. *Social insurance programs:* old-age and survivors insurance programs operating within a country's national insurance systems, which provide pensions to the insured population after retirement, provided individuals meet certain qualifying conditions.
2. *Demogrants:* pensions to the elderly solely on the basis of their demographic status, such as reaching a specified age of retirement with benefits paid to all elderly persons who reach that age.
3. *Occupational pensions:* retirement income based on rights earned at the place of employment and accumulated throughout the person's working life.
4. *Income-conditioned old-age benefits:* social assistance payments designed to guarantee a minimum level of income to the elderly in need who have no other sources of income or to supplement resources up to the guaranteed minimum level. All of these programs operate on the principle of need and use some form of means- or income-testing.
5. *Retirement savings and insurance plans:* chiefly private insurance and

savings plans designed to assure income in old age. Although operated by private insurance companies, banks, or other financial institutions, in most cases the plans are supervised by the government and are also actively encouraged and indirectly supported by the tax system.

The overall system in any country is usually dominated by one of these five programs, each of which reflects a particular value system and political approach to societal responsibility for the welfare of the elderly. Each type of program also has implications for the nature of provision, conditions of eligibility, and the level of benefits, which together shape the pattern of life of the older population.[4]

An important difference among these forms of provision is the extent to which they are based on the principle of *need* and in the form of *assistance*. In social insurance, demogrants, or occupational pensions, the right to benefits is not based on need or any individual means-testing. Persons reaching retirement age have a right to benefits if they meet the eligibility requirements as defined by law or the particular work agreement. Such benefits may be supplemented by income from other sources without penalty and thus provide a higher level of living than would be possible through the old-age benefits alone. Income-conditioned assistance benefits, however, limit recipients to this income alone, single them out from the rest of the population, and usually carry a stigma.

There are other significant differences among the various programs that are not income-conditioned. The social insurance and demogrant programs are usually universal, intended to cover the entire aged population. The occupational pension programs are more particularistic and tend to assure better coverage to the upper-level and more highly paid employees, while the lower-wage employee groups are covered less effectively. In practice, the occupational pension programs are highly selective in a sense quite the opposite to the usual meaning of the term. In the same vein, the retirement savings and insurance plans are highly particularistic and usually provide for the wealthier population groups.

The Goals and Policy Choices

Like those of most other countries, Israel's social security system for the elderly has a twofold goal: (1) to prevent poverty and economic hardship among the elderly by guaranteeing a minimum income that will enable all elderly persons to maintain a satisfactory basic standard of living without regard to their economic circumstances during their working years; and (2) to prevent a sharp decline in the standard level of living of the elderly by maintaining a reasonable relationship between a person's income before and after retirement.[5] Although the first goal reflects the universalistic and egalitarian elements of the system, the second embodies the particularistic and status-preserving elements of the system.

The policies to achieve these goals were adopted implicitly or explicitly in the early 1950s. The basis for the first universalistic tier of the system was the Old-Age and Survivors Insurance scheme introduced in 1954 as part of the first National Insurance Act. All residents are covered with the exception of those who had already reached the age of sixty at the time of their arrival to Israel. Pensionable age is seventy for men and sixty-five for women, but eligibility at this age is not conditional on retirement or the income of elderly person. Pensions for men from age sixty-five to seventy and for women from sixty to sixty-five are, however, income-conditioned. Pensions were designed to provide only a minimum to the entire elderly population by means of a universal contributory social insurance program. The government, which was responsible for this tier, accepted a subordinate, albeit important, role in the envisaged social security system for the aged as a whole and left the second tier to occupational pension plans organized chiefly by the Histadrut. As noted earlier, the government bowed to the wishes of the Histadrut, which was determined to maintain the centrality of their voluntary social insurance institutions.

The basis for the second, particularistic tier of the system consists of the employment-related occupational pension schemes, that is, all pension plans in the government, public companies, private employers, and labor unions. Responsibility for this tier is in the private sector although the government itself, as a major employer, has a substantial role in addition to granting generous tax concessions. The task assigned to this second tier is to provide the elderly population with income-related, status-preserving pensions up to a high percentage of preretirement income.

Adequacy of Benefits

In the 1960s, when it became apparent that the national insurance old-age pensions were not adequate to provide a minimum level of living, an additional selective, noncontributory, income-conditioned level was added to the first universalistic tier. This selective level, that is, the supplementary benefits, is basically a form of social assistance intended to supplement the income of recipients of national insurance old-age pensions up to a certain guaranteed minimum income. For many years, this program lacked a firm legal basis until it was incorporated in the 1980s into the Income Support Benefits Act.

A second attack on the inadequacy of the flat-rate pensions took another form. To provide a minimum level of living to the elderly population, the monthly pension level was set in the early 1950s at a fixed rate of IL 15 for a single pensioner. At that time, this sum was nearly 25 percent of the average industrial wage, but as in many other countries, the flat-rate pension was allowed to fall below the generally accepted minimum standard. The effects of inflation on the value of a fixed pension were foreseen from the start and benefits were automatically linked to the cost-of-living index. But it was not expected, however, that protecting the pensioners from inflation would give them a fixed income in real terms while other incomes leapt ahead. Inevitably, the scheme failed to maintain the original relationship between pensions and earnings. The level of the first old-age pensions paid in 1957 was already no more than 17 percent and by 1965, pensions dropped to about 10 percent of the average wage, which made it necessary to bring the flat-rate pension rate more in line with the increase in national prosperity.[6]

The subsequent increases of the flat-rate pension level did not, however, provide a satisfactory answer to the erosion of the value of the national insurance pensions in relation to earnings. Gradually it became apparent that it was necessary to abandon the flat-rate, Beveridge-type formula and to set the old-age pension rates as a percentage of the national average wage. The effort to introduce this change, supported mainly by the NII leadership, went on for more than a decade and was finally accepted in the early 1970s. An amendment to the law passed in 1973 set the pension rates starting from April that year as a percentage of the average wage. The rate for a single pensioner was set at 15 percent of the average wage, much below the level originally intended two decades earlier by the Kanev Committee and included in the 1953 law.

Eligibility and the Definition of Retirement

When the old-age and survivors insurance scheme started to pay its first old-age pensions in April 1957, after a minimum qualifying period of three years, the payment of pensions at the age of sixty-five for men and sixty for women was conditional on retirement from all employment. Because the law contained no definition of retirement, this meant the denial of pension rights to all persons who did not cease working. The main problem, however, was that the low pension rates made it very difficult for retired persons to maintain themselves on the pension alone. The NII recognized at an early stage that the pension was undoubtedly insufficient for subsistence; consequently, to require total retirement as a precondition for payment was seen as unreasonable. The crucial issue thus became whether to strictly interpret the requirement as retirement from *all* employment or to permit the pensioner, as in the United Kingdom and in the United States, to have a certain income and still retain the right to a pension.

The issue was debated throughout the years 1955 to 1956 and, in the end, a solution was adopted somewhat along the lines of the National Insurance Act of 1946 in Great Britain. An amendment to the law was passed in June 1957 (in time to apply to the first recipients of pensions), which introduced an "earning rate" and thus made possible payment of pensions to partially retired persons.[7] Minister of Labor Mordechai Namir presented the amendment to the Knesset. He emphasized its economic aspect because, in his opinion, it was aimed "to encourage old people to continue, even if only in a partial way, to maintain themselves through work, for their own good and the good of the economy."[8] There was no opposition to the amendment in the Knesset, but the case against the requirement that the pensioner's work activity be reduced, even if before retirement the pensioner succeeded in earning only a small income, was brought into the debate. G. Shocken of the Progressive Party asked: "If the insured person due to bad luck, did not earn beforehand more than IL 100 [monthly] why should he be punished and not entitled to a pension because his work was not reduced?"[9] He did not consider the proposed strictness as vital and argued that the only criterion to satisfy eligibility requirements should be that the insured person's income not exceed a certain modest accepted level. This view, however, was not accepted until 1970.[10]

The amendment authorized the NII, at its discretion, to consider an insured person as retired from any occupation, even if: "(a) [the person] works from time to time; (b) the work in his occupation is substantially reduced and does not belie the definition of retirement; and provided that his annual income from work or his said occupation does not exceed one third of the maximum income according to which contributions are paid—if he has dependents; and one fourth if he has no dependents."[11]

This liberalized concept of retirement made it possible for many persons to receive a pension while still continuing to earn some income from their occupations, but it also created many difficulties in its implementation. The extent of "substantially reduced" work as it applied to the concept of retirement was, and remained, a vague term. The discretion invested by the law gave the NII enormous power to implement this provision according to its own interpretation, and it became involved in administering extensive means tests to verify the pensioners' income from employment and to determine the number of hours they had been working.

As a result, there were enormous difficulties in applying the retirement clause equitably. After many complaints and litigations, the NII recognized that these provisions were unjust in principle and unworkable in practice and thus were finally abandoned. The liberalized policy in effect since 1970 simply allows the receipt of pensions at the age of sixty-five for men and sixty for women on condition that their income does not exceed a certain sum, which is adjusted for fluctuations in the average national wage.[12]

The Old-Age National Insurance Scheme in the 1980s:
Adequacy and Scope

The old-age national insurance scheme in operation in the 1980s provides the single pensioner a basic flat-rate pension at the rate of 16 percent of the average monthly wage. In a two-earner couple each is entitled to the full-rate pension. In a one-earner couple the pension is at the rate of 24 percent of the average wage. In addition, there is a seniority increment of 2 percent for each year in excess of ten years' insurance up to a ceiling of 50 percent of the pension. There is also a deferred retirement increment of 5 percent of the pension for each year of deferred retirement up to a ceiling of 25 percent of the pension.[13] Because of these increments the actual average old-age pension paid in 1985 for a single elderly person was 19.7 percent of the average wage and for a one-earner couple was 29.0 percent.

These pensions represent the contributory, universal first tier of the system. The flat-rate nature of the pensions allows for no variations in the income provided to pensioners, except variations resulting from size of family, seniority, and deferred retirement increments. Preretirement income is not taken into account in calculating the pensions; thus the pensions have a considerable egalitarian effect by actually providing a higher pre-retirement replacement rate to pensioners with lower earnings during their working lives. (See Table 6.1.)

The data in Table 6.1 show that persons with preretirement earnings of only half the average national wage were actually receiving pensions amounting to 32 percent of their earnings in the case of a single person; 48 percent in the case of a one-income couple; and 64 percent in the case of a two-income couple. At the same time persons with preretirement earnings of one and a half of the national average wage were receiving pensions of

TABLE 6.1   Replacement Rate of Preretirement Income of the Elderly by the National Insurance Old-Age Pensions as a Percentage of Average Wage, 1985[a]

| Preretirement Earnings | Pension Earnings | | |
	Single Person	One-Income Couple	Two-Income Couple
50	32	48	64
75	24	36	48
100	16	24	32
150	12	18	24

[a]Calculated on the basis of the uniform flat-rate pension of 16 percent of the national average wage paid upon retirement.

TABLE 6.2   Guaranteed Income of Elderly Persons by NI Old-Age Pensions and Supplementary Benefits as a Percentage of Average Wage, 1987

Type of Benefit	*Single Person*	*Couple*	*Couple and Child*	*Couple and Two Children*	*Single Parent and One Child*	*Single Parent and Two Children*
NI old-age basic pension	16.0	24.0	29.0	34.0	21.0	26.0
Supplementary benefit	9.0	13.5	13.5	13.5	13.5	13.5
Children's allowances[a]	- - -	- - -	- - -	3.0	- - -	3.0
Guaranteed total income	25.0	37.5	42.5	50.5	34.5	42.5

[a]These are the universal children's allowances paid to every family for the second and each consecutive child. The values of these allowances are given at their effective rates.

only 12 percent of their earnings in the case of a single person, and 24 percent in the case of a couple with two incomes.

Special Old-Age Pensions. Elderly persons not covered by the national insurance old-age pension scheme are covered by a non-contributory scheme and entitled to special old-age pensions financed by the government and the Jewish Agency. This scheme chiefly covers new immigrants who were too old when they arrived to be included in the contributory old-age national insurance scheme. The rates of the special old-age pensions are the same as the ordinary pensions. Entitlement to these pensions is based on the condition that the person is not receiving an equivalent old-age pension from the country of origin, and recipients are not allowed the seniority and retirement deferral increments.[14] For a breakdown of the level of income actually assured to the elderly population at the social security system's first tier, which is mostly universal and partly selective, see Table 6.2.

The *effective* rates of the monthly old-age pensions, including the supplementary benefits, that the pensions *actually* paid are frequently at a lower rate than those set by law. (See Table 6.3.) This is an almost inevitable result of the benefit-updating methods in use, which are based on the average wage for the period of the last three months for which the relevant data is available. Because there is a built-in time lag in obtaining these data, under the rapidly changing economic conditions in Israel, the pensions paid are lower than their authorized rates.[15]

It seems clear that the basic NI old-age pensions at the rates set by law (16 percent of the average wage for a single person and 24 percent for a couple)

TABLE 6.3   Effective Rates of NI Old-Age Pensions as a Percentage of Average Wage, 1965–1987

| | Single Elderly Person | | Couple | |
Year	Basic Old-Age Pension	Basic Old-Age Pension and Supplementary Benefit	Basic Old-Age Pension	Basic Old-Age Pension and Supplementary Benefit
1965	10.5	14.2	15.7	22.0
1970	11.7	16.6	17.6	25.8
1975	14.9	25.5	22.3	38.3
1980	13.6	23.8	20.4	35.7
1987	14.3	22.9	21.5	34.4

Sources: National Insurance Institute, Bureau of Research and Planning, Quarterly Statistics, various issues.

are insufficient to assure a socially acceptable minimum level of living. This was evident in the early 1960s and eventually the supplementary benefits program was adopted to raise the basic NI pensions to a more realistic level. The proposal to introduce the selective supplementary benefits was first presented in 1962 by NII Director General Giora Lotan, and he made the following arguments: First, that the proposal corresponded with the NII's aim of providing social justice and economic improvement for those elements of the population most in need, but who were unable to achieve financial security through their own efforts; and second, that it would involve only a moderate increase in cost and would not strain the scheme's finances.[16]

Lotan's proposal led to an extended debate about the merits of a universal flat-rate or means-tested pension system. Originally confined to the inner circles of the NII bureaucracy, the debate later involved the Histadrut, the political parties, and the public. The proposal encountered strong opposition among the NII officials and it took some time to persuade them to accept it and to gain the support of Minister of Labor Y. Allon, a member of Achdut-Avoda, a small, left-of-center Labor party.

The strongest opposition to the proposal came from the Histadrut on the grounds that the proposal was in conflict with the "insurance principle," that is, it discriminated among pensioners, and the selection process itself would undermine the principle of receiving a pension as a right. Moreover, the Histadrut leaders argued that the introduction of a means test would have a humiliating effect on pensioners and would transform the scheme into a social assistance program.[17] The most significant role in the debate, however, was played by the NII. After almost a decade of "educating" the public about the value of the insurance principle, it now had to change its stand and defend a departure from it. In defending his proposal Lotan argued strongly against the prevailing approach to national insurance, of which he was the pioneer, and emphasized that there was no need to see in it "a static creation based on eternal principles which are unchangeable, but a social instrument that changes its character with the changes in the society it serves."[18]

The prolonged and sometimes passionate debate was brought to an end just before the elections of November 1965 because of the government's desire to do something about pensions before the elections. The policy adopted was the payment of a "social supplement" to needy old-age pensioners, not as a part of the old- age insurance scheme, but as a social grant of the government paid out of general taxation. In this indirect way, the supplementary benefits program came into being and the element of selectivity became a part of the national insurance system.[19]

As shown in Table 6.3 the supplementary benefits significantly raised the value of the old-age pensions and improved the economic conditions of the needy aged. However, it failed to restructure the NI old-age insurance scheme so that it could more adequately serve the needs of the *entire* elderly population. The selective policy, although considered at the time to be of a temporary nature, became a permanent policy pursued by all governments since then.

The Scope of First-Tier Income Provisions for the Aged

The data in Table 6.4 reflect the rapid maturation of the first tier of the Israeli social security system for the aged population that occurred when the number of old-age pension recipients almost doubled between 1970 and 1980. In the first half of the 1980s, there was a significant slowdown in this growth, but the number of recipients still increased in this period by more than 12 percent. To the numbers of old-age pension recipients in Table 6.4 one has to add about 90,000 widows older than sixty who receive survivors pensions. These widows are an integral part of the eligible elderly population, although their pensions are not defined as old-age pensions. Nearly half of them also receive supplementary benefits in addition to their pensions.

The two main factors directly responsible for the increase in the number of recipients of old-age pensions are demographic changes and the relaxation of some of the strict insurance principles. First, the Israeli population in general has come of age and reached a more advanced age structure. In addition, the mass immigration reaching Israel in the first years of statehood included a large number of elderly persons, most of whom reached the age of retirement during the 1970s.[20] Second, during the 1970s, a considerable relaxation took place in the eligibility requirements for receiving the NI

TABLE 6.4   Recipients of First-Tier Old-Age Pensions, 1965–1988

Year	Number of Old-Age Pension Recipients			Number of Old-Age Pension Recipients with Supplementary Benefits			Percentage Receiving Supplementary Benefits
	NI Pension	Special Old-Age Pension	Total	NI Pension	Special Old-Age Pension	Total	
1965 (April)	75,388	14,800	90,188	- - [a]	- - [a]	55,771	61.8
1970 (April)	115,283	24,754	140,077	45,708	18,152	63,860	45.5
1975 (April)	175,833	34,451	210,284	71,839	31,406	103,245	49.0
1980 (annual average)	234,571	32,757	267,308	84,435	31,161	115,340	43.2
1985 (annual average)	275,589	25,492	301,081	77,474	24,203	101,667	33.7
1988 (annual average)	301,615	21,918	323,533	73,480	20,811	94,291	29.1

[a]The supplementary benefits scheme began to operate only toward the end of 1965.

Sources: National Insurance Institute, Bureau of Research and Planning, Quarterly Statistics 17:3 (October–December 1987) and 20:1 (April–June 1990).

old-age pensions, especially in the case of women, and these more flexible conditions enabled more people to receive pensions.

Demographic forecasts for the 1990s indicate that the rate of increase in the aged population, which was very rapid during the 1970s, will eventually stabilize. According to all projections, no change is expected in the proportion of persons older than sixty-five in the population until the end of the first decade of the twenty-first century.[21] Another trend which can be discerned in this first tier of income provision for the elderly is the decline in the role of its selective component, that is, the percentage of elderly people dependent on the income-conditioned supplementary benefits has been steadily declining. The ratio of those dependent on supplementary benefits dropped from 45.5 percent of all old-age pension recipients in 1970 to 33.7 percent in 1985. This drop is partially accounted for by the improvement in and maturation of the occupational pensions' programs and the subsequent increase in the receipt of these pensions among the elderly population.[22]

Attempts to Attack the Program

The political and economic uncertainties of the 1980s and the decline in the support for the welfare state encouraged numerous attempts to cut back the income provision system for the aged, especially its universalistic features. Throughout the decade repeated demands were made by Treasury officials and also by right-wing politicians to introduce more selectivity into the system and thus reduce its cost. These demands were largely influenced by the current mode of U.S. economic thinking, which inevitably reached Israel, about the need for more efficient "targeting" of social security payments.[23]

The severe cutbacks in goverment spending in the 1980s brought these demands to the fore of Israel's social policymaking process. For example, the Treasury proposed introducing a form of income testing into the NI old-age insurance pensions, and the National Unity government, with the consent of the two major political blocs taking part in it—Labor and Likud—attempted for two consecutive years to reduce the seniority and deferred retirement increments of the old-age pensions.[24] Cuts in the seniority increment would have meant that many retired persons would have had to apply for the income-conditioned supplementary benefit and that they could not receive any significant additional income beyond their minimum benefit. Although the proposal to cut the seniority increment was presented to the public as a minor change that would have little effect on the elderly population, the plan was not implemented because it was recognized that the Knesset would not pass the legislation.

The System in a Comparative Perspective

The main features of the first tier of the Israeli income provision system for the elderly that have been described are similar to those in many other countries, but how does its performance and effectiveness compare? Apart from the inherent difficulties in cross-national comparisons of this type, there are very few such studies available. A recent comparison of the performance of the first tier of the Israeli system with its Canadian equivalent is available and despite the obvious differences in size, demography, and political economy, it may provide a broader perspective on the Israeli system. The study analyzes the effectiveness of a universalistic system in

TABLE 6.5   Government Pension Systems as Guaranteed Annual Income of a Single Elderly Person Without Other Income in Canada and Israel, as a Percentage of Preretirement Income, 1984

Government Pension Systems Guaranteed Income	Persons Earning 50% of Average Earnings		Persons Earning 75% of Average Earnings		Persons Earning 100% of Average Earnings	
	Canada	Israel	Canada	Israel	Canada	Israel
Old-Age Security	28.2	- - -	18.8	- - -	14.1	- - -
Social Insurance Pension[a]	22.3	36.4	22.3	24.3	20.3	18.2
Guaranteed Income Supplement	18.7	11.6	8.7	8.7	4.7	5.8
Replacement Ratios						
Gross replacement ratio of earnings	69.2	48.0	49.8	32.0	39.1	24.0
Net Replacement ratio of earnings[b]	81.0	56.3	63.0	40.5	51.0	32.1
Guaranteed income as percent of poverty line	79.8	87.6	86.3	87.6	90.4	87.6

[a]In Canada, the Canada Pension Plan; in Israel, the Old-Age National Insurance Pension.

[b]Net replacement ratio: after deduction of income tax and national insurance contributions of preretirement earnings.

Source: A. Doron, *Income Maintenance Provisions for the Elderly in Canada and Israel: A Cross-Country Comparison* (Jerusalem: Hebrew University, Program of Canadian Studies, Occasional Paper No. 4, 1987), p. 21.

TABLE 6.6   Government Pension Systems as Guaranteed Annual Income of a Two-Earner Elderly Couple Without Other Income in Canada and Israel, as a Percentage of Preretirement Income, 1984

Government Pension Systems Guaranteed Income	Persons Earning 75% of Average Earnings		Persons Earning 100% of Average Earnings		Persons Earning 150% of Average Earnings	
	Canada	Israel	Canada	Israel	Canada	Israel
Old-Age Security	37.6	- - -	28.2	- - -	18.8	- - -
Social Insurance Pensions[a]	22.3	48.5	22.2	36.4	21.0	24.3
Guaranteed Income Supplement	18.0	- - -	10.7	- - -	4.0	- - -
Replacement Ratios						
Gross replacement ratio of earnings	77.9	48.5	61.1	36.4	43.8	24.3
Net Replacement ratio of earnings	86.8	54.5	72.0	42.7	55.0	31.0
Guaranteed income as percent of poverty line	102.0	83.1	107.0	83.1	115.0	83.1

[a]In Canada, the Canada Pension Plan; in Israel, the Old-Age National Insurance Pension.

Source: A. Doron, *Income Maintenance Provisions for the Elderly in Canada and Israel: A Cross-Country Comparison* (Jerusalem: Hebrew University, Program of Canadian Studies, Occasional Paper No. 4, 1987), p. 24.

both countries in relation to different types of families of the elderly with different preretirement levels of income.[25]

If we compare the 1984 pensions in Canada and in Israel of a single elderly person whose preretirement income ranged from one-half to the full average wage, it is clear that a pensioner with no other income was better off in Canada than in Israel. (See Table 6.5.) In both countries the universal and social insurance pension payments were not high enough to assure an income at the guaranteed minimum, and the pensioners were dependent on a supplementary income benefit provided on the basis of need. In all cases, however, the Canadian pensioners received a higher rate of their preretirement incomes.

Although the guaranteed income of the single pensioner as a percentage of the poverty line in both countries seems to be more or less identical, the poverty line for a single person in Canada is calculated at the rate of 43.4 percent of the average industrial wage while in Israel it is set at a rate of only 25 percent of the average wage. The poverty line for a couple in Canada is 57.2 percent of the average wage; in Israel it is 40 percent. Consequently, the guaranteed income for the individual pensioner is in fact much lower in Israel than in Canada.

Likewise, if we compare the 1984 pensions in Canada and in Israel of an elderly couple, both of whom worked before reaching retirement age, whose combined preretirement income ranged from three-quarters to one and a half times the average wage, the relative circumstances of the Canadian couple were much better than those of the Israeli one. (See Table 6.6.) In all cases the Canadian couple was eligible for an income-conditioned, need-related supplement, while the similar Israeli couple entitled to the old-age national insurance pension was not eligible for any income-conditioned supplement. In all cases the Canadian couple received a higher rate of its preretirement income than did the Israeli couple, and the Canadian couple was assured of an income above the accepted poverty line, while the Israeli couple received an income below the accepted poverty line.

These conclusions may not be surprising in view of the great differences in the resources available for social expenditure in Canada and Israel and the sharp contrasts in their sociopolitical environment. Nevertheless, the contrast in the extent and adequacy of the public-income provision for the aged in the two countries points to the long road Israel still has ahead of it to improve the living conditions of its elderly population.

Notes

1. Abraham Doron, "National Insurance in Israel—Patterns of Structure and Change," *State, Government, and International Relations* 13 (Winter 1979) (Hebrew).

2. Central Bureau of Statistics, *Statistical Abstract of Israel 1989*, No. 40 (Jerusalem, 1990), p. 79.

3. Ibid., pp. 142–143.

4. Arnold J. Heidenheimer, Hugh Heclo, and Carolyn Teich-Adams (eds.) *Comparative Public Policy: The Politics of Social Choice in Europe and America*, 2nd ed. (London: Macmillan, 1983), pp. 203–205; Martin Rein, *From Policy to Practice* (Armonk, NY: Sharpe, 1983), pp. 29–31.

5. Joseph A. Pechman, Henry J. Aaron, and Michael K. Taussig, *Social Security: Perspectives for Reform* (Washington, DC: Brookings Institution, 1968), pp. 55–56.

6. Joseph Lavon, *The Level of Living in Israel* (Tel Aviv: Ha'vaad Hapoel, Institute for Social and Economic Research, March 1969) (Hebrew).

7. *National Insurance Law, 1953 (5714)*, Section 5(1) amended as of 31 July 1957.

8. *Divrei Haknesset* (Parliamentary Records), Vol. 22, May 28, 1957, p. 2006.

9. Ibid., p. 2016.

10. The same solution was also recommended by William C. Fitch, Social Insurance adviser to the NII, in *National Insurance Program in the State of Israel*, Report to the government of Israel (Tel Aviv: USA Operations Mission to Israel, October 1956), pp. 10–11.

11. *National Insurance Law* (Haifa: Israel Business Books Ltd., 1961), p. 2.

12. The income permitted to an elderly person without dependents equals 50 percent of the average wage. Elderly persons with one dependent are permitted an income of 67 percent of the average wage and 6 percent for each additional dependent. In calculating the permitted amount, income from occupational pensions is not taken into account. *National Insurance Law (Consolidated Version) 1968 (5728)*, Section 12(a) amended as of 1 April 1970.

13. Abraham Doron, Nira Shamai, and Yossi Tamir, *Income Maintenance from a Family Policy Perspective: Description and Analysis of Programs in Israel* (Jerusalem: Hebrew University, Paul Baerwald School of Social Work, and National Insurance Institute, 1981), pp. 10–11.

14. Ibid., p. 11.

15. See, for example, L. Achdut (ed.), *Annual Survey 1986* (Jerusalem: National Insurance Institute, Bureau of Research and Planning, December 1987), pp. 10–11 (Hebrew).

16. National Insurance Institute, *Annual Report 1961–1962* (Jerusalem, May 1963), p. 14.

17. The Histadrut attitude is well represented in a series of articles by Aaron Ephrat, "National Insurance on the Agenda," *Al Hamishmar*, 24 and 31 January 1965 and 15 February 1965 (Hebrew).

18. *Davar*, 7 January 1965 (Hebrew).

19. National Insurance Institute, Special Research Unit, *Summary of Developments and Trends in Social Security 1965–1969* (Jerusalem, 1970), pp. 11–12.

20. Yaakov Kop (ed.), *Socio-Economic Indicators, Israel 1988* (Jerusalem: Center for Social Policy Studies, 1988), pp. 25–27.

21. Central Bureau of Statistics, *Israel's Statistical Monthly* 4 (1987), p. 16.

22. L. Achdut (ed.), *Annual Survey 1984* (Jerusalem: National Insurance Institute, Bureau of Research and Planning, 1985), p. 53 (Hebrew).

23. See Public Committee to Set Priorities in Public Spending and the State Budget, *Report Submitted to the Minister of the Treasury* (Jerusalem, November 1985), pp. 23 and 30 (Hebrew); L. Achdut (ed.), *Annual Survey 1986* (Jerusalem: National Insurance Institute, Bureau of Research and Planning, December 1987), Introduction by Director General Mordechai Tzipori and pp. 30–31 (Hebrew); L. Achdut and G. Yaniv (eds.), *Annual Survey 1987* (Jerusalem: National Insurance Institute, Bureau of Research and Planning, September 1988), pp. 26–27 (Hebrew).

24. See, for example, Edna Aridor, "National Insurance on the Treasury's Target," *Haaretz*, 11 March 1987 (Hebrew); Gideon Eshet, "Transfer Payments To Means Test", *Yedioth Akharonot*, Mamon—Weekend Supplement, 9 December 1988 (Hebrew); Ministry of Labor and Social Affairs, *Budget Proposal for the Fiscal Year 1986* (Jerusalem, January 1986), p. 103 (Hebrew).

25. Abraham Doron, *Income Maintenance Provisions for the Elderly in Canada and Israel: A Cross-Country Comparison* (Jerusalem: Hebrew University, The Program of Canadian Studies, Occasional Paper No. 4, 1987).

7

Pensions for the
Elderly Population:
The Second Tier

This chapter is concerned with the second tier of the income provision system for the elderly in Israel, which was explicitly designed to provide relatively high income-related pensions on top of the first-tier minimum-level NI pensions. This second tier includes a variety of special schemes for different occupational groups affiliated with the Histadrut, for employees of large corporations, the government, public services, and other enterprises. As a result the system's earnings-related benefits transpose the relative position that the recipients acquired in the labor market into the realm of social security, which preserves rather than modifies the existing pattern of social inequality.[1] Initially, this second tier was expected to play a major role in the income provision system for the elderly as a whole, although its evolution over the years has not always followed its prescribed path. In the following analysis we examine the actual functions performed by this second tier and conclude with a cross-national evaluation of the social security and occupational welfare system for the aged in Israel. This second tier of the Israeli income provision system for the elderly consists of three sets of programs: (1) Histadrut-affiliated pension plans, (2) company pension plans, and (3) budgetary pension plans.

Histadrut-Affiliated Pension Plans

The Histadrut—the General Federation of Labor—is the major carrier of occupational pension plans in Israel, which stems from its pioneering role in this field during the pre-state period. (See Chapters 2 and 3.) In addition, its domination is based on political decisions made in the early 1950s, as described in Chapter 6, when the old-age national insurance scheme was assigned a subordinate role to provide only minimum-level pensions and left the field of the complementary, occupational pensions open to the Histadrut.

The Histadrut-affiliated pension plans operate through seven large insurance funds representing the special interests of various occupational groups that have been in the process of being amalgamated into one major fund. In line with social insurance funding principles, employers and employees both participate in paying insurance contributions to these funds: Employee contributions were usually 5 percent of their wages and the employer's share was 12 percent, but in the late 1980s, the combined contributions rate was raised to 18 percent. All the plans are designed to provide their members earnings-related pensions after retirement and similar pensions to their survivors; the amount varies according to the length of membership in the fund and the pension rights accrued during that time.[2]

It is only possible to join a pension plan in accordance with the existing work agreement between the employer and the particular pension fund which covers all the employees at that workplace. Neither an individual employee nor a group of employees can join such a pension plan without having all other employees also join. The collective action of all employees is based on the principle of mutual aid and meant to prevent discrimination against individual employees. However, an employee who stops working at a particular firm also ends membership in the pension plan connected with that employment.[3]

Eligibility for an old-age occupational pension is conditional upon a minimal qualifying period of membership. An employee who has been insured for at least ten years and has reached retirement age—usually sixty-five for men and sixty for women—is eligible for a partial pension commensurate with the rights accumulated in the particular fund. An employee who has been insured in a pension fund for a period of thirty-five years is eligible for a full retirement occupational pension, that is, 70 percent of preretirement wages. Persons insured more than thirty-five years are entitled to a one-time, additional lump-sum payment based on the number of years of membership in the fund more than thirty-five years up to the age of retirement.

Until recently, the earnings base for calculating the pensions was the employee's average wages in the three years prior to retirement. This was a simple method that was easy to implement, but it worked against employees in those branches of the economy where earnings tend to decline during the years preceding retirement, such as industry, construction, and agriculture. At the same time, it was advantageous to those who worked in branches of the economy where earnings reached their peak just before retirement. This provision was changed and pensions are now calculated on the basis of lifetime earnings. For every year of employment (and membership in the fund), the ratio between the person's earnings and the average wage is calculated. This "wage ratio" for the entire period covered by membership in the pension fund constitutes the base for calculating the pension. This averaging method has been gradually adopted since the 1980s by all Histadrut pension funds and has resulted in greater flexibility in including various wage components to calculate the pensions earning base.

The long-term value of the old-age occupational pensions is preserved by their linkage to the consumer price index whereby pensions are uprated when the cost-of-living increment is paid to all employees. This method of maintaining the long-term value of pensions was instituted during the 1980s and superseded the earlier method by which the pensions were linked to the wage grade reached at the point of retirement. The old method was meant to assure the relative value of the retired person's pension in line with the preretirement rank and thus reinforce the system's status-preserving features.

In practice, however, the old method was not able to prevent the erosion of the relative value of these pensions because its recipients did not benefit from the natural "creeping of wages," such as rise in rank, and from various wage increments that had not existed in the pensioner's wage rank before retirement. In contrast, the current method is intended to assure only the real value of the pensions. Consequently, it lacks the earlier, strong status-preserving element embodied in the attempt to maintain the relative rank value of pensions over time.

The Histadrut-affiliated pension plans cover 60 percent of all wage earners in Israel, although in a survey conducted in the early 1980s by the Central Bureau of Statistics (CBS), it found that only about 50 percent of all employees and members of cooperatives were insured in these pension funds.[4]

Company Pension Plans

These plans operate only in large enterprises such as the Egged Bus Company, Hadassah Medical Organization, Israel Electric Corporation, the Jewish Agency, and similar workplaces and cover 9.5 percent of the wage earners. The separate pension funds that they maintain provide for their employees after retirement and they usually operate on principles similar to the Histadrut-affiliated funds. The company and the employees share in the insurance contributions paid to the fund, and the accumulated resources are expected to provide the needed funds for the payment of pensions.

What characterizes most of these plans is that they have the backing either of strong industrial concerns or large public organizations, and consequently they contribute to the fragmentation of the overall system of income provision for the elderly. They are also an expression of the existence of private welfare states in Israel that preserve the social, economic, and employment advantages of the better paid worker groups.[5] The terms for joining these pension plans, conditions for eligibility in them, and methods of calculating pensions and maintaining their value over time are ordinarily patterned on the Histadrut pension models.

Budgetary Pension Plans

The third type of pension plan operates mainly in the public services and covers all civil servants, local government employees, employees of government-owned companies, and employees of large public corporations, which amount to about 22 percent of the employee population. In contrast to the other pension plans, these plans do not require the employer or the employees to participate in a separate pension plan. Under this type of arrangement, the employer takes the full responsibility for paying the pensions to the retired employees from the current budget. Obviously, only the public services that have a claim on tax revenue can undertake such a long-term responsibility.

These plans operate principally on the basis of statutory rules and regulations, as in the case of the civil servants, or on the basis of wage agreements, which generally follow the civil servants' pension pattern. The pensions in these plans are determined on the basis of the person's last preretirement earnings and the length of time served with the employer.

Limits of the Occupational Pension System

The second-tier occupational pension system in Israel covers in its various plans more than 80 percent of the country's employee population, a much higher ratio than in other countries.[6] Coverage in itself is, however, insufficient in evaluating effectiveness. In spite of some important improvements introduced into this tier during the 1980s, the system still suffers from three main deficiencies: coverage, vesting and transferability (or portability) of pension rights, and their maturation.

Inadequate Coverage. Practically none of the second-tier occupational pension plans, with the exception of the civil servants' pension scheme, are rooted in any binding legislation; rather, they are all based on specific work agreements between the employers and their employees. Since the mid-1960s numerous attempts were made to introduce a form of compulsory pension legislation to assure coverage for all. Many government committees issued reports on this matter and most of the ministers of Labor tried to launch national pension insurance schemes during their stay in office; but these attempts failed because of opposition from the Histadrut, the Employers Association, the Treasury, or a coalition of these organizations.[7] The reluctance of the affected interest groups to produce some sort of compromise proposal is an expression of the conflict of social and economic interests on the issue of pensions.

The existing voluntary arrangements make it practically impossible to extend coverage in this tier to the entire employed population; as a result, at least 20 percent of the employed are not covered by any of the pension plans. The groups excluded from coverage in pension plans are mostly among the poorer sectors of the employee population. The marginal position of poorer employees in the labor market pushes them inevitably into jobs that, in addition to low wages, provide very limited work-related benefits and rarely include participation in a pension plan. The contrast between the poorer and the better-off employees is a consequence of a voluntary, in fact free-for-all, system.

Vesting and Transferability. The reported data on the extent of coverage by the various types of occupational pension plans reveal coverage only at a particular time. Participation in a pension plan at one time does not assure coverage during the entire or most of the person's working life. Only continuous participation is able to assure a full pension at the time of retirement, unless adequate vesting and transferability arrangements are built into the system. In practice, vesting refers to the provision in pension plans of an assurance that employees who terminate their employment before eligibility for regular retirement will be able to retain the pension credits accrued to them. Transferability involves the possibility that persons may transfer accumulated pension credits from job to job that eventually combine into a single pension at the time of retirement.[8]

All the occupational pension plans described above assure the person's coverage in the pension plan as long as the person continues to be employed at a workplace that participates in a pension plan. In many cases, when a worker changes jobs, membership in the pension plan is terminated; the worker may also lose accumulated pension rights when (1) there are no adequate arrangements for vesting or for transfer of these rights to the new workplace; (2) there is no pension plan in the new workplace to which one can transfer the accrued rights; or (3) when the person is no longer employed. Job mobility and crossing occupational status lines are necessary in a modern economy, but in Israel they have a negative effect on the ability of employees to maintain the continuity of their pension insurance over time.

During the 1980s significant changes have been made to facilitate continuity of coverage and transferability of accumulated pension rights among all the Histadrut-affiliated pension plans and also between them and some of the workplaces that have their own pension plans or have budgetary pension plans. The new vesting and transferability arrangements greatly improved the chances of the population insured in the occupational pension system to acquire full pensions when reaching retirement age. Nevertheless, some of the pension funds still allow insured persons, in certain circumstances, to withdraw their accumulated funds when they cease their membership in the plan. In most of these cases, the withdrawn funds are used for immediate consumption and not for the purpose of the pension savings plans.

In spite of these changes, the actual arrangements to assure continuity of coverage and tranferability of accrued rights have remained complicated because of technical difficulties in determining transfer values and in equating pension credits among different plans. Moreover, in most cases the initiative in this respect must come from the employee, who has to negotiate the transfer procedures. As a result, a considerable loss of accrued pension rights occurs among the insured workers, which subsequently reduces their chances of receiving a full pension upon retirement.

Maturation Period. Full occupational pension is normally obtained on the condition that pension rights have accumulated over a period of thirty-five years, which is almost an entire working life. The relatively long maturation period accentuates the importance of suitable arrangements to preserve continuity of coverage, which is problematic because of the relatively short duration of most of the existing occupational pension plans in Israel. Most of them were established in the 1950s and 1960s, and many of their currently insured members joined these occupational plans only in the 1970s and 1980s. Because these plans are only now beginning to reach full maturation, the majority of the insured who have retired or who are on the verge of reaching the age of retirement, could only accumulate partial rights, and they will receive a small pension relative to their length of membership in these plans.[9] In time, it may be expected that as the plans reach full maturation, the coming generations of pensioners will receive more adequate pensions.

The Scope of Occupational Pension Recipients

The data available on the scope of occupational pension recipients are rather limited, partly because of the fragmented nature of the system and also because of the reluctance or inability of some of the organizations to release current information. Data released by the Histadrut-affiliated pension funds show that all these funds together (excluding the Makefet Pension Fund) paid pensions to 42,681 persons in December 1986. Most of the pensions paid were at a rather low level, with 86 percent of them being lower than half of the national average wage; only between 2 to 3 percent of all the pensioners were receiving pensions at the level of the national average wage or higher.[10]

Broader data on the the ratio of occupational pension recipients are only available from a survey conducted by the NII in 1978 among the entire population that claimed old-age pensions. In this survey it was found that only 39 percent of all the NII pension claimants who were employees, self-employed, and others were also recipients of a second-tier pension. Among the employee group, the percentage of occupational pension recipients was significantly higher at 53 percent.[11] Although the NII estimates that the number of occupational pension recipients among the retiring employee population has grown considerably since 1978, no definite figures are available.

The survey confirms the small size of the pensions: More than half (54 percent) of the persons entitled to a pension received one that was less than half of the average wage, and only 7 percent of the recipients received pensions that were higher than the average wage. The level of pensions received by men was higher than that of women: Only 17 percent of the eligible men received a pension whose value was less than 25 percent of the average wage, while 40 percent of the women received pensions at this low rate.

Although there are insufficient data on the scope of pension recipients in the second tier of the income provision system for the aged, it is evident that the number of second-tier old-age pension recipients is small compared to the number of recipients of NI old-age pensions. The relatively small number of recipients and the low level of pensions they receive, particularly among women, illustrates the major weaknesses of the occupational pension system. Other deficiencies of the system derive from inadequate coverage, problems of maturation, and lack of proper vesting and transferability arrangements. Some of these limitations will eventually be corrected due to the reforms that have been made in the system during the 1980s. A more comprehensive solution, however, will be found only with a more radical overhaul of the system as a whole.

Savings Plans for Old Age

There is still another tier of income provision for the elderly population that includes a wide variety of savings plans, most of which are private and nongovernmental, but they all have broad government support and receive generous tax concessions. They include provident funds and life insurance.

Provident Funds. These are savings plans in which the participants— and in the case of employed persons, their employers also—deposit monthly sums or a certain percentage of their wages, into a fund. They are not pension plans, which provide regular payment of benefits after retirement; rather they assure the accumulation of savings, which are available after retirement in a lump sum or, in some cases, in monthly payments until the sum accrued is depleted. Such savings plans are widespread in Israel and are available through commercial institutions such as banks, which are a major channel of saving for a high proportion of self- employed persons, or on a nonprofit basis by organized groups of employees in many companies.[12]

In a survey conducted by CBS in 1980 it was found that about 114,000 employees save in provident funds, which represents 16.6 percent of all employed persons who were covered by some form of old-age insurance.[13]

Life Insurance. These are traditional savings and insurance plans operated by private insurance companies, which offer a choice of savings for old-age and also receive government encouragement and support. The various private savings and insurance plans mainly serve the more affluent sector of the employee population and of the self-employed population. These groups obtain significant tax advantages through the use of these savings plans, which reflect the government's desire to increase private savings in the economy in general and for old age in particular. These savings plans, intended to complement the two-tier structure of income provision for the elderly population, are chiefly designed to enable the middle- and upper-class population groups to maintain their standards of living after retirement; in this way, they constitute an important extension of the particularistic and status-preserving components of the system as a whole.[14]

The Effectiveness of the Income
Provision System for the Aged

Having now described the multilevel income provision system for the elderly in Israel, we can evaluate its effectiveness by examining it in a cross-national perspective. To what extent did Israel succeed, compared to other countries, in achieving its twofold goal of preventing economic hardship among the elderly without regard to their economic circumstances prior to retirement? The data in Table 7.1 show that the elderly in Israel maintain a relatively high level of adjusted disposable income compared to the elderly in six other countries. Indeed, the 75+ age group in Israel has the highest relative level of disposable income compared to the other countries; for example, the Israeli elderly are much better off than the elderly in Britain, who are the lowest on the ladder of the countries compared.[15]

TABLE 7.1   Adjusted Disposable Income of the Elderly in Relation to National Mean and Poverty Rates[a]

	Adjusted Disposable Income[b]		Poverty Rates[c]	
	65-74	*75+*	*65-74*	*75+*
Canada	.94	.81	11.2	12.1
Germany	.84	.77	12.7	15.2
Israel	.92	.96	22.6	27.1
Norway	1.01	.79	2.7	7.3
Sweden	.96	.78	0.0	0.0
U.K.	.76	.67	16.2	22.0
USA	.99	.84	17.8	25.5
Mean	.92	.80	11.9	15.6
S.D.	.08	.08	7.5	9.2

[a]The data are for 1979 except for Canada and Sweden where the data are for 1981.
[b]Disposable income: gross income minus income tax. The adjustment of disposable income for family size is based on the following equivalence scale:

No. of family members	1	2	3	4	5
Equivalence factors		.50	.75	1.00	1.25	1.50

[c]Proportion (percent) persons belonging to families with an adjusted disposable income below half of the median for all families.

Source: Peter Hedstrom and Stein Ringen, *Age and Income in Contemporary Society* (Luxembourg: Luxembourg Income Study, LIS-CEPS Working Paper Series, 1985), pp. 19 and 23.

Although income from earnings and capital are included in the data, public transfers and occupational pensions account for at least half of the gross income of the elderly and this share increases with age. Such income constitutes a larger proportion of family income of the elderly in the European countries than in the United States, Canada, and Israel and indicates the strong inegalitarian effect of the status-preserving elements in the Israeli system. Additional evidence is found in the fact that Israel has the highest rates of poverty among the elderly population—almost double the mean rate in the other countries. These data indicate the very high extent of inequality in the distribution of income among the elderly in Israel and the relative failure of the egalitarian components of the income provision system to achieve its avowed goals.[16] The extent of inequality is shown even more vividly in Table 7.2; the inequality of income distribution in the oldest group, including measurement by the Gini coefficient, is highest in Israel.

TABLE 7.2 Shares of Income Within Age Group of Family Heads (Equivalent Net Income)

	Norway	Germany	U.K.	Sweden	Israel	USA	Canada
65-74							
Bottom quintile	0.5	7.1	10.9	14.1	7.7	6.6	8.7
Top quintile	35.3	36.7	37.6	28.5	43.7	40.8	39.7
Gini coefficient	0.2495	0.2981	0.2656	0.1426	0.3599	0.3416	0.3092
75+							
Bottom quintile	11.4	5.6	12.0	15.1	7.4	7.0	10.0
Top quintile	34.6	39.7	36.8	27.3	50.4	42.9	39.6
Gini coefficient	0.2293	0.3395	0.2403	0.1258	0.4288	0.3554	0.2807

Source: Lea Achdut and Yossi Tamir, *Retirement and Well-Being Among the Elderly* (Discussion Paper No. 34) (Jerusalem: National Insurance Institute, Bureau of Research and Planning, 1986), p. 27.

Summary and Evaluation

The income provision system for the elderly in Israel has to its credit some remarkable achievements, but at the same time it has serious weaknesses that keep it from fulfilling its major task of assuring an adequate income to the elderly population as a whole. This does not mean only a minimum for subsistence because a minimum, generous as it may be, inevitably leads to a steep decline in the standard of living of those among the elderly who have to subsist on this income alone.

The significant accomplishments of the system are chiefly in its first, universalistic tier, which includes universal coverage and the provision of a social minimum for all. The existing income provision arrangements for the elderly in the first, mainly governmental tier, which include the old-age national insurance scheme and the special noncontributory old-age pensions, cover the entire population. The selective, supplementary benefits in this tier also assure a guaranteed minimum level of income to all elderly whose incomes fall below this minimum. In these two areas, the system is effective, and it has succeeded in preventing severe economic hardship among the elderly population in Israel.

The existing arrangements are, however, much less effective in achieving the wider social goals of the system and preventing a steep decline in the standard of living of the elderly. Originally, the two-tier system was intended to assure a combined retirement income close to what had been previously maintained, but in practice the two tiers of the system both fall short in achieving their objectives in this respect. The old-age national insurance scheme was originally planned to assure a modest income to the entire population by providing pensions at the level of about 25 percent of the average wage to a single person and of 37.5 percent to a couple. This goal has not been achieved. The value of the NI old-age pensions actually paid fell below this original target and none of the amendments over the years changed this situation. To enable a significant part of the elderly population to maintain even a minimum level of living, a selective, income-conditioned element had to be added to the first-tier, universal system. Had it not been for the selective supplementary benefits, the condition of about 40 percent of the elderly would have been extremely precarious.

Neither has the second-tier occupational pension system succeeded in fulfilling its objectives. First, the various plans did not manage to cover the entire employee population. Second, most of the plans have not succeeded in assuring adequate pensions to most of those reaching retirement age. It is also doubtful whether under the existing circumstances the occupational pension system as a whole can significantly improve its effectiveness in the future. The principal deficiency of the second-tier occupational pension system is its essentially private and voluntary character. Its mode of operation requires a long period of maturation that under conditions of rapid economic change and increased labor mobility are difficult for employees to meet in a voluntary system. In addition, the legal, financial, and administrative problems of vesting and transferability contribute to a continuing loss of accumulated pension rights, a loss that cannot be easily remedied. As a result, more than one-third of the elderly who recently reached retirement age were not entitled to any second-tier occupational pension, and those who were eligible generally received very small pensions.

Yet the most conspicuous weakness of the system lies in the total lack of integration between its two tiers. In spite of various attempts over the years to create linkages between them, the two tiers continue to operate separately without any real points of contact between them.[17] The result is that, on the one hand, the system as a whole fails to assure most retirees an income close to the one they had during their working life, and on the other hand, the more influential population groups manage to receive incomes equal to those they had while working, or even exceeding their preretirement income, by using to their advantage the lack of integration in the existing system. In other words, the fragmentation of the system creates, and perhaps even increases, the extent of inequality and the economic gap among the retired elderly population. This is the consequence of the dominance of the particularistic and status-preserving elements in the Israeli income provision system for the elderly.

These limitations have been recognized for many years, and since the mid-1960s, there has been a public debate on how to remedy these serious shortcomings. It is generally accepted that a reform of the system requires a statutory binding base for the second-tier occupational pension system and linkages between the two tiers so that they are integrated in a more coherent whole with a clearly defined common goal. Proposals for such a reform have been on the public agenda since the 1970s, mostly in the form of alternative national pension insurance schemes, but none of them received sufficient political support to be adopted by the Knesset.

The difficulty in finding a generally agreed-upon approach for reforming the income provision system for the elderly lies in the deep political and economic divisions on this issue in Israeli society. The second-tier occupational pension system is rooted in economic and political interests that go far beyond a concern for the welfare of the elderly. The Histadrut, which operates the main pension funds, and the private, profit-making organizations in the field all have enormous stakes in preserving the present system. Any significant change in the existing arrangements has the potential of endangering the political and economic advantages they derive from the present structure.

The Israeli political system has been incapable or unwilling to mobilize its power to reform the pension system. Although the lack of concerted action is partly related to the complexity of the problems in any such reform, the major obstacles are political because of the redistribution of power in Israeli society that would have to occur. Other democratic welfare states, such as Great Britain and Sweden, have for many years experienced similar difficulties in their attempts to reform their pension systems.[18] In any event, a future decision to reform the country's pension system is unavoidable if Israel wants to realize the goal it set for itself in the early 1950s of assuring an adequate income to all of its elderly people.

Notes

1. Jens Alber, "Some Causes of Social Security Expenditure Developments in Western Europe 1949–1977," in Martin Loney, David Boswell, and John Clarke (eds.), *Social Policy and Social Welfare* (Milton Keynes: Open University Press, 1983), p. 162.

2. Shlomo Cohen and Ya'akov Antler, "The General Characteristics of Israel's Pension System," *Bitachon Sotziali* (Social Security), No. 27 (1985) (Hebrew); Abraham Doron, "The Income Maintenance System for the Aged Population in Israel," in S. Bergman and I. Margulec (eds.), *Aging in Israel: Selected Topics in Gerontology* (Tel Aviv: Am Oved, 1984) (Hebrew). Also Yehuda Kahane, *The Handbook of Life Insurance, Pension Funds, and Retirement Saving Programs in Israel* (Hertzliya: Ateret Publishing, 1988). Unless otherwise stated, the following data on the Histadrut and the other pension plans are based on these publications.

3. See, for example, Mivtahim, Workers Social Insurance Institute, *Comprehensive Pension Insurance Regulations*, April 1980 (Hebrew).

4. Central Bureau of Statistics, "Retirement Insurance by Employers," reprint from *Statistical Bulletin of Israel—Supplement* 3 (1982).

5. On "private welfare states" in Israel, see Abraham Doron, "The Histadrut: Social Policy and Equality," *Jerusalem Quarterly* 47 (Summer 1988), pp. 131–144.

6. Shlomo Cohen, "Reforming the Israeli Pension System—Proposals of the National Insurance Institute and the Ministry of Labor and Social Affairs," Memorandum to E. Sharon, director general of the Treasury, 12 May 1987 (Hebrew)

7. See National Insurance Institute, "Plan for Graded Old Age Pension," *Annual Report 1964–1965* (Jerusalem, July 1966); "Almogi's Plan to Introduce a National Pension," *Shaar* 28 (January 1972) (Hebrew); "The Pension Law: Proposed Legislation," *Labor and National Insurance* 27:7 (July 1975) (Hebrew); Office of the Minister of Labor and Social Affairs, "Legislating a Pension Law," March 1978 (Hebrew); "Pensions in Israel—A Survey of the Existing System and Principles for the Proposed Reform" (National Insurance Institute, Bureau of Research and Planning, January 1987) (Hebrew). On the opposition to the proposed legislation see, for example, Eli Danon, "Keisar [The Secretary General of the Histadrut]: We Will Fight the National Pensions Law as Proposed by Katzav [Minister of Labor and Social Affairs]," *Maariv*, 3 February 1987 (Hebrew).

8. Max Horlick, *Private Pension Plans in West Germany and France* (Washington, DC: U.S. Department of Health and Human Services, Social Security Administration, Research Report No. 55, 1980), pp. 41–43.

9. Shlomo Cohen, op. cit., pp. 5–7.

10. Histadrut—General Federation of Labor, Executive Committee, "Selected Points from the Full Actuarial Report for December 1986," 28 December 1987 (Hebrew).

11. Nahum Steigman and Eitan Hamburger, *Level and Composition of the Incomes of New Applicants for Statutory Old-Age and Survivors Pensions 1978* (Jerusalem: National Insurance Institute, Bureau of Research and Planning, Survey No. 29, 1980) (Hebrew).

12. Yehuda Kahane, op. cit., Part 3.

13. "Retirement Insurance by Employers," op. cit.

14. Yehuda Kahane, op. cit., Part 6.

15. Peter Hedstrom and Stein Ringen, *Age and Income in Contemporary Society* (Luxembourg: Luxemburg Income Study, LIS-CEPS Working Paper Series, 1985). See also, P. Hedstrom and S. Ringen, "Age and Income in Contemporary Society: A Research Note," *Journal of Social Policy* 10:2 (April 1987), pp. 227–234.

16. *Age and Income in Contemporary Society*, op. cit., p. 26.

17. Cohen and Antler, op. cit., p. 8.

18. See, Hugh Heclo, *Modern Social Politics in Britain and Sweden: From Relief to Income Maintenance* (New Haven: Yale University Press, 1974), pp. 227–283.

8

Children's Allowances

In this chapter our concern is with benefits in cash provided to families with children. These benefits, generally known as children's allowances, reflect the recognition in virtually all contemporary welfare states that the well-being of children is a matter of national concern that cannot be left only to parents, voluntary action, or private charity. Children's allowance programs express state intervention into the economic circumstances of families with children and the legitimation of socializing some of the costs of bringing up children.[1] The underlying principle, as developed in the Beveridge Report, is that an adequate income for families with children could not be secured in industrialized societies that maintain a wage system based on the product of a person's labor rather than on family size.[2] Children's, or family, allowances thus became "a means by which an individual wage is converted into a family wage by being adjusted to the number of persons who must live on it."[3]

In addition to their egalitarian objectives, children's allowance programs, which differ significantly from country to country, may have additional aims such as promoting a positive demographic policy (that is, to check the fall in the birthrate or to encourage it directly); strengthening health policies by raising the standard of living of large families; and sustaining the family "as the vital nucleus of the social order."[4]

The children's allowances program evolved in Israel over a long period of time, in a piecemeal way, and in a variety of forms. Although there was considerable agreement about the necessity of the programs, their establishment was generally accompanied by a protracted debate about goals, costs, and consequences. In most cases, the struggle to launch a particular program was not confined to the political arena but spilled over to the public bureaucracies and involved issues of administrative feasibility and organizational responsibility. The various phases in the evolution of the program will be described in chronological order.

The Social and Institutional Background

During the time of the British Mandate, when the introduction of a state children's allowances program was not considered feasible, the main effort of the labor movement was directed toward securing a wage system that would be related in some way to the size of family. Motivated by its egalitarian socialist philosophy, the Histadrut was partially successful in securing a system of wages that was not based entirely on productivity but also on family size. Until the mid-1950s, the wages of all Histadrut employees—excluding those employed in its industrial sector—were uniform and related only to family size.[5] Outside its own institutions, however, and even within its own industrial enterprises, the Histadrut failed to achieve this degree of egalitarianism.[6]

Nevertheless, the Histadrut did succeed in establishing the principle of a family supplement as a basic component of the wage structure in Israel. Toward the end of the Mandate period, a supplement to the basic wage for the spouse and first three or four children had already been adopted as part of most wage agreements. This principle was also favored by the Mandate government; its Wages Committee of 1942, which was set up to determine the standard wage of industrial and unskilled workers, recommended the adoption of the system of family allowances in industry.[7] Though the Wages Committee qualified its recommendation with the statement that a family allowance scheme would be practical "provided that the competitive position of the employer is not immediately threatened by additions to labor costs," it supported the existing family supplements attached to wages and even assisted in their expansion.

The system of wage-connected children's allowances underwent considerable change after independence when social and economic changes gradually brought about a modification of the egalitarian philosophy of the labor movement. In the mid-1950s, the Histadrut abandoned its own uniform wage scale and adopted a conventional hierarchical wage system.[8] Children's allowances were not abandoned as a component of the wage structure, but they became a less important part of wages. In a study carried out in 1962, the NII found that 77 percent of all working families were receiving children's allowances for the first three children up to the age of fourteen. The average monthly allowance per child was IL 4.65, but this amounted to only about 1.4 percent of the average monthly wages.[9] Moreover, though they covered practically all families employed in the public sector and about 90 percent in industry, a substantial percentage of families in other parts of the economy were not covered. In sectors that the Histadrut did not reach, no family supplements were paid at all. The insignificant size of the allowance and its inadequate coverage finally precipitated state intervention into the field of family allowances.

The Large Families Insurance Scheme

Children's allowances did not play an important part in the early social insurance plans and they were expected to be introduced only in the last stage of the plan's implementation.[10] In the social insurance plan prepared in 1949 by the Interministerial Committee headed by Kanev, family allowances were again relegated to the third and last stage. This time Kanev argued that for financial reasons it would be impossible to introduce such a scheme at an early stage.[11] Though no special urgency was attached to family allowances by the social insurance planners, demands for their introduction were made from time to time by various political groups in the Knesset and in the press. From the early 1950s, however, the ultra-orthodox religious groups led by the Agudat Israel Party became the strongest advocates for a family allowance scheme.

The interest of the orthodox groups in such a scheme was based on the high proportion of large families among them. Because of their religious beliefs, they practiced no family planning and they were opposed to the use of contraception. In addition, they were also interested in encouraging an increase in the birthrate of the Jewish population, which had been on the decline and in their view was endangering the survival of the Jewish people. Knesset member Rabbi S. Lorenz of Agudat Israel, who repeatedly raised the question of family allowances in the Knesset, introduced a private bill in 1956 to establish allowances for families with two or more children, but the government rejected the bill.[12]

Meanwhile the government itself started to consider the introduction of an allowance for large families, which it hoped would reduce the gap in the level of living between the population of European origin and that of the Asian and North African immigrants, among whom large families were the rule rather than the exception. In 1957 a special ministerial committee was set up to study the problem and, early in 1958, Minister of Labor Namir announced in the Knesset that the committee had agreed in principle to introduce a children's allowance, and he expected that although the question of finance had not yet been settled, the scheme would probably come into existence within the year.

A year later, however, Namir could not add much to what he had promised in 1958 because the Histadrut had strongly opposed the proposed system of financing. It was estimated that the proposed scheme would require contributions at the rate of 1 percent of wages and that the cost be divided equally among the government, employers, and employees, with each paying one-third of the estimated cost.[13] The Histadrut objected, however, to the imposition of any financial burden on the workers. Within the Histadrut, some officials who represented the new immigrant groups campaigned against the official position, but the Histadrut leadership could not be persuaded.[14]

A compromise was finally reached whereby the chief demand of the Histadrut—that no part of financing the scheme should be imposed on employees—was accepted; but, at the same time, the rate of the basic allowance was substantially reduced from IL 10 to IL 6. This was indeed a Pyrrhic victory because it did not help the immigrant groups to save a few pounds a year in contributions, while allowances were denied to families most in need of them. In addition, the Histadrut's intransigence resulted in the postponement of the introduction of the scheme for almost two years.

In June 1959 the cabinet formally approved the bill to introduce monthly children's allowances for large families with four or more children. This was done no doubt with an eye on the forthcoming elections, which were to take place in three months, but sudden developments gave the proposal even greater urgency. At the beginning of July 1959, riots broke out in the Wadi Salib quarter of Haifa and spread to several other towns inhabited mainly by immigrants from North Africa. The violence originated in longstanding intergroup tensions between the North African immigrants and other parts of the community.[15] A special committee, which was set up by the government to inquire into the causes of the riots, reported a month later that the social difficulties of absorbing these immigrants were the main source of the outbreaks. The report also emphasized the fact that the difficulties of absorption were much greater because of the large number of families with many dependent children.[16]

The bill contained a proposal to introduce a large families' national insurance scheme that would provide monthly allowances for all families with four or more children who had not attained fourteen years of age. The allowance was to be paid for the fourth and each subsequent child on an increasing scale beginning with IL 6 per month for the fourth child and reaching IL 10 for the eighth and each additional child.[17]

In the Knesset, Minister of Labor Namir outlined the new scheme's aims as follows:

1. To lighten the social conditions of weak parts of the population.
2. To check the negative trends in demographic developments.
3. To remove some anomalies in the field of employment and the distribution of wages within enterprises in relation to the family situation of the workers.[18]

Though some of the speakers criticized the timing of the bill to coincide with upcoming elections, none objected to the contents. Namir and others referred to the role that the new scheme would play in removing the discontent that had led to the recent demonstrations, but the opposition demanded that the scheme be widened. Eventually, on August 3, 1959, at its final reading, the bill was passed unanimously.

This unanimous passage of the bill in the Knesset did not mean that there was no opposition to it. The classical arguments against family allowances were raised and debated in the press and in public. The fear was voiced that the new scheme would cause a weakening of parental responsibility, especially among groups in which this responsibility was perceived as already in decline. It was also claimed that the allowances would contribute to the proliferation of children among parts of the population that were least capable of supporting them.[19]

During its first six years, until 1965, the large families' insurance scheme paid allowances each year to nearly 50,000 families for more than 100,000 children. The majority of the allowances—about 66 percent—went to families with four or five children, about 20 percent went to families with six children, about 10 percent to families with seven children, and between 4 and 5 percent to families with eight children or more. The majority of the recipients were, as expected, among immigrant groups. About 75 percent of the allowances went to families of North African and Asian origin, 4 percent to Jews born in Israel and 6 percent to families of European origin. About 15 percent of the allowances went to the Arab population, though it constituted only about 10 percent of the total population.[20]

The large families' insurance scheme represented the first use of children's allowances to deliberately modify the income distribution pattern and to reduce the extent of inequality among families in Israel. It had been the declared purpose of the scheme to lessen the gap between the levels of living of large and small families and, at the same time, between those who came from Europe and the new immigrant population, which originated in Moslem countries. In the years following its introduction, the question was constantly raised: To what extent had the scheme actually fulfilled this goal?

There was little doubt that its provisions were not adequate to make a significant impact on the economic well-being of large families. There were, therefore, continuous pressures throughout the 1960s to extend the scheme's provisions, and as a result, the allowances were raised a number of times, and in 1965, the eligibility age was raised from fourteen to eighteen years. Nevertheless, even with these improvements, the allowances continued to provide only a small fraction of the ordinary cost of maintaining a child in a family.

Employed Persons' Children's Insurance Scheme

Although the large families' national insurance scheme somewhat modified the income inequalities among families with a large number of children, the problems of those with less than three children were still unsettled. Two alternatives had been examined: either to establish a national insurance scheme that would pay children's allowances or to set up an equalization fund that would more equitably spread the existing wage supplements among all employers. In June 1963, Minister of Labor I. Allon appointed a planning committee to prepare the introduction of a family allowance scheme for employed persons; and he appointed Giora Lotan, director of the NII, as chairman of the committee, which was composed of representatives of the government, the Histadrut, and the Manufacturers' Association.

The government and the Histadrut agreed that the total cost of the allowances should be carried entirely by the employers. The Manufacturers' Association, which naturally opposed this view, argued that children's allowances were part of a demographic and social welfare policy and that there was therefore no justification for putting the entire cost on employers and adding to the cost of production. In the association's view, the only proper way to finance the allowances was to secure a substantial contribution from the Treasury that would cover at least all costs in excess of the already existing wage-connected children's allowances.[21]

In 1964 the unresolved issues became a part of the negotiations for a common political platform of the "Alignment" coalition between the Mapai and Achdut Avoda parties.[22] By the end of 1964 an agreement was finally hammered out on all of the major points, and on December 1 the Ministerial Committee on Economic Affairs approved the plans for the family allowances scheme. Three months later the bill on the employed persons' children's insurance scheme was ready to be put before the Knesset.

The bill granted coverage to children up to age eighteen in the families of employed persons, irrespective of whether the children were working. The final amount of the monthly allowance of IL 10 was to be introduced in three stages from 1964 through 1967. The allowance was to be paid together with wages by employers who were later to be reimbursed by the NII. Allon explained that this method of payment was adopted "to simplify the administrative procedures involved in payments to thousands of employees."[23] This was, however, only part of the reason. The suggested method of payment was adopted mainly on the insistence of the Histadrut because the new allowance could be made to appear as the Histadrut's own achievement. The NII did not object to paying the allowances through the employers because this solved the problem of confirming the employee's status. The allowances were to be considered taxable income and the scheme was to be financed entirely by contributions from the employers. The scheme was discussed in the Knesset in the preelection atmosphere of 1965, but perhaps because there was little attention given to the whole issue by the public or the press, there was practically no opposition to the bill in the Knesset. All participants in the debate, however, deplored the fact that only children of employed persons were included.

Because it involved the payment of allowances for nearly 650,000 children through thousands of employers, the administrative difficulties in implementing the new scheme were enormous. There were also important social policy decisions at stake. For example, the scheme provided for the payment of the allowance not only to persons actually employed but also to those in search of employment. The law deliberately avoided the use of the term "unemployed" and the term "work seekers" was used instead, with the latter term limited to only those registered in an official labor exchange. As a result, the policy was inconsistent with the social insurance basis of the scheme. It constituted an equalization fund—the kind established in Europe in an earlier period—by organizations of employers, with almost no redistributive component between income groups. The scheme mirrored, to a large extent, the predisposition of trade unionism in Israel, which as elsewhere sought chiefly to improve the condition of its already better-off members.[24]

In the next decade, from 1965 to 1975, the problem of the inclusion of children of nonemployees continued to be an important social as well as political issue. It was clear that the need for children's allowances was greater among the nonemployee families than among the employees because most of the former belonged to the lowest income groups in Israel. The main policy issue was, however, how to finance the inclusion of these children in a broader children's allowance program.

It was apparent that the majority of nonemployee families would not be able to carry the burden of such a scheme if it were financed only through their own insurance contributions. Although in principle, the Treasury appeared to be ready to participate in the coverage of such costs, a campaign against a "new tax" was initiated by the well-to-do and better-organized groups among the nonemployee population, especially the smallholder settlements movement (the moshavim).[25] Although the whole moshavim movement was built on the idea of mutual help, when it came to children's allowances, which would benefit some of their own members, the better-off among them refused to participate in the costs. Given the circumstances of Israeli society in the 1960s, they also had the political power to impose their views on the government.

No comprehensive solution was found to this problem until 1975; however, some indirect measures were taken to provide at least a partial solution. In 1972 the large families' insurance scheme was extended to cover the third child of nonemployee families, and in 1972, the same measure was applied to the third child of employee families. By the middle of the 1970s, only the first and second child of nonemployee families were not covered by any of the children's allowances program.

The Veterans' Family Allowances Scheme

Another phase in the extension of the children's allowances program occurred in July 1970, with the introduction of the veterans' family allowances scheme. There were a variety of complex social and political motives that brought this scheme into existence. On the one hand, the aftermath of the Six Day War brought a period of rapid economic growth and an increase in national prosperity and personal affluence. On the other hand, it also led to considerable social unrest; for example, the Black Panthers movement, increased awareness of the growing social gap—the *paar hevrati*—between the population groups of Oriental and European origin, and the realization that extensive poverty existed among the underprivileged.[26] The accepted view within social policy circles was that the social gap could, at least in part, be handled effectively by improving the country's social security system and, in particular, by extending the children's allowances program and raising the level of these cash benefits.[27]

The main policy proposal under consideration was to raise the level of the children's allowances paid to large families on whom the social gap and poverty problems were focused. This proposal, however, encountered strong opposition because it would disproportionately benefit the Arab population, which contained many large families. Increased universal allowances to all large families, it was argued, would miss the main target population and transfer a considerable part of total resources to the Arab population. The overwhelming opposition cut across political party lines; and rooted in nationalistic attitudes against increasing benefits to the Arab population, these arguments won the day.

To avoid the charge of discrimination against the Arab citizens of Israel, a scheme was developed to circumvent the payment of the increased allowances to them. It was decided to pay the increased allowances only to the large families of veterans, that is, families in which one of its members had served in the Israel Defense Forces (IDF) or other national security service. The scheme was not defined as a part of the national insurance program but put within the context of veterans' benefits and included in the Demobilized Soldiers' Return to Work Law. Although it was to be implemented by the NII, as the other children's allowance schemes, its costs were to be covered entirely by the Treasury.[28]

After a prolonged debate, the new scheme finally came into effect in July 1970. Basically, it added an additional layer of benefits to large families with four or more children on top of the already existing allowances. In strictly legal terms the new allowances were nondiscriminatory because eligibility to them was open to all who served in the Israeli armed forces and was not restricted to the Jewish population. The Druze and some of the Bedouin who serve in the IDF were thus eligible for the benefits, but in practice, it effectively excluded from coverage most of the Arab population.

Subsequently, some minor changes were made in the scheme, but its major premises remained intact. In September 1971, payment of its benefits was extended to families receiving social assistance and to new immigrant families, the latter being financed by the Jewish Agency. In 1974 the whole scheme was extended to also cover the third child.[29] Additional changes were introduced during the 1980s to allow families of persons who devote all of their time to study in rabbinical institutions (yeshivot) to be eligible for the allowances. This occurred as part of the negotiations for inclusion of the orthodox religious political parties whose participation was required by the coalition government.

The Reform of the Children's Allowances Program in 1975

As a result of the developments in the previous decade, three major children's allowances programs were operating in Israel in the early 1970s: two insurance schemes—one for large families and one for employed persons—and allowances for the families of veterans. In addition to the direct cash benefits paid to families, there was also an extensive system of personal deductions for children in the income tax system. There was, however, little coordination among the various schemes or between the direct cash benefits paid by the NII and the tax benefits granted by the income tax authorities. Consequently, measures taken in one part of the overall system often contradicted those in another part.

To remedy this situation, the almost unanimous thinking at the time within the government was that it was imperative to consolidate the existing schemes and integrate them into the tax system. Such a reform, it was thought, would strengthen the fragmented children's allowances program as a whole and improve the economic circumstances of families with children, especially those in large families. Initial steps in this direction were already taken in the early 1970s by increasing the level of children's allowances and reducing the personal deductions for children in the income tax system.[30] The thinking embodied in this proposal and the measures subsequently taken were strongly influenced by similar trends in other European countries and reflected a pattern of cross-national, societal learning.[31]

At the same there were growing pressures in the country to bring about a radical reform in the direct tax system. Since the mid-1960s the tax system had become increasingly inequitable because of the serious erosion of the tax base that resulted from myriad deductions and other tax exemptions for selected groups of taxpayers. In December 1974, the government finally appointed a committee of experts to deal with the issues of tax reform, which was headed by Hayim Ben-Shahar, an economist and president of Tel Aviv University. The task of the committee was, among others, to recommend changes that would: (1) lead to a fair distribution of income in the economy; and (2) prevent distortions and their adverse influences on productivity and tax behavior. In addition the committee was given full authority to recommend, at its discretion, changes in the income protection system.[32]

The Ben-Shahar committee submitted its recommendations to the minister of the Treasury at the end of March 1975. The recommendations encompassed a comprehensive reform not only in the tax base and taxation rates but also in the system of deductions, credits, and family allowances. The main recommendations regarding children's allowances were as follows:

1. Cancel all deductions for children in the direct tax system and replace them with a uniform system of universal children's allowances. This should be accomplished by establishing a credit points system that would serve as a basis for personal credits as well as allowances on account of children.
2. Link the credit points on which the allowances would be based to the consumer price index.
3. Make the status of the self-employed equal to that of employees by granting children's allowances for the first two children of the self-employed (and nonemployed) families as well.

The committee's recommendations on children's allowances were fully accepted by the government and put into effect almost immediately, from July 1975.[33] The most important change in child benefits was the cancellation of all personal deductions for children in the direct tax system and the introduction of a universal children's allowances program, which covered the entire population and replaced the large families' and employed persons' children's insurance schemes. Under the new program all families in Israel were entitled to the allowances paid by the NII for every child until the age of eighteen. For the first time, the payment of children's allowances actually became universal in Israel, but veterans' allowances continued and the differences in the level of allowances received by various families remained unchanged.[34]

In place of the tax deductions for children, which had been canceled, a credit points system was established that served as a base for personal tax credits and the payment of children's allowances. The value of a credit point set in July 1975 was IL 100, which at the time was equivalent to 5 percent of the average wage. The first and second child were entitled to 1 credit point each, and each subsequent child to one and a quarter points.

In addition, under the veterans' allowances scheme, three-quarters of a credit point was paid for the third child, 1 credit point for the fourth and fifth child, and one and a quarter points for the sixth and each additional child. The credit points were linked to the consumer price index.

In summary, the new universal children's allowances program that followed the reform came to play a dual role: It was the equivalent of a "negative income tax" for families whose income was below the tax threshold level, and it served as a tax credit for families with incomes exceeding the tax threshold.[35]

In practical terms the 1975 reform of the children's allowances program had two major effects: First, it increased the number of families receiving children's allowances from about 400,000 to 500,000, and the number of children for whom allowances were paid from about 1 million to 1,400,000. Second, it made the system somewhat more progressive and enhanced the egalitarian effect of the social security system as a whole. The goals of the reform reflected the spirit of the time and the willingness to use social policy measures to influence the income distribution pattern in favor of selected underprivileged groups. This mood was, however, to change very soon.

Developments in the 1980s

The continuous trend in Israel's social policy since 1959 to extend the program to cover wider population groups and to increase the level of the allowances came to an end in the early 1980s. The change not only came about as a result of the country's economic crisis, which required retrenchment in public spending, but it also reflected the change of mood after the Lebanese War and the general decline of support for the welfare state.[36]

A series of successive steps was taken to reduce the scope and level of benefits; for example, in 1984 the allowances for the first two children became taxable in families with up to three children where the marginal tax paid by the main breadwinner was 50 percent. In July 1985 this measure was extended to the allowance for the third child in families of up to three children. At the same time, the allowance for the first child in families with up to three children was discontinued.[37]

Although it adopted these measures, the government did not want it to appear that it was neglecting the needs of low-income population groups so it continued the allowance for the first child to these groups on a selective basis. For example, working families in which the earnings of the main breadwinner did not exceed 80 percent of the average wage (90 percent from 1988) continued to receive the allowance through their employers. Other low-income families, including recipients of income support benefits and other national insurance benefits, were entitled to receive the allowance directly from the NII. In practice, however, the actual take-up of the allowance for the first child by the low-wage earner families remained very low; almost half of the eligible families, about 50,000, did not receive the allowance.[38] The limits of selectivity and the use of income testing were self-evident in this case.[39]

All these measures reflected a substantial change in the approach toward the children's allowances program as well as the social security system as a whole. Mainly, it marked a significant departure from the principle of universality, which was the basis of the 1975 reform, and a return to selectivity. In addition to the low rate of take-up, it also had an adverse effect on the well-being of other small families that lost their right both to children's allowances and to the tax benefits for their children.

Despite these restrictive measures, some steps were taken during the 1980s to improve the benefits of the veterans' family allowances scheme. As of April 1983, the allowances paid for the fourth and each consecutive child were increased by 1 credit point, and in July 1984, one-half credit point was added for the third child in families with four children or more. The purpose of these steps was to restore the value of the allowances paid to large families, which were considerably eroded by the prevalence of double-digit inflation. Another consideration was the demand of a minor but important partner in the governing Likud coalition, the Tami Party, representing mostly the Eidot Hamizrach of North African origin. Tami insisted on introducing these changes, and the Government, somewhat reluctantly, accepted the Tami demands.

A more serious threat to the entire children's allowances program appeared in 1987 in the context of the government's policy to reduce the direct tax rates. A committee of experts, headed by an economist, E. Sheshinsky, was appointed in June 1987 to reform the income tax system for individuals. The Sheshinsky committee seriously considered abolishing the entire children's allowances program and replacing it with a system of income tax credits, while retaining the payment of direct allowances only to families outside the labor market. The deliberations of the committee were widely reported in the media, which aroused very strong opposition and as a result, the committee abandoned the idea.[40] At the same time, the Sheshinsky committee was very critical of the government's policy regarding the payment of children's allowances to small families. It stated clearly that the cancellation of the allowance for the first child and taxation of the allowances for the second and third child were grossly unfair and had a negative effect on the horizontal equality among families with similar levels of income but with different numbers of persons in them. The committee's recommendation to reinstate the allowance for the first child and revoke taxation of the allowances for the additional two children was, however, rejected by the government.

The Children's Allowances Program in the Late 1980s

The children's allowances program in operation toward the end of the 1980s provided NII benefits for every child in Israel younger than eighteen and consisted of two main schemes: the universal children's allowances and the veterans' family allowances, with both schemes fully integrated in the direct tax system. The cash benefits paid by them to families with children were at the same time tax credits built on a credit point system. Linked to the consumer price index and raised four times a year since 1981, the value of a credit point in 1987 prices was New Israel Shekel (NIS) 28.7 and was equal to 3.2 percent of the average wage.[41]

In 1986 a total of NIS 832 million were paid in children's allowances (including about 631 million in universal allowances and 201 million for veterans' family allowances). This outlay constituted about 2 percent of the GNP and 23 percent of all benefit payments made by the NII. The following table shows the scope of payments of children's allowances in the years 1970 to 1986, in 1985 constant prices. The data in Table 8.1 show that until 1982, there was a continuous upward trend in the scope of children's allowances payments. The great jump in payments in 1975 does not, however, reflect an entirely real increase in benefits because a considerable part represents substitution of direct children's allowances for the personal tax deduction for children, which was abolished following the 1975 reform of direct taxes and children,s allowances.

From 1975 until 1986 the children's allowances payments as a proportion of the GNP had remained more or less stable, at around 2 percent. The proportion taken by the children's allowances payments of all NII payments was at its highest in 1975—almost 34 percent; it fell to its lowest at 22 percent in 1984 and rose again to almost 23 percent in 1986.

The data in Table 8.2 show the development of the value of the children's allowances since the program was reformed in 1975. The aim of the reform was to raise the credit point to the level of 5 percent of the average wage, but in 1975 the annual average value of a credit point was only 4.4 percent. Since then the value of the credit point, both in real terms and relative to the average wage, eroded steadily and reached its low point of 2.2 percent in 1984. From 1975 to 1984 its purchasing power fell by about 30 percent, and its value in relationship to the average wage fell by 50 percent.

These increases in the absolute and relative values of the credit point in 1985 and 1986 naturally benefited only those families that were not affected by the abolition of allowances for the first child and the taxation of allowances for the second and third child. The situation became especially difficult for families with three children who did not receive an allowance for the first child. The children's allowances for these families fell from a level of nearly 18 percent of the average wage in 1975 to only 10 percent in

TABLE 8.1   Range of Children's Allowances Payments, 1970–1986

Year	Payments of Children's Allowances (NIS Million—1985 Prices)			Proportion of Children's Allowances as Percentage of		Annual Change (Real Terms) of Children's Allowances in %
	Children's Allowances	Veterans' Allowances	Total	Total NII Payments	Gross National Product	
1970	135.7	8.4	144.1	23.2	0.9	--
1975	404.4	75.8	480.2	33.6	2.1	a
1980	427.1	75.0	502.1	27.0	1.8	4.5
1981	427.4	81.7	556.1	25.8	1.8	10.8
1982	465.6	78.6	544.2	23.2	1.7	-2.1
1983	412.5	106.8	519.2	23.3	1.7	-4.6
1984	396.7	103.5	500.2	21.7	1.5	-3.7
1985	429.0	131.7	560.7	23.1	1.9	12.1
1986	479.4	154.4	634.4	23.2	2.0	13.1

[a]The changeover in 1975 from tax deductions for children to direct payments of children's allowances makes the rate of change in this year meaningless.

Source: Esther Sharon, *The Children's Allowances System in Israel: 1959–1987* (Jerusalem: National Insurance Institute, Bureau of Research and Planning, 1987), p. 17 (Hebrew).

TABLE 8.2 Average Value of Children's Allowances (Including Veterans' Family Allowances), 1975–1986

Year	One Child[a]		Two Children		Four Children		Five Children	
	1985 Prices (NIS)	As % of Average Wage	1985 Prices (NIS)	As % of Average Wage	1985 Prices (NIS)	As % of Average Wage	1985 Prices (NIS)	As % of Average Wage
1975	28.1	4.4	56.2	8.8	175.5	27.4	238.7	37.3
1980	21.9	2.8	43.7	5.6	136.6	17.7	185.7	24.0
1981	23.8	2.8	47.6	5.6	148.9	17.6	202.6	23.9
1982	22.9	2.6	45.7	5.3	142.3	16.5	194.3	22.4
1983	20.3	2.4	40.5	4.8	150.9	18.0	218.6	26.1
1984	19.5	2.2	39.1	4.4	151.1	16.9	215.0	24.2
1985	24.7	3.1	28.0	3.6	191.6	24.7	271.2	35.1
1986	28.3	3.2	28.3	3.2	219.7	25.3	311.9	35.8

[a]Entitlement to children's allowances is built on a credit point system; the number of credit points increases with an additional child in the family.

Source: National Insurance Institute, Bureau of Research and Planning, *Annual Survey 1986* (Jerusalem, 1987), p. 22 (Hebrew).

1986. On the other hand, for families with four children, there was a sharp drop in the allowances from 1980 to 1984, but from 1985 onward the allowances rose to 25 percent of the average wage, which is close to what they were in 1975.

Of the 640,000 families with children in Israel in 1987, 513,000 of them, or 80 percent, received children's allowances. This was a direct result of the departure from the principle of universality and the cancellation of the allowance for the first child. Of the 520,000 families with one to three children, only 160,000, or 30 percent, actually received an allowance for the first child. Children's allowances were paid for about 1,250,000 children of whom the majority—nearly 500,000—were the second child. The veterans' family allowances were paid for about 300,000 children; the majority of them—nearly 200,000—were the third child in the family. (See Tables 8.3 and 8.4.)

The Program in a Comparative Perspective

The children's allowances program in Israel has many similarities to children's allowances in other countries. The allowances have essentially evolved into a legal entitlement that is not income conditioned and is paid to all families with children. In most countries the benefits vary only with the number and age of children in the family, but part of the benefit in Israel is also contingent on the family's veteran status. As in other countries, the program is viewed as a policy strategy whereby society as a whole

TABLE 8.3   Families Receiving Children's Allowances and Veterans' Family Allowances, According to Family Size (May 1987)

| | Number of Children in Family | | | | | | |
	1	2	3	4	5	6	Total
Families receiving children's allowances	36,194	204,460	149,844	62,854	26,796	33,134	513,282
Also receiving veterans' allowances	- - - -	- - - -	124,739	46,307	15,191	13,266	199,503

Source: Esther Sharon, The Children's Allowances System in Israel: 1959–1987 (Jerusalem: National Insurance Institute, Bureau of Research and Planning, 1987), p. 25 (Hebrew).

TABLE 8.4 Number of Children for Whom Children's Allowances and Veterans' Family Allowances Were Paid, by Order of Child in Family (May 1987)

Type of Allowances	First Child	Second Child	Third Child	Fourth Child	Fifth Child	Sixth Child	Total
Children's allowances	219,765	477,088	272,628	122,784	59,930	69,216	1,221,441
Veterans' family allowances	- - - -	- - - -	199,503	74,764	28,457	26,293	329,017

Source: Esther Sharon, *The Children's Allowances System in Israel: 1959–1987* (Jerusalem: National Insurance Institute, Bureau of Research and Planning, 1987), p. 25 (Hebrew).

shares in the cost of rearing children. Despite this goal, children's allowances in Israel and in other countries as well do not cover the full financial costs of bringing up a child. At best, they provide a small supplement to family income, which serves as partial compensation for the real economic burden of rearing children. The relative value of this partial compensation is usually worth more to families with many children or with low incomes.[42]

What is the value of this income supplement and how do families with children in Israel fare in comparison with similar families in other countries? In other words, to what extent did the children's allowances program in Israel succeed in sharing the cost of child rearing in families? The data in Table 8.5 show that in 1979 the allowance for a first child ranged in value from a low of 1.9 percent of the net average production worker's wage (APWW) in Australia to a high of 13.4 percent in France, where the child must be younger than three and family income cannot be too high. In Israel the allowance for the first child was somewhere in the middle—higher in value than in the Federal Republic of Germany (FRG), Canada, and Australia. However, since the cancellation of the allowance for the first child in the mid-1980s and the restriction of the allowance to low-income families only, the relative position of Israel with regard to the first child has considerably deteriorated.

For a family with four children, the benefit value in relation to the APWW ranges from a low of 8.2 percent in Canada to a high of 45.4 percent in France. The value of benefits to these families in Israel fell below those in France and in the FRG, but was higher in value than in the other countries, including Sweden. The relatively high position of Israel in this case reflects the priority Israeli social policy has given throughout the years to large Jewish families in the population. Note that the level of cash benefits is the

TABLE 8.5   Intercountry Comparison of Children's Allowances as a Percentage of Net Average Wage,[a] 1979

Country	Number of Children in Family		
	1	2	3
Sweden	6.2	12.4	24.9
FRG	3.1	9.3	34.0
France[b]	13.4	20.8	45.4
Canada	2.1	4.1	8.2
Australia	1.9	4.6	11.1
U.K.	5.6	11.2	22.4
Israel	4.3	8.6	28.1

[a]Net Average Wage : the net average production worker's wage (APWW).
[b]The benefit for one child is an income-tested benefit limited to families with one child younger than three years or more children younger than a specified age.

Source: Alfred J. Kahn and Sheila B. Kamerman, *Income Transfers for Families with Children: An Eight-Country Study* (Philadelphia: Temple University Press, 1983), p. 202. © 1983 Temple University; reprinted by permission of Temple University Press.

only basis for comparison in this and the subsequent tables; their real value is, of course, influenced by the availability of other in-kind benefits, such as medical care, food, transportation and housing vouchers, and so on.

The data in Table 8.6 show that the value of the children's allowances in a two-parent family with one earner at the APWW level is worth less than 10 percent of total family income in all countries except France. This most common type of family did better in Israel than in Canada and Australia, but not as well as in the European countries. Again, with the cancellation and taxation of the children's allowances for these families in the mid-1980s there was a further drop in the value of the cash benefits paid to them. Two-parent, one-earner families *with four children* fared much better in Israel. It is this larger family to whom children's allowances as a deliberate social policy strategy are particularly addressed. The value of children's benefits paid to these families in Israel compared well with the more advanced welfare states in Europe such as France and the FRG and was higher than in Sweden and the U.K.

It is evident that the level of cash benefits for children's support varies greatly in the countries included in the comparison. It is also clear that the countries vary in their generosity toward different types of families, a pattern that reflects the policy priorities of each country. In comparison with the European countries, Israeli children's allowances are much less generous toward small families, which is a trend that has become even

TABLE 8.6   Children's Allowances as a Percentage of Family Income, 1979

| | Two-Parent Family and One Earner at APWW with | | | |
| | Two Children | | Four Children | |
Country	FI[a] as % of APWW	CI[b] as % of FI	FI as % of APWW	CI as % of FI
Sweden	133.1	9.4	164.1	15.0
FRG	119.7	7.7	148.0	22.9
France	136.9	15.2	172.6	26.3
Canada	114.2	3.6	123.5	6.7
Australia	107.2	4.9	113.7	9.8
U.K.	120.4	9.3	131.6	17.0
Israel	112.9	7.6	132.4	21.2

[a]FI: family income; includes, in addition to earnings, all types of cash benefits and tax credits.
[b]CI: children's allowances.

Source: Alfred J. Kahn and Sheila B. Kamerman, *Income Transfers for Families with Children: An Eight-Country Study* (Philadelphia: Temple University Press, 1983), p. 16. © 1983 Temple University; reprinted by permission of Temple University Press.

more obvious in the last decade. The Israeli program, however, compares well in its generosity as far as most large families are concerned, and this has been a characteristic feature of the program from its beginning.

Summary

The children's allowances program has undergone many changes since its inception in 1959, and throughout the years it has been under continuous review and reform. Its pattern of evolution reflects the difficulty of reaching a consensus about the role of the program and a long-term social policy strategy for the support of families with children. In view of the social, economic, and political changes affecting Israeli society in recent years and the persistence of deep ethnic, religious, and social class cleavages, the prospect of reaching such a consensus seems remote. The established pattern of incremental change will apparently continue in the years ahead.

In spite of the inherent instability, the program in its various forms has attained over the years a number of significant social achievements. First, the program achieved universality of coverage. The program began in 1959 with benefits for only large families with four and more children, but in 1975 the program became universal and expanded to cover all children in Israel without exception. The universalization of the program suffered some setbacks in the mid-1980s, but there are pressures, including the report of the Sheshinsky committee, to reverse this trend.

Second, the program has achieved, at least partly, some of its egalitarian objectives by narrowing the income inequality between large and small families and has reduced the extent of poverty among families with children. In 1986, the allowances supplemented the income of families with four chidren at the rate of 25.2 percent of the average wage and families with five children at the rate of 35.8 percent, in constant 1985 prices. This constituted a very significant increase in the disposable incomes of these families, and it also contributed to the country's integration objectives as most of these families are from the Eidot Hamizrach.

The data in Table 8.7 show the extent to which the payment of children's allowances succeeded in reducing the incidence of poverty among families with children until the allowances lost effectiveness in the early 1980s. As shown earlier, the decline in the effectiveness of the children's allowances was mostly the result of the erosion of the value of the credit points on which the program operates. In addition, the growth of unemployment in those years and the increase in wage differentials also played an important part in this process. As far as large families are concerned, however, the value of children's allowances stopped decreasing in the mid-1980s.

Third, the performance of the Israeli children's allowances program fared comparatively well with that of other countries, including advanced welfare states such as Sweden and France. It would, however, be presumptuous to draw any definite conclusions from these limited comparisons because of the great differences in the social, political, economic, and demographic structure of these countries. In any event, the program's benefits to large families are well within the parameters of an international standard.

TABLE 8.7   The Decrease in the Incidence of Poverty Among Working Jewish Families with Children, 1979–1984, as a Percentage (after Taxes and Children's Allowances Payments)

	1979	1981	1982	1983	1984
Families with 1–3 children	26.7	18.4	15.0	7.8	7.6
With 4 or more children	47.1	23.0	28.4	23.6	24.0

Source: National Insurance Institute, Bureau of Research and Planning, *Annual Survey 1984* (Jerusalem, 1985), p. 40.

A controversial and disturbing aspect of the program remains, however, in its effective exclusion of a large segment of the Arab population in the State of Israel from receiving a substantial part of the allowances paid to large families. Although in principle the exclusion is nominally based not on ethnic grounds but on service in the armed forces, similar to services to veterans in the U.S., in practice it is only the Israeli Arabs who do not serve in the IDF and are therefore not entitled to benefits conditioned on such service. The rationale usually given for this policy is that the long period of active reserve service in the IDF, up to age fifty-five, entails a very significant loss of earnings, and therefore the partial compensation provided to veterans' families is economically justified. This explanation has some merit, but it is doubtful whether it is sufficient to legitimate the controversial practice. The debate on this issue will continue, but within the context of the historical Arab-Israeli conflict there seems to be insufficient popular support in Israel to expect a change in this policy.

The children's allowances program in Israel has become a major part of the structure of the country's social security system, and it has also become deeply integrated into the social and political structure. Israeli society as a whole has been significantly transformed by it, which makes it unlikely that the program's opponents in and out of the government will succeed in reducing it significantly. The debate about the program will, however, remain high on the public agenda.

Notes

1. Sheila B. Kamerman and Alfred J. Kahn, *Child Care, Family Benefits, and Working Parents: A Study in Comparative Policy* (New York: Columbia University Press, 1981), pp. 34–35; Jonathan Bradshaw and David Piachaud, *Child Support in the European Community* (London: Bedford Square Press, 1980), p. 13.

2. Sir William Beveridge, *Social Insurance and Allied Services* (Beveridge Report) (London: HMSO, Cmd. 6404, November 1942), p. 154.

3. T.H. Marshall, *Social Policy* (London: Hutchinson University Library, 1965), p. 66.

4. Ibid., p. 67. See also Bradshaw and Piachaud, op. cit.; Sheila B. Kamerman and Alfred J. Kahn (eds.), *Family Policy: Government and Families in Fourteen Countries* (New York: Columbia University Press, 1978); Sheila B. Kamerman and Alfred J. Kahn, *Child Care, Family Benefits, and Working Parents*, op. cit.

5. Fanny Ginor, *Socio-Economic Disparities in Israel* (Tel Aviv: David Horowitz Institute for Research on Developing Countries and Transaction Books, Rutgers University, 1979), p. 104.

6. See Zvi Zussman, *Wage Differentials and Equality Within the Histadrut* (Tel Aviv: Massada, 1974) (Hebrew). This study shows the significant wage differentials that existed during the Yishuv period in spite of the official egalitarian ideology.

7. Palestine, *Report of the Wages Committee*, No. 9 of 1943 (Jerusalem: Government Printer, 1943), pp. 35–37.

8. *Encyclopedia Hebraica*, Vol. 15 (Jerusalem: Encyclopedia Publishing Company, 1962), p. 40 (Hebrew).

9. National Insurance Institute, *Survey of Family Allowances in Israel, 1962*, Memorandum prepared by A. Nitzan, January 1963. It should be noted that the average concealed the actual spread of the allowances which ranged from IL 2 in agriculture to IL 15 in the merchant navy.

10. I. Kanevsky, "A Social Insurance Plan for the State of Israel," *Khikrei Avodah* (Labor Studies) 2:1–2 (June 1948) (Hebrew).

11. *A Social Insurance Plan For Israel*, Report of the Interministerial Committee for Social Insurance Planning (Ministry of Labor and Social Insurance, 1950), p. 92 (Hebrew).

12. *Divrei Haknesset* (Parliamentary Records), Vol. 21, November 14, 1956, p. 261 (Hebrew).

13. National Insurance Institute, Memorandum of G. Lotan to the Minister of Labor, 30 December 1957 (Hebrew).

14. See, for example, letters of M. Ben-Porat, head of the Or-Yehuda Local Council, to Cabinet Ministers (24 December 1958) and to local Histadrut Worker Councils and other public figures (23 January 1959) in which he attacked the Histadrut position and demanded its abandonment (in the files of the National Insurance Institute) (Hebrew).

15. Meir Avizohar, *Money for All: The Development of Social Security in Israel* (Tel Aviv: Yariv and Hadar, 1978), pp. 68–71 (Hebrew).

16. Government Press Office, *Excerpts from the Report of the Wadi Salib Inquiry Committee Presented to the Government on 17 August 1959* (Jerusalem: August 1959) (Hebrew).

17. *Reshumot* (Official Gazette), Law Proposals, No. 401, July 13, 1959 (Hebrew).

18. *Divrei Haknesset* (Parliamentary Records), Vol. 27, July 21, 1959, p. 2639 (Hebrew).

19. Ibid., 22 July 1959, p. 2668. See also Eleanor Rathbone, *Family Allowances* (London: Allen & Unwin, 1949), Chapter 6, "The Case of the Opposition."

20. Giora Lotan, *National Insurance in Israel* (Jerusalem: National Insurance Institute, 1969), pp. 61–64.

21. Objections of the Manufacturers' Association to the Report of G. Lotan on Family Allowances, 18 June 1964 (in the files of the National Insurance Institute) (Hebrew).

22. In 1964 these two Labor parties agreed to a "Ma'arakh," that is, to align themselves on the basis of an agreed political platform for the Knesset elections in 1965.

23. *Divrei Haknesset* (Parliamentary Records), Vol. 42, March 23, 1965, p. 1625 (Hebrew).

24. On the Histadrut's neglect of the lower-paid workers in its wage policy, see Abraham Doron, "The Histadrut: Social Policy and Equality," *Jerusalem Quarterly* 47 (Summer 1988), pp. 135–138; Michael Shalev, *Labor and the Political Economy of Israel* (London: Oxford University Press, 1992).

25. *Haaretz*, 7 June 1966 (Hebrew).

26. See Menahem Hofnung, "Public Protest and the Public Budgeting Process: The Influence of the Black Panthers on Allocations for Social Welfare," (M.A. thesis, Hebrew University, November 1982) (Hebrew)

27. Esther Sharon, *The Children's Allowances System in Israel: 1959–1987*, Study No. 38 (Jerusalem: National Insurance Institute, 1987), p. 7 (Hebrew).

28. Meir Avizohar, op. cit., pp. 79–80.

29. Esther Sharon, op. cit., p. 7.

30. Rafael Roter, "Reform of Children Allowances in Israel," *Bitachon Sotziali* (Social Security), Nos. 4–5 (July 1973) (Hebrew).

31. See, for example, Eveline M. Burns (ed.), *Children's Allowances and the Economic Welfare of Children*, Report of a Conference (New York: Citizens' Committee for Children of New York, Inc., 1968); Vera Shlakman, *Children's Allowances* (New York: Citizens' Committee for Children of New York, Inc., n.d.); Bradshaw and Piachaud, op. cit., pp. 40 and 94.

32. *Recommendations for Changes in Direct Taxation*, Report of the Committee on Tax Reform (Jerusalem: Summer 1975) (Hebrew).

33. The rapid acceptance of the Ben-Shahar committee's recommendations was due to the government's a priori commitment to implement the committee's proposals, even though it was reluctant to do so. This action was unprecedented in Israel and never recurred. Later, inflation, the Lebanese War, and the lack of Treasury support brought about the gradual erosion of this program.

34. Esther Sharon, op. cit., pp. 10–11.

35. Rafael Roter and Nira Shamai, "The Reform of Taxation and Transfer Payments in Israel, July 1975," *Bitachon Sotziali* (Social Security), Nos. 12–13 (March 1977) (Hebrew).

36. Actually, by late 1970, the first Likud government Treasury minister, Simha Ehrlich, had already declared his intention to eliminate all children's allowance payments. See Meir Avizohar, op. cit., p. 85.

37. Esther Sharon, op. cit., pp. 11–13.

38. Ibid., p. 31.

39. See, for example, Charles Hoffman, "Tami Will Present Its Own Economic Scheme to Knesset," *Jerusalem Post*, 27 December 1983.

40. See, for example, Dov Genihovski, "Are Children a Joy?" *Yediyot Aharonot*, 10 November 1987 (Hebrew); "Sheshinsky—Signs of Opposition," *Hadashot*, 10 November 1987 (Hebrew). The Sheshinsky Report is the *Report of the Experts Committee on the Income Tax Reform for Individuals*, submitted to the minister of the Treasury (Jerusalem, February 1988), p. 44 (Hebrew).

41. L. Achdut and G. Yaniv (eds.), *Annual Survey 1987* (Jerusalem: National Insurance Institute, Bureau of Research and Planning, September 1988), p. 14 (Hebrew).

42. See Alfred J. Kahn and Sheila B. Kamerman, *Income Transfers for Families with Children: An Eight-Country Study* (Philadelphia: Temple University Press, 1983).

9

The Struggle for Unemployment Insurance

As in many other countries, unemployment insurance was not among the first forms of income protection to be included in Israel's social security system. In Germany, the cradle of modern social insurance, it took almost half a century from the inception of its social insurance program in the 1880s to the establishment of the first unemployment scheme in 1927.[1] In Israel it took two decades from the introduction of national insurance in 1953 until the first unemployment insurance program came into effect in 1973. The long delay in adopting social security measures to resolve the problems of income protection for the unemployed stemmed from the fact that unemployment insurance has been the most politically controversial and socially explosive issue in the evolution of modern social policy.[2]

The strong objections to unemployment insurance were deeply rooted in the economic and political thought of contemporary capitalist industrial society. For more than a century, mainstream classical and neoclassical economic theory was fundamentally opposed to unemployment insurance on the grounds that any widespread lack of work opportunities in modern industrial societies was mainly the result of excessively high wages; hence, lower wages were considered to be the only effective remedy for unemployment.[3] In this view, government intervention into the labor market through unemployment insurance would not only fail to solve the problem, it would only aggravate conditions leading to unemployment.[4]

Both conservative and liberal politicians were strongly influenced by this line of economic thought. A parallel, conventional view was that unemployment was mainly due to the weakness of individual character, of personal failures, and not the impersonal outcome of poorly adjusted markets. Because the fault was in the unemployed themselves and not in the society as a whole, the responsibility for unemployment was viewed as a private and not a public matter. Although the left-wing parties opposed these views, they were not in favor of supporting unemployment insurance. Instead, they continued to cling to the belief that some form of work provision to the unemployed was morally and economically superior. The traditional demands of the international labor movement were mostly formulated in terms of "the right to work," that is, the maintenance of employment status under nonpunitive conditions. Not until 1910, at the Congress of the Second Internationale in Copenhagen, was a resolution adopted in favor of "general obligatory (unemployment) insurance, the administration of which should be left to the workers' organizations and the costs of which should be borne by the holders of the means of production."[5]

In Sweden, for example, the Social Democratic Party for many years favored an attack on unemployment through government relief work. Even after the party's election victory in 1932, unemployment insurance was given a priority second only to a public works program.[6] The British Labour Party in its formative years also opposed unemployment insurance calling it "a shallow and fake remedy"—in contrast to a truly curative socialist policy—and party members pressed their proposals for "right to work" legislation. In and out of Parliament, the British left—including the Fabians—played no direct part in this fundamental extension of modern social policy.[7]

In general, governments rejected cash support in favor of the provision of relief work to deal with the economic plight of the unemployed. This policy had the support of neoclassical economic theory, especially when it paid below-market wages and was therefore efficient in its low cost; according to theory, the policy was also beneficial if it helped to reduce general wage levels. Relief work programs could also rely on popular support, including the working classes themselves: Relief work programs were at least preferable to Poor Law relief because of their lesser stigma. Relief work was also considered superior in a moral sense because it did not reduce the incentive to work and did not contribute to the weakening of the character of the poor.

In the context of these deeply rooted attitudes, the adoption of unemployment insurance was a prolonged and laborious process. The transformation of the principle into practice in Israel and most other countries was essentially a product of the work of liberal reformers within the higher echelons of the civil service; these technipols acted on the fringe of the political arena. It was these civil servants who became the agents of change rather than the politicians who were more bound to their traditional ideas and attitudes.

The actual programs were developed as a reaction against the recurrent economic crises and rising levels of unemployment, a process that had begun in the 1920s and the 1930s but gained momentum during the post-World War II period. With the following decades of practically full employment lasting until the mid-1970s, unemployment insurance schemes became increasingly recognized not only as poverty relief measures, as in the past, but also as complements to economic policy and as a vital technique for managing the economy.

The growing distinction in the post-war period between unemployment insurance as an antipoverty measure and as a tool of economic and labor market management smoothed the transition of unemployment insurance into an integral part of the social security systems of all advanced industrialized countries. An additional factor that facilitated this transition was the change in economic thinking, supported by Keynesian theory, that removed the conventional economic opposition to unemployment insurance, at least for a limited time. With the advent of the economic crisis in the 1970s and 1980s, which again brought with it very high levels of unemployment, most countries had comprehensive unemployment insurance schemes in operation to deal with the recurring problem of joblessness. The political interest in unemployment insurance, however, has not diminished with the times; unemployment insurance continues to be an explosive issue in in the social and political arena in most contemporary welfare states.

The struggle to introduce unemployment insurance in Israel can best be understood against the background of the evolution of modern social policy in this field in other countries. The protracted debates in Israel about unemployment insurance, in spite of the particular local circumstances, mainly reflected the same social and political controversies on this issue as in most other contemporary capitalist societies; it is from this perspective that the development of unemployment insurance in Israel is analyzed.

The First Two Decades: 1948–1967

Since the beginning of Zionist settlement, unemployment was one of the most serious problems that the Yishuv—the Jewish community in Palestine—and the labor movement within it had to cope with. Toward the end of the Mandate regime it became obvious that with the growth of the Yishuv the government would probably have to accept some measure of responsibility for the unemployed and that this should take place within the framework of a broader social insurance program. The Histadrut had voiced this view since the mid-1940s and repeatedly demanded that the

Mandate government introduce a compulsory social insurance program that included unemployment insurance. At the end of 1945 Zvi Berinson, the legal adviser of the Histadrut (later judge of the Israeli Supreme Court), submitted a memorandum to the government in which he argued for a social insurance program:

> It would be impossible for a social insurance program not to deal with the problems of want resulting from unemployment. Almost everyone is aware of the fact that idleness and want deriving from worklessness cannot be explained by the personal failings of the affected people as they are a direct result of the faulty organization of society. Unemployment is a social disease and it has to be solved by society as a whole. Individual or collective action by those affected themselves or by the working class alone is not sufficient. Freedom from want resulting from unemployment cannot be achieved as long as there is no concerted attack against this form of want taken by the combined forces of the workers and employers, and is supported energetically and effectively by the government. [8]

In 1948, when Israel gained independence, there was considerable support for unemployment insurance within the existing Jewish community that found its expression in a variety of ways. The labor movement was in principle committed to establishing unemployment insurance and in the first social insurance plan prepared by Kanev in 1948, unemployment insurance played a prominent role.[9] The first elected government promised in 1949 "to introduce in progressive stages a system of social insurance and mutual aid institutions against unemployment."[10] The interministerial committee headed by Kanev that prepared the 1950 social insurance plan also recommended the introduction of unemployment insurance in the first stages of implementation.[11] It was at this point, however, that the first cracks in the front began to appear.

The consensus among the majority of the Kanev committee members was to postpone the unemployment insurance scheme until some later date or to eliminate it entirely. The chief exponents of this view were the representatives of the Treasury and the Ministry of Labor who argued that the main task of the government in the years ahead was the absorption of the new immigrants in work and not to "provide for those at work in the event they become unemployed."[12] Surprisingly, the Ministry of Commerce and Industry took an entirely different position. They were prepared to support unemployment insurance, which in their view would assure income security to the entire working population, on the condition that the practice of providing severance payments was abolished. H.

Grunebaum, director general of the ministry, outlined this view in a 1950 memorandum submitted to the committee:

> The lack of planned and systematic unemployment insurance is a destructive factor having effects in all directions. The weakest worker, i.e., the unskilled worker and the worker who holds no steady job and has no possibility to save, suffers from it particularly.
>
> ... The organized workers have succeeded in assuring for themselves during periods of unemployment, financial help in the form of severance payments, paid for 12 working days (4 percent of the yearly wages) or one month's salary for each year of employment. These payments constitute a one-sided burden on the employers to benefit the most well-off workers. To our knowledge there is no parallel for this in any other country in the world. ...
>
> The small amount of security given to workers through severance payments is in inverse proportion to the burden it puts on industry.
>
> ... On the basis of all these considerations I ask the Committee to reconsider its decision ... to postpone unemployment insurance. We see as one of the most pressing tasks of the Committee the introduction in the near future of regular unemployment insurance and bringing to an end of the unjust system of severance payments.[13]

It was not likely that these proposals could have been accepted because they were a direct attack on the Histadrut, which considered severance payments as one of its most important achievements. When the matter was brought to the attention of Golda Meir, the minister of Labor and Social Insurance, it was decided not to mention proposals to abolish severance payments in the committee's report.[14]

In this atmosphere the recommendation to introduce unemployment insurance that was included in the report of the Kanev committee had very little meaning other than as a gesture to make the social insurance plan look comprehensive. The implicit consensus within the committee was that it would be better for the government to provide relief work for the unemployed than to give them assistance in cash. In fact, the decision adopted was to postpone the establishment of unemployment insurance to some indefinite point in the future.

As a result of the position taken by the Kanev committee, unemployment insurance was not even considered when the drafts of the first national insurance bills were prepared in the early 1950s. The problem, however, did not disappear from the agenda. In 1951, Giora Lotan analyzed in the *Monthly Review of Labor* the arguments for and against introducing unemployment insurance, and he concluded that "all considerations bring us to the conclusion that unemployment insurance should be included in our social insurance program."[15] In principle, the labor movement was still fully committed to establishing unemployment insurance, but within the government another position had been evolving, which was clearly stated in June 1953 by Meir in the Knesset. She said: "We are not preparing an unemployment insurance law and for the while we have no intention to prepare such a proposal. We see in the creation of work for the unemployed a much better and more effective measure to deal with the problem of worklessness than unemployment insurance."[16] From 1953 and until after the 1967 War, this was the policy preferred by the government and it received throughout this period the full support of the ruling Labor parties.

The reluctance of the Labor parties to change their attitudes toward unemployment insurance was influenced by both ideological and practical considerations. Manual labor always had an important place in the Socialist-Zionist hierarchy of values, and from those values came the belief that provision of such labor would contribute to the integration of the new immigrants into the social as well as the economic life of Israel. Then, too, the large number of unemployed in the early 1950s (which reached nearly 10 percent of the labor force) and the structural nature of unemployment made it very difficult and costly to introduce unemployment insurance.

After 1954 unemployment steadily decreased. Between 1960 and the end of 1965 the country's economy was in a state of almost full employment. On the one hand, only 3.6 percent of the civilian labor force was unemployed in 1965, and the average number of persons who were registered as unemployed in the official labor exchanges was 3,200. However, full employment, as reflected in both these averages, concealed the concentration of heavy pockets of unemployment among the new immigrant groups. The unskilled workers, who came mainly from these groups, constituted about 60 percent of all unemployed. In the new development towns, in which the new immigrants constituted more than 90 percent of the total population, the extent of the unemployed civilian labor force was higher than 10 percent, or three to four times higher than the national average. Moreover, the number of persons employed in relief work in these towns was very high. Thus, during the period from 1954 to 1965, unemployment became predominantly, if not entirely, a problem of the new immigrant population, particularly in the development towns.[17]

The improved employment situation, which lasted until 1965, did not remove either the need or the pressures for unemployment insurance. The radical left-wing groups, such as the communists and some members of Mapam, repeatedly introduced private bills in the Knesset on unemployment insurance. William Fitch, a U.S. expert who served in 1956 as an official adviser on social insurance to the NII, prepared a report in which he recommended the introduction of unemployment insurance.[18]

At the same time, the position of the Histadrut and the ruling Labor parties opposing any form of unemployment insurance was reinforced by the growing difficulties of absorbing immigrants from Moslem countries. It was feared that unemployment insurance payments, which were identified with the "dole," would only aggravate the presumed lack of motivation to work among the new immigrant groups. Though no study has ever substantiated this belief, it was a widely held assumption.

These views were expressed frankly in the Knesset by the various Labor ministers in the late 1950s and early 1960s. In January 1958, for instance, Labor Minister M. Namir (a former secretary general of the Histadrut) stated:

> The Histadrut is not at present supporting unemployment insurance by means of financial assistance. . . . The overwhelming majority of the unemployed are new immigrants. The greatest revolution in our society and . . . in . . . every new immigrant, is the problem of bringing them into the path of work and the habits of manual labor. What then is the logic and educational reason for us, to take new immigrants, who have never worked in their lives, and who have to pass here the first class of the school of work, and tempt them by handing out money by financial assistance, after which they would have to consider whether it is worthwhile for them to go to work or whether it is worthwhile to content themselves with a lower income and a life of idleness.[19]

Two years later, in April 1960, Labor Minister G. Yosephtal reaffirmed the government's position:

> I am certain that in a state such as ours there is no better method than the existing one of ensuring work for the unemployed. We do not think that money payment without exchange is the right method. . . . Paying assistance in cash could turn the unemployed into everlasting seekers of assistance and not into workers. I do not assume that anybody thinks that it is possible to introduce two insurance systems, one for the settled population and another one for the new immigrants. The fact is that among those looking for relief work or employed in relief works, there are only perhaps 2 percent of oldtimers.[20]

Y. Allon, minister of Labor at the end of 1965, held the same views as those formulated by his predecessors. In his opinion, "there was no point in paying benefits for not working." However, he entertained the idea of introducing legislation that would establish a statutory right for relief work. Though this was discussed for a long time within the Ministry of

Labor and other government circles, no action was taken upon it.[21] In the context of these prevailing attitudes, the provision of relief work became an integral part of government policy to deal with the problem of the unemployed. Since 1955 these work projects had been substantially expanded and the average number of persons employed in the decade from 1955 to 1965 was about twenty thousand. The projects were financed chiefly by the Treasury, although some local authorities participated in the financing of individual projects carried out in their communities.[22]

Relief work was distributed on the basis of a family means test and the capacity to perform manual labor. The eligible unemployed were entitled to a number of working days per month, ranging from eight days for a single person to twenty-five days for a head of family with eight or more persons. Special relief work was provided for unemployed persons with physical handicaps and for older age groups, chiefly in agriculture and afforestation and similar manual labor. In the large cities, relief work for the handicapped was more diversified and included gardening projects, maintenance of buildings, collection of wastepaper and the like. The only concession to the handicapped, who constituted 75 percent of all relief workers, was a five-hour working day, which resulted in lower pay—the equivalent of one third of the average monthly wage at the time. The wage rates paid to persons on relief work were equivalent to the ordinary rate for unskilled workers in agriculture. In the 1950s the Histadrut, however, agreed to introduce an even lower wage scale for those employed in relief work. These special lower wage rates were canceled by the end of the decade after demands from within the Histadrut itself.[23]

The entire relief work program, though it was part of government policy, was not based on any specific legislation, and the Ministry of Labor, which administered the program, had an enormous degree of discretion in its actual operation. The unemployed had no right to claim relief work, and no clear legal rules were established regarding the conditions under which work should be granted. All particulars of the program were decided by the administrative authority and at the discretion of the Ministry of Labor and its officials and public control and supervision of the program was at a minimum.

The relief work program was, therefore, by its very nature no substitute for unemployment insurance. Relief work was not provided to every unemployed person capable and available for work, nor was it a source of alternative income to the involuntarily unemployed. As a form of social assistance that provided a minimum level of help to the needy unemployed, the relief work program had all of the punitive and deterrent characteristics of similar aid programs. To actually receive relief work, a person had to undergo a family means test; as an additional deterrent, the work included mostly physical labor in places that required lengthy and tiring travel.

Anyone who could obtain other work, even at lower wages, preferred it to relief work.

Moreover, the relief work program did not provide any protection to skilled workers or professionals who were out of work for a short time while changing jobs or in cases of frictional unemployment. The only collective provision available to these groups was severance payments; since the 1930s, employers have been responsible for providing severance pay when an employee is dismissed from a job. The extent of such payments ranged from one week's to one month's wages for each year of work at a particular job. They were originally based on a custom that in 1940 had already been recognized by the courts as binding in principle. Severance payments were gradually incorporated into the collective wage agreements and by 1960 covered most branches of the economy. In 1963 the Dismissal Compensation Law was enacted, which made it compulsory for all employers to pay severance payments at a rate of two weeks' wages for every year of employment for wage earners and one month's salary for each year of employment for salaried employees. The severance payments clearly benefited the better-off groups in the working population, and the relatively liberal rates of severance payments supported these groups through short periods of unemployment.

Although the provision of relief work and severance payments mitigated some of the problems of unemployment, those provisions did not entirely remove the need for unemployment insurance. Despite the government's official opposition to unemployment insurance, the issue was still debated throughout the period from 1954 to 1965. Within the government, the problem was examined several times in attempts to find an acceptable solution. In December 1961, Minister of Labor Allon appointed a committee to study the possibility of introducing unemployment insurance; the committee was headed by O. Messer, director general of the Ministry of Labor. During its two-year period, the committee systematically examined all the arguments for and against unemployment insurance under the specific conditions of Israeli society. In its report of February 1964, the committee did not produce any new ideas but recommended that the right to relief work should be made a statutory right and that in this way the unemployed should be ensured a minimum income.[24] In this recommendation the committee served chiefly as a mouthpiece for the minister of Labor: The effect of implementing this recommendation would have been to provide a statutory basis for the existing system of relief work without bringing about any essential change in its character.

The lack of any significant difference between the proposed recommendations and the existing system was pointed out by Hanna Weinberg, the Bank of Israel's representative on the committee. She dissented from the recommendations approved by the majority and proposed instead to introduce an unemployment insurance scheme: "Relief work could not be a proper solution to the problems of frictional unemployment. In my opinion, those problems need to be solved by the establishment of an unemployment insurance scheme which would provide for every dismissed worker a decent level of living until he would find a new job."[25] These views were not, however, in line with the prevalent official attitude and, as a result, were rejected.

The need for unemployment insurance became more urgent during 1966 and 1967, the period just preceding the Six Day War. The severe economic recession that Israel underwent in this period brought the problem of unemployment inevitably to the fore. The unemployment peak in the winter of 1967 totaled nearly 12.5 percent of the labor force and affected the unprecedented number of 116,000 persons.[26] It was the first time since independence that unemployment affected not only the new immigrant population but also the more established population groups such as young skilled workers and professionals. Although they were relatively small in number, the influence of the unemployed among the established population was greater than that of the much larger groups of unemployed among the new immigrants. The combination of large numbers of unemployed and the increased political strength of particular groups among them eventually forced the government, however reluctantly, to look for new solutions.

After a lengthy period of procrastination the government announced in October 1966 that it authorized the minister of Labor to appoint a committee to study proposals to introduce legislation that would provide an assurance of work and an unemployment insurance law. The committee was to report no later than the beginning of April 1967. It was appointed at the end of December under the chairmanship of Knesset member Moshe Bar'Am (Labor) and included more than twenty members from virtually all political parties and government ministries.[27] To many observers, it appeared that by appointing such a committee the government intended to gain time and postpone a decision rather than deal seriously with the problem.

In the atmosphere of an expanding economic crisis, however, the appointment of the committee was not enough. The left-wing Mapam Party, a junior coalition partner, conditioned its further stay in the government by demanding immediate provision of cash relief payments to the unemployed, as if an unemployment insurance law was already in effect. Reluctantly, the government gave in to these demands and agreed to pay unemployment grants beginning in April 1967. This forced decision to pay cash grants to the unemployed was a turning point in the social policy toward the unemployed that the government had pursued since 1948.[28]

The unemployment grants program began to operate as an expedient in April 1967, but it was far from satisfactory. The established eligibility conditions were excessively restrictive and clearly intended to limit as far as possible the number of the unemployed entitled to the grant. The amounts paid were very low and hardly sufficient even for a minimum level of living. As in the relief work program, payment of the grants was based on the income of all members of the family, and not as a right of the unemployed person. Not surprisingly, the number of eligible persons who actually applied for and received the grant was very small.

The immediate result of introducing the unemployment grant payments was that the committee appointed earlier to consider the adoption of an unemployment insurance law was no longer under pressure to deal with the problem, and it decided, therefore, to postpone its recommendations. The continuing resistance to unemployment insurance of the main Labor parties and the ambivalent position of the government were clearly evident within the Bar'Am committee. Under these circumstances, payment of the grants, however restricted, made it easier for the committee to avoid any clear decision.

In the meantime, the growing tensions on the borders of Israel in April and May of 1967 and in June during the Six Day War and its aftermath entirely changed the economic and employment conditions in the country and, for the time being, removed the pressure from the government to act. Eventually, the Bar'Am committee submitted its report in June 1968 in which it did not depart from the accepted orthodoxy in its recommendation to establish a legal right to relief work.[29]

Despite the groundwork covered by the various committees and governmental bodies that had studied the problem of unemployment since 1948, by the end of the second decade of independence, in 1967, the introduction of an unemployment insurance scheme still seemed far away. The predominant view of the majority of the dominant political groups in Israel was that it was still premature to introduce unemployment insurance. This persistent view was undoubtedly influenced by the Israeli establishment's difficulty in identifying with the needs of the unemployed who were mostly new immigrants originating from Arab countries. A change in policy toward the unemployed had to wait for the coming decade.

The Breakthrough

The breakthrough that finally made possible the introduction of an unemployment insurance scheme took place in the third decade of Israel's independence. Many factors combined to produce this change: First, there was a significant improvement in the economy, which began with the abrupt end of the economic recession of 1966 and 1967 that followed the Six Day War in June 1967. The subsequent recovery moved the country into a new phase of rapid economic growth in which the gross domestic product increased at an average rate of 11.7 percent per year between 1968 and 1971—one of the highest in the world at that time. The number of unemployed as a percentage of the labor force declined steadily and reached the low level of 3.5 percent in 1971, or practically full employment. This favorable change in economic circumstances gave an impetus to new thinking about the problem of unemployment.[30]

Second, the decrease in the unemployment rate brought about a steady decline in the relief work program. At the peak of the economic recession, in May 1967, nearly 25,000 persons were employed in the relief work program, but in 1969 their number had dwindled to about 3,000. The government was actually considering closing the program entirely as more officials admitted the serious shortcomings of relief work. Minister of Labor Joseph Almogi stated openly in 1968 that the relief work program would have to be closed at any cost because it was "bad for the country and bad for the person employed in them. It paid no worthwhile wages and provided inadequate conditions of work. Local authorities are interested in relief work programs when they are financed from the national budget."[31]

Third, the country's leading economists increasingly recognized that relief to the unemployed was not merely an anti-poverty measure but an important part of economic and labor market management. David Horowitz, governor of the Bank of Israel, declared in 1968 that:

> Unemployment insurance is necessary not only as a matter of social justice but also on economic grounds. Relief work created to deal with the problems of unemployment tends dangerously to become unproductive. It is desirable to have a pool of unemployed that their livelihood is assured so that the economy has the maneuvering capacity to increase production. Unemployment insurance requires a small financial effort from the state and it carries with it the advantage of an anti-cyclical policy.[32]

Fourth, within parts of the Labor Party establishment, there was a significant change in attitude toward the immigrant population, old and new. Again, it was Almogi who stated in 1969—while expressing his support for unemployment insurance—that the danger had passed that new immigrants would prefer cash relief instead of choosing to work. In his view, the immigration of the past with its particular demographic composition had come to an end, and newly arriving immigrants from more affluent societies would not accept work with a spade. Inadvertently,

Almogi revealed the strong bias within the labor movement toward the immigrants from Arab countries from 1948 to 1952—a bias that had prevented the introduction of unemployment insurance.[33]

Fifth, the late 1960s was a period of social unrest in which the socially underprivileged groups of the Eidot Hamizrach, the Sephardic Jewish community, increased their efforts to assert their rights and improve their positions within Israeli society. In response to these pressures, there was more wilingness within the dominant, mainly Ashkenazi, political establishment to respond to the needs of these groups and to introduce social reforms in the country's social security system.

Finally, the pragmatic fiscal policy considerations of the late 1960s tipped the scales in favor of unemployment insurance. In 1969 and 1970, there was a sharp fall in the country's foreign currency reserves, mostly as a result of increased defense expenditures. At the same time, both the wage and price systems showed signs of breaking down in the face of the declared national policy of a price and wage freeze. The economy faced the danger that a large general wage rise, which was the likely result of new wage agreements due to be signed at the end of 1969, could cause a further worsening of the balance of payments, intensify inflationary pressures, and produce an imminent economic crisis.[34]

It was against this background that a "package deal"—the name of a broad agreement between the government, the Histadrut, and the Coordinating Committee of Economic Organizations on wages, prices, and taxation—was signed in January 1970. As part of this typical "neo-corporatist" package deal, the parties agreed to increase significantly the employers' and employees' national insurance contributions with the tacit understanding that the additional funds were to be used to introduce an unemployment insurance scheme. In this indirect and opportunistic way, unemployment insurance was finally to become a reality.[35]

The decision to collect unemployment insurance contributions beginning in April 1970 also made it imperative to establish the parallel right to unemployment benefits. Minister of Labor Almogi appointed an unemployment insurance committee in March 1970, headed by Rivka Bar-Yosef, a sociologist from Hebrew University in Jerusalem. The committee's task was to prepare the general principles for an unemployment insurance scheme, and it was to submit its proposals within a three-month period in line with the "arrangements dictated by the package deal."[36]

At the beginning of August 1970 the committee was ready with its report. The basic assumptions of its recommendations were that the goal of the proposed unemployment insurance scheme was "to insure workers against the loss of wages during periods of temporary unemployment of a frictional or cyclical nature." In addition, the scheme was to be compulsory with wide coverage based on social insurance principles and not provided as a service. The committee assumed that its benefits were to "protect the standard of living of the insured against any drastic reduction during the period of unemployment" and declared that "the rights of the unemployed will be formulated in such way as to reduce as much as possible any negative work incentives."[37]

As unemployment insurance was already a fait accompli, the Bar-Yosef committee's proposals were accepted by the government without much debate. The unemployment insurance bill was approved by the Ministerial Committee on Legislation in December 1970, and it was tabled in the Knesset in February 1971. In the parliamentary debate on the proposed legislation Yoram Aridor of the right-wing Herut Party noted that the bill was a victory for the liberal-national school of thought, which always supported the broadening of social legislation, while the conservative-socialistic school was hesitant in these matters. Almogi, the minister of Labor, defended Labor's record and explained the reasons that prevented the introduction of unemployment insurance earlier.[38] Although the bill was finally passed by the Knesset in March 1972, it did not end the struggle for unemployment insurance.

The Unemployment Insurance Scheme in Operation

The unemployment insurance scheme, which has been in operation since January 1973, covers all employed person in the country. An unemployed person who has completed the required qualifying period is eligible for unemployment benefits if between the ages of twenty and sixty (for women) or sixty-five (for men). To qualify for a benefit, the unemployed person is required to register with the local employment service, be available for employment, and be willing to accept suitable work when it is offered. Entitlement to unemployment benefits begins after a waiting period of 5 days, and the benefit is paid for a maximum period of 175 days per year for an unemployed person forty-five or older, or a breadwinner with three dependents. The maximum period is 138 days in all other cases.

Unemployment benefits are also paid to participants in vocational training courses who have met the eligibility requirements. In these cases, the benefit constitutes only the difference between the living allowance they are receiving during the period of training and the full amount of unemployment benefit to which they are entitled. The daily rate of unemployment benefit is calculated on the basis of the unemployed person's average wage in the immediate period prior to unemployment and the average wage in the country. The benefits are progressive; for example, the ratio of the benefits to the unemployed person's previous income is lower whenever the income is higher. (See Table 9.1.)

The increase in the extent of unemployment benefit payments in the

TABLE 9.1   Calculation of Unemployment Benefits

Unemployed Person's Wage Prior to Unemployment	*Benefits as a Percentage of Prior Wage*
On part of wage less than half of average daily wage	80
On part of wage from 50 percent to 75 percent of average daily wage	50
On part of wage from 75 percent to all of average daily wage	45
On part of wage more than average daily wage, up to maximum wage	40

Source: National Insurance Law (Consolidated Version) 1968 (5728) (Haifa: A.G. Publication, Ltd., 1986), p. 109.

1980s shows the important changes that occurred in the Israeli economy in this period, and it also reflects the performance of the unemployment insurance scheme. (See Table 9.2.) The year 1980 was to a large extent a turning point in the level of employment in Israel. For the first time since the 1960s, the rate of the unemployed among those in the civilian labor force rose above 4 percent and reached 5.4 percent in the last quarter of 1980. Unemployment increased again in 1984 and its rate went up from 4.5 percent in 1983 to 5.9 percent in 1984 to 6.7 percent in 1985 and to 7.1 percent in 1986. The increase in the unemployment benefit payments showed the scheme's limited capability to respond to the changing employment circumstances by providing income protection to those dependent on it. Because of the various eligibility conditions, including work availability tests, only a small percentage of the unemployed in the civilian labor force—that increased from 11.0 percent in 1980 to about 14.0 percent in 1985–1986—were entitled to benefits.[39]

Another important issue in the payment of unemployment benefits was the erosion of their real level toward the end of the 1970s. A number of changes introduced in the calculation of benefits and improvements in the updating methods of NII benefits in 1980 remedied this situation in the early 1980s. Again, the trend of declining benefit levels in the years from 1983 to 1985 was halted in 1986 with the real rise in wages and the fall of inflation following the economic reforms of 1985.

The unemployment insurance benefits remained throughout the years a very small part of the total NII benefit payments (contributory and

TABLE 9.2   Unemployment Benefits, 1973–1987

Year	Total Number of Unemployment Benefit Payments	Average Daily Unemployment Benefits as a Percentage of Average Wage	Average Number of Days of Unemployment Benefit Payments
1973	3,062	42.0	- -
1975	6,832	38.0	- -
1977	14,780	36.3	- -
1979	17,949	29.8	- -
1980	111,793	39.6	- -
1981	140,214	42.6	75
1982	132,351	43.1	75
1983	119,643	39.8	75
1984	183,190	36.1	80
1985	235,325	39.9	84
1986	228,211	43.6	88
1987	220,504	47.7	- -

Sources: National Insurance Institute, Bureau of Research and Planning, *Quarterly Statistics* 18:1 (April-June 1988), Table L/1; National Insurance Institute, Bureau of Research and Planning, *Annual Survey 1986* (Jerusalem, December 1987), p. 59.

noncontributory). Until 1980 these benefits constituted less than 1 percent of total payments. With the increase in unemployment, they rose in 1980 to 1.7 percent and reached 2.6 percent in 1986 when the number of unemployed receiving benefits reached its peak. As a percentage of the GNP these payments constituted only 0.09 percent in 1980 and rose to 0.20 percent in 1986. In financial terms, therefore, the unemployment insurance scheme did not become a heavy burden on the country's social security system or on its resources, as many had feared.

The Unemployment Insurance Scheme in a Comparative Perspective

Unemployment benefits are an important part of social security systems in most advanced industrialized countries. They are designed to replace a proportion of wages lost as a consequence of involuntary unemployment. The question is how do unemployed families in Israel fare in comparison with similar families in other countries? The type of family compared in Table 9.3 has the characteristic profile for which unemployment insurance benefits were created. The main earner in the family is available and ready

TABLE 9.3 Intercountry Comparison of Unemployment Benefits Received by a Two-Parent Family with Two Children and an Unemployed Breadwinner, as a Percentage of Net Average Wage, 1979

Country	Benefit as a Percentage of Net Average Wage[a]
Sweden	91.6
FRG	69.9
United States (New York)	31.5
United States (Pennsylvania)	42.4
France	68.0
Canada	62.6
Australia	59.8
United Kingdom	49.5
Israel	40.0

[a]Net average wage: the net average production worker's wage (APWW).

Source: Alfred J. Kahn and Sheila B. Kamerman, *Income Transfers for Families with Children: An Eight-Country Study* (Philadelphia: Temple University Press, 1983), p. 222. © 1983 Temple University; reprinted by permission of Temple University Press.

to work and the family has no earned income. The data show that with exception of the United States (New York), Israel ranks below all the countries compared and provides this family a replacement rate of only 40.0 percent of the APWW. The four high-ranking countries in this respect are Sweden with a replacement rate of 91.6 percent, the FRG with 69.9 percent, France with 68.0 percent, and Canada with 62.2 percent. In terms of generosity of provision, Israel ranks very low.

The wage replacement function of the unemployment benefits is to a certain degree in constant tension between the desire to provide an adequate level of benefit and at the same time to protect the motivation to work. As benefits rise, the income gap between the working and the unemployed person and family decreases, which creates a situation with the potential for producing disincentives to work. There is no simple solution to this problem and, of course, behavioral responses to such a situation may vary from country to country. However, as the data in Table 9.3 show, Israel has chosen a deterrent policy by providing rather low replacement rate benefits.

The data in Table 9.4 compare the net family income packages, which include—in addition to the unemployment benefits—income of other cash benefits such as children's allowances and refundable tax credits. The data

TABLE 9.4 Intercountry Comparison of Unemployment Benefits Received by a Two-Parent Family with Two Children and an Unemployed Breadwinner, as a Percentage of Net Family Income, 1979

Country	Benefit as a Percentage of Net Family Income[a]
Sweden	75.5
FRG	78.5
United States (New York)	45.0
United States (Pennsylvania)	63.2
France	67.3
Canada	81.5
Australia	92.8
United Kingdom	67.0
Israel	58.9

[a]Family income includes all types of cash benefits and tax credits.

Source: Alfred J. Kahn and Sheila B. Kamerman, *Income Transfers for Families with Children: An Eight-Country Study* (Philadelphia: Temple University Press, 1983), p. 221. © 1983 Temple University; reprinted by permission of Temple University Press.

show that the unemployment insurance benefits play different roles in the income packages provided in different countries. The value of the unemployment benefits range from a high of 92.9 percent of net income in Australia to a low of 45.0 percent in the United States (New York). Three more countries provide benefits at more than 75 percent of net income: Canada, FRG, and Sweden. Again, Israel ranks very low (58.9 percent), below nearly all other countries compared.

The cross-country comparative data reflect the policy choices with regard to the unemployed that were adopted by various countries. It is clear, however, that Israeli policy priorities regarding the unemployed are much less generous than the other countries included in the comparison.

The Continuing Debate
on Unemployment Insurance

Throughout the more than fifteen years of operation of the unemployment insurance scheme, the controversial issues associated with it were never removed from the public agenda. The debates became even more sharp in the 1980s with the worsening of the Israeli economy and the significant growth of unemployment. Politicians, economists, and some industrialists repeatedly blamed unemployment insurance for actually creating disincentives to work and artificially increasing the number of the unemployed. Numerous public and governmental committees again dealt with the matter in the late 1980s; a few bills were tabled in the Knesset to change the existing legislation, and in a number of instances the law was actually amended. For example, efforts were made to change the definition of "suitable employment," and there were repeated attempts by the government since the early 1980s to restrict the eligibility of young persons for unemployment benefits. This was aimed primarily against young men in their early twenties recently discharged after three years of compulsory military training who, it was believed, would prefer to remain idle rather than work. Although there was no evidence supporting this accusation, eligibility conditions were tightened, and the benefit rate was deliberately lowered to make receipt of unemployment insurance less attractive to these veterans.

Yet in spite of this ongoing debate, in times of high unemployment, unemployment insurance has become an integral and accepted part of the country's social security system. No one suggested the return to the earlier relief work programs, and no one seriously contemplated abolishing unemployment insurance. The arguments concentrated predominantly on changing specific parameters of the existing arrangements, and perhaps this is a sign that unemployment insurance has finally become fully absorbed into the institutional structure of Israeli society.

Notes

1. Unemployment insurance as a continuing, critical issue in social policy is discussed in Peter A. Kohler and Hans F. Zacher (eds.), *The Evolution of Social Insurance 1881–1981: Studies of Germany, France, Great Britain, Austria, and Switzerland* (London: Frances Pinter and New York: St. Martin's Press, 1982); Jens Alber, "Government Responses to the Challenge of Unemployment: The Development of Unemployment Insurance in Western Europe," in Peter Flora and Arnold J. Heidenheimer (eds.), *The Development of Welfare States in Europe and America* (New Brunswick, NJ: Transaction Books, 1981); E. Ashford, *The Emergence of the Welfare States* (Oxford: Basil Blackwell, 1986); John A. Garraty, *Unemployment in History, Economic Thought, Public Policy* (New York: Harper & Row, 1978); Derek P.S. Hum, *Unemployment Insurance and Work Effort: Issues, Evidence, and Policy Direction* (Toronto: Ontario Economic Council, 1981).

2. Hugh Heclo, *Modern Social Politics in Britain and Sweden: From Relief to Income Maintenance* (New Haven: Yale University Press, 1974), pp. 66–68.

3. The classical economists' objections to unemployment insurance are discussed in Jose Harris, *Unemployment and Politics* (New York: Oxford University Press, 1972).

4. Heclo, op. cit., pp. 66–67.

5. Goran Therborn, *The Working Class and the Welfare State: A Historical-Analytical*

Overview (Paper for the First Nordic Congress of Research in the History of the Labor Movement, Murikka, Finland, August 23–27, 1983), p. 5.

6. Hugh Heclo and Henrik Madsen, *Policy and Politics in Sweden: Principled Pragmatism* (Philadelphia: Temple University Press, 1986), p. 156.

7. Heclo, op. cit., pp. 83–90.

8. Memorandum submitted to the director of the Department of Labor of the Palestine government, 31 December 1945 (in the files of the Jewish Agency Political Department, General Zionist Archives, Jerusalem).

9. I. Kanevsky, "A Social Insurance Plan for the State of Israel, *Khikrei Avodah* (Labor Studies) 2:1–2 (June 1948) (Hebrew).

10. *Israel Government Yearbook, 1951–1952* (5712), p. LII.

11. *A Social Insurance Plan for Israel*, Report of the Interministerial Committee for Social Insurance Planning (Tel Aviv: Ministry of Labor and Social Insurance, 1950) (Hebrew).

12. Ibid., p. 41.

13. Memorandum of the Ministry of Commerce and Industry to the Interministerial Committee for Social Insurance Planning, 15 November 1949 (in the files of the National Insurance Institute) (Hebrew).

14. Ibid.

15. Giora Lotan, "Unemployment Insurance," *Monthly Review of Labor* 3:1 (January 1951), p. 3 (Hebrew).

16. *Divrei Haknesset* (Parliamentary Records), Vol. 14, June 30, 1953, p. 1759 (Hebrew).

17. Ministry of Labor, Manpower Planning Authority, *Manpower in Development Towns*, December 1964 (Hebrew).

18. William C. Fitch, *National Insurance Program in the State of Israel*, Report to the government of Israel (Tel-Aviv: U.S. Operations Mission in Israel, October 1956), pp. 8–9.

19. *Divrei Haknesset* (Parliamentary Records), Vol. 25, January 28, 1958, p. 993 (Hebrew).

20. Ibid., Vols. 28–29, April 4, 1960, p. 1093.

21. "Opposes Unemployment Insurance," *Haaretz*, 10 March 1966 (Hebrew).

22. "New Directives Concerning Relief Work," *Labor and National Insurance* 16:7 (July 1963), pp. 279–280 (Hebrew).

23. In the mid-1950s, a special lower wage rate agreed to by the Histadrut was maintained for the persons on relief work. As a result of pressure from the left-wing Labor parties, this wage rate—known as "Sakhar Dahak"—was abolished in later years.

24. *Report of Committee on Unemployment Insurance*, 13 February 1964 (in the files of the National Insurance Institute) (Hebrew).

25. Ibid.

26. Abraham Doron, "The Struggle for Unemployment Insurance in the State of Israel," *Molad* 2:10 (220) (June 1969), pp. 445–446 (Hebrew).

27. "An Interministerial Committee Will Examine the Issues of Unemployment Insurance," *Haaretz*, 15 November 1966; Rafael Eldor, "The Unemployment Insurance Committee Was Composed," *Maariv*, 21 December 1966 (Hebrew).

28. Dan Mirkin, "Relief to the Unemployed—Soon," *Haaretz*, 24 November 1966; "Mapam Will Vote for the Budget—Eshkol and Sapir Accepted Part of Their

Demands," *Maariv*, 24 November 1966; and "Yaari: Mapam's Remaining in the Government is Conditioned on Providing Assistance to the Unemployed," *Haaretz*, 5 January 1967 (Hebrew).

29. "Report of Committee on Legislation Proposals to Provide Employment and Unemployment Insurance," *Labor and National Insurance* 21:8 (August 1968), pp. 255–258 (Hebrew).

30. Ephraim Dovrat, "Israel's Economy in the 1970s," *Economic Quarterly* 16:62 (July 1969), p. 129 (Hebrew).

31. "A New Alignment—Need of the Hour," *Labor and National Insurance* 20:12 (December 1968), p. 394 (Hebrew).

32. "Horowitz Supports the Introduction of Unemployment Insurance," *Haaretz*, 8 April 1968 (Hebrew).

33. Dan Margalit, "Procrastination in Welfare Affairs," *Haaretz*, 1 July 1969 (Hebrew).

34. David Bigman, "Developments in the Sphere of the Balance of Payments During 1970–1971," *Economic Quarterly* 19:73–74 (March 1972) (Hebrew).

35. "The Comprehensive Agreement between the Government, the Histadrut, and the Coordinating Committee of Economic Organizations on the Matter of a Policy for Wages, Prices, and Taxes for 1970 and 1971," January 1970 (known as the "Package Deal"); see also Amira Galin and Yanai Tab, "The Package Deal—A Turning Point in Labor Relations in Israel," *Economic Quarterly* 18:69–70 (July 1971) (Hebrew).

36. *Report of the Committee on Unemployment Insurance*, (Jerusalem, 10 August 1970), p. 2 (Hebrew).

37. Ibid., p. 5.

38. *Divrei Haknesset* (Parliamentary Records), Vol. 60, March 15, 1971, pp. 1824 and 1846 (Hebrew).

39. Liora Apel and Yehoshua Hendles, "Development of Unemployment in Israel," *Economy and Labor* 6 (October 1989), pp. 22–27 (Hebrew).

10

The Social and Economic
Impact of Social Security

The rapid growth of the Israeli social security system reflects the course of social and economic development in the quarter century between the 1950s and the mid-1970s. The development of social security shows not only the political willingness to allocate increased resources for this purpose but also the increase in the country's affluence that made these allocations possible. Moreover, the increase in social security spending reflects the political choice of programs that were thought to be effective in their contribution to social protection and to social cohesion. At the same time, achieving these goals also involved increased significance to the economy. Our intention in this chapter is to describe and analyze some of the most important socioeconomic effects of the evolution of Israel's social security system.

The Cost of Social Security

The cost of social security includes the receipts and expenditures of the NII, the chief state agency responsible for the operation of the country's national insurance programs and other noncontributory cash benefit programs. There are some small government benefit programs for the victims of Nazi persecution administered directly by the Treasury and an important benefit program for ex-service men and women and their families in the Ministry of Defense. Although these government programs are not included in the following account, this will have a minor effect on the overall picture presented. This contrasts with the outlays for private occupational pension plans that are also excluded because they are mostly outside the realm of national accounting, but which have considerable importance.

The gradual expansion of the scope of Israel's social security system since the mid-1950s has also significantly increased its costs, as seen in

Table 10.1. *Contributions* collected to finance the contributory national insurance programs have risen from 2 percent of the GNP in 1955 to 2.6 percent in 1965, 4.6 percent in 1975, 5.7 percent in 1980, and 6 percent in 1988. The receipts of the NII for both the contributory and noncontributory programs increased from 2.5 percent in 1965 to 5.6 percent in 1975 and to about 8.0 percent of the GNP in 1988. Concurrent with the rise in national insurance contributions and other NII receipts, there was also an immense growth of social security *benefits* paid by the NII to various eligible groups. Contributory national insurance benefits have risen from 0.7 percent of the GNP in 1955 to 1.7 percent in 1965, 5.1 percent in 1975, 5.5 percent in 1980, and 7.1 percent in 1988. Benefits paid by the NII in both the contributory and noncontributory programs have increased from 2.1 percent of the GNP in 1965 to 6.5 percent in 1975, 6.7 percent in 1980, and 8.2 percent in 1988. This growth in benefits in the 1970s and 1980s does not reflect in its entirety a real increase. Part of this increase can be accounted for by the substitution of national insurance cash benefits for certain income tax allowances that were cancelled in 1975, and another part, such as the children's allowances, is a result of the transfer of social assistance payments from the Ministry of Social Welfare to the NII. In any event, the growth of social security benefits in relation to the GNP is noteworthy.

TABLE 10.1   NII Receipts and Benefits as a Percentage of GNP, 1955–1988

Year	NI Receipts[a]	NI Benefits[b]	All NII Receipts[c]	All NII Benefits[d]
1955	2.00	0.70	- - -	- - -
1965	2.60	1.70	2.50	2.10
1970	4.90	2.90	5.10	3.80
1975	4.66	5.14	5.66	6.54
1980	5.71	5.47	7.51	6.75
1986	5.37	6.35	8.05	8.00
1987	5.60	6.48	7.73	7.84
1988	6.00	7.10	8.40	8.20

[a]Receipts collected as contributions for the various national insurance programs.
[b]Benefits paid by the various contributory national insurance programs.
[c]All receipts, including contributions, government participation in the cost of national insurance programs, and governmental financing of noncontributory benefit programs.
[d]All contributory and noncontributory benefits paid by the NII.

Sources: National Insurance Institute, Bureau of Research and Planning, *Annual Survey 1980* (Jerusalem, September 1981), p. 1; *Annual Survey 1988* (Jerusalem, October 1989), pp. 5–6 (Hebrew), with administrative expenditures excluded.

The Pattern of Social Security Expenditures

Although the overall proportion of social security expenditures to GNP has grown, there is considerable variation among the major programs that shaped the pattern of these expenditures from 1965 through the mid-1980s. As in practically all industrialized countries, the expenditures on old-age and disability pensions also dominate the picture in Israel, where they account for about 50 percent of the total social security expenditures. (See Table 10.2.) Since the introduction of the general disability insurance scheme in the mid-1970s, the combined share of old-age, survivors, and disability expenditures has remained stable. In the mid-1980s, about 4.0 percent of GNP was devoted to only this item of social security expenditure. (See Table 10.3.) It has also risen faster than any other item, from somewhat higher than 1 percent in 1970 to nearly 3.4 percent in 1980, and reached 4.0 percent in 1986. The main factors explaining this development are demographic and programmatic: The demographic factor reflects the long-term trend of a 50-percent increase in the proportion of people older than sixty-five in the total population since 1965, from 6 percent in 1965 to about 9 percent in 1988, which is still relatively low compared to most European countries.[1] The programmatic factor represents the maturation of the old-age and survivors insurance scheme that came into effect in 1954 and the general disability insurance that was initiated in the 1970s; the programmatic factor also includes the fact that with the passage of time, more of the insured persons reached retirement age, experienced disability, or experienced the death of a working spouse. In addition, the incremental improvements in the old-age benefits introduced from the mid-1960s to the mid-1980s also contributed to this development.

The second largest social security expenditure is children's allowances, which accounts for nearly a quarter of the total social security expenditures. In the mid-1970s, at the time when the program underwent a major reform, the share for children's allowances increased significantly, but since then it declined again and returned to its earlier level in the 1980s. In this respect, Israel compares well with countries such as France, Belgium, and New Zealand, which have extensive children's allowances programs and devote more than 20 percent of their social security expenditures to them.[2] In the mid-1980s, nearly 2 percent of the GNP was devoted to this item of expenditure, which is slightly lower than its share was in 1975.

Unemployment benefits constitute a relatively small proportion of the total social security expenditures, which account on the average for no more than about 2 percent of the total. In this respect, Israel is similar to many other industrialized countries, although the actual share of these benefits in other countries is higher than in Israel. The rise of the unemploy-

TABLE 10.2 Expenditure on Social Security Programs as a Percentage of Total Social Security Expenditures, 1965–1988

Year	Old-Age and Survivors	General Disability	Employment Injury and Hostile Border Action Casualties	Maternity	Children's Allowances	Unemployment Benefits	Reserve Service	Income Support Benefits	Others
1965	42.2	--	15.2	12.2	23.5	--	6.3	--	0.6
1970	38.1	--	9.4	6.9	23.3	--	19.2	--	3.1
1975	38.5	2.4	5.9	5.1	33.6	0.6	13.6	--	0.3
1980	39.7	10.2	5.6	5.4	26.6	1.7	10.7	--	0.1
1983	39.6	11.6	5.1	5.1	23.0	1.5	12.7	1.9	.1
1986	38.5	11.6	5.2	5.2	23.1	2.6	10.8	3.3	.4
1987	39.1	10.8	5.2	4.6	22.0	2.8	12.1	2.8	.6
1988	38.6	10.7	5.8	4.8	20.4	4.1	11.8	2.5	1.3

Sources: Years 1965–1975 were calculated from National Insurance Institute, Bureau of Research and Planning, Quarterly Statistics 18:1 (April-June 1988), Table A-2; Years 1980–1988 were calculated from National Insurance Institute, Bureau of Research and Planning, Annual Survey 1988 (Jerusalem, October 1989), Table 3.

TABLE 10.3   Expenditure on Main Social Security Programs as a Percentage of GNP, 1965–1988

Year	Old-Age and Survivors	Disability	Children's Allowances	All Other Programs	Total
1965	0.90	- - -	0.50	0.70	2.10
1970	1.10	- - -	0.70	1.00	2.80
1975	2.52	0.16	2.20	1.66	6.54
1980	2.68	0.69	1.80	1.58	6.75
1986	3.10	0.90	1.80	2.20	8.00

Sources: Percentages calculated from National Insurance Institute, Bureau of Research and Planning, *Quarterly Statistics* 18:1 (Jerusalem, 1988–1989), Table A-2; National Insurance Institute, Bureau of Research and Planning, *Annual Survey 1986* (Jerusalem, December 1987), Table 1; and *Annual Survey 1987* (Jerusalem, September 1988), Table 1.

ment rates in Israel in the 1980s also increased the relative share of these expenditures and brought them up to 4.1 percent in 1988.

Social assistance payments have also remained a relatively small social security expenditure. Since the transfer of these payments to the NII under the Income Support Benefits Law in 1982, however, expenditures have been growing and increased from 1.3 percent in 1983 to 3.3 percent of total social security expenditures in 1986. Even at this level expenditures constituted less than 0.3 percent of GNP. All other social security programs, including maternity, work injury, reserve service, and the whole range of other small programs absorbed in the mid-1980s constitute no more than 2.20 percent of GNP.

The Redistributive Effect

With the growth of its economic significance, the Israeli social security program has also been playing an increasingly important role in the prevention of economic hardship and poverty and has contributed to a slightly more equal pattern of income distribution.

The Prevention of Poverty. Studies carried out over the years have shown consistently that social security benefits have played a major role in the reduction of poverty and in the improvement of the relative condition of the weakest population groups in the country. The data in Table 10.4 indicate that between 1968 and 1975 there had been almost no change in the incidence of poverty before receipt of social security benefits among families in the employee population. Despite the growth of national prosperity in this period, the rigidity of the market wage and income structure prevented any reduction in the scope of poverty. Since the mid-1970s, with the advent of the economic crisis, growing unemployment, high inflation, and stagnation of the Israeli economy, there has been a continuous rise in the incidence of poverty before receipt of social security benefits among these families, from 9.7 percent in 1977 to the peak of 14.0 percent in 1984, an increase of about 45 percent. It seems reasonable to conclude that social security benefits contributed over the years to significantly reduce the actual incidence of poverty, with poverty defined as 40 percent of the median income for a family of four.

The improvement of the social security benefits system from 1968 to 1977 brought about a marked decrease in the incidence of poverty after receipt of benefits in this period, from about 6.0 percent of families in the employee population in 1969 to only 3.6 percent in 1975. The social security benefits were especially instrumental in the reduction of poverty among the elderly population. In 1969 the old-age pensions brought about a 50-percent decrease in poverty among the elderly, from 27.8 percent before receipt of benefits to 14.2 percent. In 1975 the equivalent decrease was nearly 90 percent, from 24.5 percent before benefits to only 2.7 percent. This situation changed considerably from the late 1970s to the mid-1980s, a period that was marked by an increase of pre-transfer poverty (before receipt of benefits), and in the wake of galloping inflation, the social security system was much less effective in preserving the real value of its

TABLE 10.4   The Percentage of Employee Families Living in Poverty Before and After Receipt of Social Security Benefits, 1968–1987

Year	Before	After	% of Decrease
1969	10.1	6.0	40.6
1975	10.4	3.6	65.4
1977	9.7	2.8	71.1
1979	11.2	4.7	58.0
1982	12.7	5.6	55.9
1984	14.0	7.5	46.4
1987	11.3	5.4	52.2

Sources: Years 1969–1975: Yossi Tamir, *The Changing Patterns of Poverty Within the Employee Population in Israel, 1969–1975* (Jerusalem: National Insurance Institute, Bureau of Research and Planning, 1977), p. 10 (Hebrew); Years 1977–1987: National Insurance Institute, Bureau of Research and Planning, *Annual Survey 1984* (Jerusalem, December 1985), p. 32 (Hebrew); and *Annual Survey 1987* (Jerusalem, September 1988), p. 65 (Hebrew).

benefits. As a result, social security benefits were much less effective in the reduction of poverty.

The Effect on the Pattern of Income Distribution. The desire for a more equal pattern of income distribution is particularly important in a country such as Israel where socioeconomic disparities strongly overlap the differences in ethnic origin. In an immigrant society, the lessening of these differences is essential to further social integration.[3] Social security insurance benefits have had a somewhat equalizing effect on the patterns of income distribution in Israel, especially in the decade from 1968 to 1977.

Until 1969 the impact of social security benefits on the income distribution patterns was rather small. A study of the redistributive effect of the national insurance program in 1969 showed that it reduced the overall inequality in the country by 5.7 percent, as measured by the Gini coefficient.[4] Even after allowing for the regressivity of the national insurance contributions, the net reduction of inequality remained 4 percent by the Gini coefficient. The net benefit (benefits minus contributions) was positive for the lower five deciles in the population, while only the four highest deciles were negatively affected.

From the early 1970s, the impact of social security on the income distribution pattern increased considerably. As shown in the Table 10.5, social security benefits had reduced inequality within the total population in 1968 by only 6.82 percent, as measured by the Gini coefficient, but the reduction of inequality rose to 11.52 percent in 1975. Within the employee population, social security benefits had reduced inequality in 1969 by 5.9 percent, in 1977 by 14.7 percent, and in 1984 by 11.2 percent.

The Effects on Social Structure

The gradual institutionalization of social security has strongly influenced the economic stability of the total population, and over the years, it has brought about a far-reaching transformation of Israeli society. The impact of this evolution can be seen in three main areas: First, the progressive extension of the system to a wide range of programs that cover the entire population against the most frequent risks of loss of income has contributed to personal security and indirectly improved the quality of life for many citizens. Second, the comprehensive program of children's allowances has brought about some redistribution of income to families with children and has reduced some of the inequalities resulting from family size in a market society where wage income is unrelated to the family responsibilities of the breadwinner. Third, universal coverage for a minimum level of living and the institutionalization of this right as an entitlement have contributed to the integration of new immigrants and other low-income persons into the mainstream of life in Israeli society.

TABLE 10.5   Patterns of Income Inequality in Israel as Measured by the Gini Coefficient[a]

	Economic Income[b]	Economic Income + Benefits	% Reduction of Inequality[c]
Total population			
1968	.4235	.3946	6.8
1975	.4028	.3564	11.5
Employee population			
1969	.3568	.3359	5.9
1975	.3453	.3076	10.9
1977	.2838	.2418	14.7
1979	.3075	.2709	11.9
1981	.3202	.2812	12.2
1982	.3246	.2804	13.6
1983	.3217	.2792	13.2
1984	.3475	.3086	11.2
1987	.3803	.3464	9.8

[a]Gini coefficient: a measure of overall inequality. This coefficient ranges between 0 and 1; the higher the coefficient the greater the degree of inequality.

[b]Economic income: income before payment of taxes and the receipt of social security benefits.

[c]Reduction is defined as the difference between the indexes of total income and economic income divided by economic income.

Sources: Total Population: L. Achdut, Y. Geva, and Y. Tamir, *Changes in Poverty Patterns in Israel 1968–1975: In View of the Development of the Income Maintenance System* (Jerusalem: National Insurance Institute, Bureau of Research and Planning, 1979), pp. 41–42 (Hebrew). Employee Population: For 1969–1975, Y. Tamir, *The Changing Patterns of Poverty Within the Employee Population in Israel, 1969–1975* (Jerusalem: National Insurance Institute, Bureau of Research and Planning, 1977), p. 28 (Hebrew). For 1977–1987, National Insurance Institute, Bureau of Research and Planning, *Annual Survey 1984* (Jerusalem, December 1985), p. 42 (Hebrew); *Annual Survey 1987* (Jerusalem, December 1988), p. 73 (Hebrew).

In more concrete terms, social security benefits have become an important component of the incomes of practically the entire population. At any time, a substantial part of the population is dependent on social security benefits for all or part of its net income. In 1986, for example, about 85 percent of household units received some net income in the form of social security benefits, not including children's allowances. About 16 percent of all households (including the recipients of old-age NI pensions with supplementary benefits, income support, and alimony payments) were receiving almost their entire net income in social security benefits. The

TABLE 10.6   The Effect of Social Security Benefits on the Distribution of Income Among the Employee Population, 1986–1987

| | Share of Each Decile in Total Income | |
Deciles	Economic Income[a]	Economic Income + Benefits
Lowest	1.93	2.79
2	3.53	4.13
3	4.63	5.11
4	5.95	6.29
5	7.35	7.51
6	8.80	8.82
7	10.55	10.40
8	12.94	12.62
9	16.65	15.93
Highest	27.67	26.41
Ratio between incomes of highest and lowest deciles	14.30	9.50

[a]Economic income: income before payment of taxes and the receipt of social security benefits.

Source: National Insurance Institute, Bureau of Research and Planning, *Annual Survey 1987* (Jerusalem, September 1988), p. 73 (Hebrew).

one-time slogan of the Beveridgean welfare state—that the state will care for everyone from the cradle to the grave—has thus become a reality. In fact, every child is born in Israel with the help of maternity insurance that provides free maternity hospital care for the mother and a cash grant for a layette for the newborn baby. And at the end of the life cycle, every deceased person is buried with an old-age insurance grant that covers burial costs.

The achievements of the Israeli social security system should be viewed in perspective, with an awareness of its serious limitations. Although it has significantly broadened the field of social protection, its impact on equality has been quite limited. (See Table 10.6.) In particular it has not succeeded in abolishing relative poverty and it has failed to make significant progress in reducing class inequality.

The Impact on the Arab Population

The establishment of a universal social security system that covers all population groups and provides everyone with uniform benefits had in it the potential to contribute toward the closure of the deeply embedded cleavages between Israel's Jewish majority and Arab minority. However, the trends that evolved over the years in the Israeli social security policies that affect the Arab population have resulted in diverse outcomes, some of which are unfortunate.[5]

The question of how to bridge the gap between the Jewish and Arab population in the context of a national social security system posed a difficult problem for the planners of the first social insurance program in 1948. One view was that programs such as national insurance and social assistance should be established on a separate autonomous basis for the two communities because the state could not undertake the burden of immediately providing the Arab population with the same level of services that the Jewish community had already attained through its efforts in the Yishuv. Giora Lotan said at that time:

> With all the political importance of equality in the basic services, we will have to leave some of these outside the scope of services provided by the state. I refer to social insurance and social assistance, even in the limited form in which they exist now. . . . To provide the Arab population with the services the Jewish population is receiving at present would mean doubling the existing financial burden. The conclusion from this must be that the Va'ad Leumi (Council of the Jewish Community) should continue to exist to provide certain services for the Jews exclusively.[6]

This view had, however, only limited support. The majority of the planning committee members accepted the principle that all services should be extended to the whole population, without regard to nationality. The supporters of this view also argued that the extension of services to the Arab population would help close the existing social and economic gap between the two communities. I. Ronen, an economist (and later a senior Treasury official), said, "As to social insurance benefits for the Arabs in the Jewish state, it seems that in this matter we do not have much choice; not only from the political-legal point of view, but also from the economic standpoint, we will be interested in putting an end to the two standards of living prevailing in Palestine. . . . Social insurance in this matter will be a tool of first magnitude."[7]

This argument prevailed during the critical period of the establishment of the national insurance program in the early 1950s. All national insurance programs established at the time, including old-age and survivors, work injury, maternity, and large families' allowance schemes, were all universal in their coverage and nondiscriminatory in their provision of benefits. As predicted, the extension of the newly established national insurance benefits to the Arab population improved the level of living of this population group and brought it somewhat closer to the standard of living of the Jewish population. For example, the actual impact of this policy can best be seen in the implementation of the maternity insurance benefits that provide free hospital care for women at childbirth. The percentage of hospital births among the Jewish population before the introduction of the scheme was already higher than 90 percent, while at the same time in 1954, only 5 percent of the non-Jewish population gave birth in hospitals. A decade later, more than 80 percent of the Arab women were using hospitals for childbirth, and the initial gap between the two populations closed entirely during the 1970s.[8]

The social assistance program that was in operation during the first years of statehood was nondiscriminatory in principle, as its poor quality of service affected both Jews and Arabs equally. Although the rules and regulations regarding social assistance and the legislation that was adopted in 1958 did not make any explicit distinction between Jews and Arabs, in the late 1950s claims began to be made that in practice Arabs were receiving lower assistance payments. During the 1958–1959 annual budget debate in the Knesset on the Ministry of Social Welfare, Joseph Khamis (Mapam) openly complained that the assistance rates applied to the Arabs were lower than those applied to the Jews, and he provided evidence to support this claim.[9]

This type of discrimination became formalized in an indirect way in the 1960s. Partly as a result of the Klein Report, the Ministry of Social Welfare set official assistance rates for the population in need and published them in "Taas," its administrative instructions manual. The assistance rates were set at two levels: the regular level for the urban population and a lower level for the rural population, which was about two-thirds of the regular rate. The rationale for this substantial difference was that the cost of living in the rural areas was significantly lower than in urban areas, and therefore there was no justification for having the same assistance rates in the two areas.

Although this explanation had some basis in fact, it was not the real reason for setting different rates. In practice, the lower assistance rates were applied only in Arab rural localities; they were never applied in Jewish rural localities. Throughout the 1960s, the representatives of the Arab localities pressured the ministry to change this policy, but with little success. It remained in force until the early 1970s and was finally abolished in April 1973.[10] Since then, the same assistance rates have been applied throughout the country, and these unified rates were later included in the Income Support Benefits Law of 1980, which replaced the old, locally administered social assistance program. The 1980 law integrated this last-resort safety net on a national basis for the entire population and finally removed the distinction between assistance for Jews and for Arabs. The new program administered by the NII represents a policy change, as is evident from the relatively large numbers of Arab recipients of income support since the inception of the program.[11]

This trend to remove any differentiation of or discrimination against the Arab population suffered a reversal, however, in 1970, in the children's allowances program. The veterans' family allowances scheme introduced that year increased the children's allowances for veterans' families with four or more children, while it excluded most large families in the Arab population from receiving this supplement. In strictly legal terms, the new supplementary allowances were nondiscriminatory because, like similar veterans' benefits in other countries, entitlement to them was limited only to those who served in the Israeli armed forces. In practice, however, most Arabs do not serve in the armed forces, so they are effectively excluded from receiving the additional allowances.[12]

This disturbing aspect of the overall children's allowances program, although highly controversial, has remained intact over the years and was actually reinforced when coverage was extended to the third child in the family. Under the continuing circumstances of strained relations between Jews and Arabs, this practice continues to receive strong support within the Jewish community, while it has come to be seen among Arabs as the epitome of discrimination.[13] The problem is that the discriminatory practice in the children's allowances program overshadows the fact that Israel's Arab citizens have nominal equality with Jews in all other social security programs. It is regrettable that the absence of an entitlement to part of the children's allowances program distorts the record of the social security system in improving some of the conditions of the Arab population and in reducing the social and economic gap between Arabs and Jews.

Notes

1. Central Bureau of Statistics, *Statistical Abstract of Israel 1989*, No. 40 (Jerusalem, 1990), pp. 599–600.

2. Margaret S. Gordon, *Social Security Policies in Industrial Countries: A Comparative Analysis* (London and New York: Cambridge University Press, 1988), pp. 282–284 and 348–350.

3. Rivka Bar-Yosef, "Welfare and Integration in Israel," in S.N. Eisenstadt and Ora Ahimeir (eds.), *The Welfare State and Its Aftermath* (London: Croom Helm, 1985), pp. 247–261.

4. Jack Habib, *Redistribution Through National Insurance in Israel by Income and Demographic Groups* (Jerusalem: National Insurance Institute, Bureau of Research and Planning, 1975).

5. A critical view of these policies can be found in Aziz Haidar, *Social Welfare Services for Israel's Arab Population* (Tel Aviv: International Center for Peace in the Middle East, 1987).

6. *Khikrei Avoda* (Labor Studies) 2:1–2 (June 1948), p. 123 (Hebrew).

7. Ibid., p. 150.

8. National Insurance Institute, Bureau of Research and Planning, *Statistical Abstract 1968/69* (Jerusalem, 1970), p. 21 (Hebrew); Central Bureau of Statistics, *Statistical Abstract of Israel 1983*, No. 34 (Jerusalem, 1983), p. 722.

9. *Divrei Haknesset* (Parliamentary Records), Vol. 21, March 17, 1958, pp. 1359–1360 (Hebrew).

10. Ministry of Social Welfare, Taas (Administrative Instructions Manual), *Assistance Rates from April 1973*, Instruction No. 311/73 (Jerusalem, April 1973) (Hebrew); See also the statement of M. A. Kurtz, director general of the Ministry of Social Welfare in the Knesset Finance Committee, Minutes of the Committee, No. 548, February 12, 1973 (Hebrew).

11. Ora Haviv, *Recipients of Income Support Benefits by the Place of Residence for the Years 1986–1987*, Survey No. 64 (Jerusalem: National Insurance Institute, Bureau of Research and Planning, April 1989), p. 3 (Hebrew).

12. One of the justifications for not requiring military service from the Arab citizens of Israel is the continuing state of war maintained by Arab states. Other non-Jewish citizens such as Druze, Bedouin, and Circassians do serve in the Israel Defense Forces.

13. In his critique of the "dualist" character of social protection in Israel, Michael Shalev notes that although Arab citizens are strongly discriminated against, the discrimination is typically indirect and its magnitude is less in income maintenance than in other public services. See *Labor and the Political Economy in Israel* (Oxford: Oxford University Press, 1992), Chapter 6, "Policy Outcomes: Dualism and Disorder."

11

Summary
and Conclusion

The evolution of social security that we have described may be considered both as an important chapter in the country's history and as a case study in social policy development that may shed some light beyond the Israeli experience. In this concluding chapter we summarize the multiple factors and interactions that played a major role in this process. Douglas Ashford's conclusion also seems appropriate here: "Perhaps the welfare state was neither pushed nor pulled into existence by inexorable economic and social forces as much as it was the product of institutionalized searching, experimentation, and accumulation within the democratic framework of each country."[1]

It was in the context of the nation-building process, rapid economic development, and modernization that the institutional backing and financial resources for the evolution of a social security system evolved within the Israeli polity. Long before statehood in 1948, the social institutions of the Jewish community in Palestine were organized as a state-on-the-way, with a democratic foundation that included universal suffrage and parliamentary responsibility. Political structures were carried over to the period of statehood despite the enormous difficulties in the absorption of an unprecedented mass immigration and a prolonged war of independence. After statehood was achieved, the fundamentals of social security were almost immediately established and rapidly expanded, along with the accompanying strains and conflicts, which is an indication of the adaptability of the Israeli political system—despite its structural rigidities —in responding to the social needs and the circumstances of a changing society.

Although there are divergent views about the importance of the level of economic development in the evolution of social security, it seems clear that the rapid growth of the Israeli economy until the Yom Kippur War of

1973 provided the necessary resources for the establishment and maintenance of a comprehensive income maintenance system, even at a low level
of adequacy.[2] At the same time, the national insurance and occupational
pension plans were also a significant source of the capital savings that
served to stimulate the growth of the Israeli economy. Throughout the
1950s and 1960s, the relatively large accumulated reserve of social security
funds was invested by the Treasury and constituted a substantial component in the country's economic and fiscal policies. Israel is another example
of the way in which social security and economic growth have been highly
interrelated and supportive of each other.[3] In addition to these basic political and economic factors, five other elements had considerable influence
on the evolution of the Israeli social security system: the process of cross-
national, societal learning; the public policy planners' network; the internal
conflicts within the labor movement in the early stages; later, the interclass
strains regarding reforms and improvements in the system; and the periodic elections as they affected the timing and change of policy.

The basic form and content of the Israeli social security system is similar
in most respects to those found in more developed industrial societies.
Although Israel did not have a legacy of Poor Laws or an anti-State,
laissez-faire tradition to overcome, its social policy development recapitulated in condensed form most of the patterns and sequences that occurred
as social security programs were adopted in older, richer countries such as
England and the United States. The progressive extension of benefits to
additional population groups and coverage of a broader range of risks
characterize most social security systems, regardless of the type of economy
or polity. Much of this can be accounted for by the processes of institutional
and societal learning, with elites serving as agents of institutional change
and interest groups facilitating societal change.[4]

In Israel, cross-national learning occurred through the medium of a
network of committed, professionally educated and cosmopolitan public
policy planners whom we have described as technipols, that is, technocrats
or experts with political influence. Mostly located in the National Insurance
Institute and the Hebrew University, they maintained close contact over a
period of many years with their counterparts in Britain and the United
States. Their goals and policy preferences often conflicted with a similar
group of civil servants and economists in the Treasury who in turn were
influenced by opposing theories and policies in Europe and in North
America. In the nation-building and consolidation phases of social security
development, the network of technipols had a strong commitment to
reform and improvement of social security rooted in their belief that the
system had the capacity to deal more effectively with the problems of
income insecurity in the Israeli economy. By keeping abreast of developments in other, more advanced countries, they drew on these experiences

and used this information to help shape the growth and development of the Israeli system.

If there was one attribute that characterized the formative years of the Israeli social security system, it was the ideological zeal of Labor Zionism that dominated the social and political thinking of the Jewish community in Palestine during the period of the British Mandate and in the early years of statehood. Subsequently, social security developed as a response of democratic governance to social needs in a rapidly developing industrial society and in the course of a power struggle between conflicting social, economic, and political interests.[5] Hence, the existing array of programs and benefits should be evaluated not only for their ability to meet the population's needs but also by taking into account what was possible in the Israeli context.

Like many other countries that gained independence after World War II, Israel was faced with the challenge of putting into practice the lofty ideals espoused before statehood. In contrast to other countries, however, in Israel the conflicts concerning social security were played out mainly *within* the labor movement and the Histadrut itself, rather than against the vested interests of employers or conservative political groups in the society. It was not until the 1970s that the struggle for social security took on an inter-class character. As is the case with other forces believed to be primarily responsible for the development of the welfare state, the role of the trade union movement is complex and reflects the strain between its ideals and its organizational interests. As the powerful organization of Zionist labor unions in Israel, the Histadrut had to favor the establishment of a comprehensive national social security program. This was both a matter of ideology and practical necessity because of the needs and demands of the working population.[6] In practice, however, the Histadrut acted much more selectively from the beginning and supported only those parts of the Kanev reform program that did not threaten its own previously established benefit programs. For example, it had no difficulty in supporting the industrial injuries insurance scheme because it had no stake in the existing workers' compensation program; only the private insurance companies were affected by the proposed transfer to the government.

The Histadrut also supported the maternity insurance scheme for the same reason. To the extent that its sick fund (Kupat Holim) provided some services to mothers, the Histadrut would benefit from the new scheme. In contrast, however, the Histadrut gave conditional support to the old-age insurance scheme only insofar as it did not interfere with its own retirement and pension funds. As a result, the policy that was finally adopted permitted the state to provide only minimum subsistence pensions with provisions beyond that level left chiefly to the Histadrut's own pension funds.

No such solution could be found for medical care. A national health insurance plan seriously threatened Kupat Holim and the Histadrut, as membership in the Kupat Holim was one of the major incentives for joining the Histadrut. Although a national insurance program was eventually adopted, medical care to this day has not been included principally because of the opposition of the Histadrut. Finally, even though unemployment benefits in no way thwarted the interests of the labor movement or the Histadrut, the struggle for unemployment benefits was fought on ideological grounds for more than two decades before being adopted. In this case, the Histadrut clung to the socialist principle that only work should be provided for the unemployed. With regard to both health and unemployment insurance, the Histadrut acted in ways similar to those of unions in other countries where "leaders . . . were particularly opposed to sickness and unemployment insurance, largely for fear of weakening union influence over workers and increasing workers' dependence on the government."[7] Yet, British labor leaders had concluded as early as 1908 that "the introduction (in Germany) of state insurance of workmen against sickness, invalidity, and old age had in no way exercised an injurious effect on the Trade Unions of the country."[8] Nearly a half century later, the Histadrut leaders thought otherwise, and because they had—in the formative years of nation- and institution-building—the power to block any legislation, the national insurance program at every step represented a compromise that was acceptable to the Histadrut and to the Labor Party, which largely controlled the Histadrut.

Opposition to the establishment of a national insurance program was not limited to the Histadrut alone. Special interest groups such as the private insurance companies and conservative groups within the civil service, particularly among the Treasury's economists, fought continuously against state action in the field of social security. In the 1980s, Treasury economists—some of whom were students of Milton Friedman—gained a dominant position on the Israeli political scene and have been able to limit the expansion and improvement of some social programs. It is ironic that although Israel did not have to overcome a nineteenth-century, laissez-faire resistance to social security and state intervention, it faced similar constraints on public policy from the revival of neoconservatism in the 1970s. Yet the Israeli experience also illustrates the possibilities and limits of social reform in a democratic society without radical change in its political and economic structure.[9]

In this context, the role of elections in Israel could hardly be overestimated. As the record shows, the necessity to face the electorate approximately every four years was a powerful incentive in the introduction of new schemes and the improvement and reform of existing ones. From 1953 onward, *practically every major improvement in the country's social security system was carried out shortly before an election.* Although the need for these changes existed long before the elections, only the requirement to face the voters could evidently force the Knesset members to finally make crucial policy decisions that had long been deferred because no consensus could be reached. To paraphrase Benjamin Franklin, there is nothing like an election to concentrate a politician's mind. Elections were a stimulus for change and innovation in social security that reflected the capacity of the political system to respond to the pressures for social reform.

A reasonable assessment of the social security system in Israel would probably come to this conclusion: Despite the enormous economic and political constraints of absorbing mass immigration and coping with the external threats to its security, Israel succeeded, after only forty years of statehood, in building a comprehensive system of social protection that includes national insurance, social assistance, occupational, and other statutory benefit programs. The scope, if not its adequacy, is impressive when one notes that by the end of the 1980s, the entire population was covered by old-age, survivors, disability, maternity, and children's allowances schemes; in addition, all employed persons were covered by unemployment and industrial injuries insurance. Social assistance became a national responsibility, and long-term care insurance covered some of the most important needs for social care of the elderly. All of these programs matured very quickly and provided a wide range of cash and in-kind benefits to very large population groups.

From the perspective of social security providing care "from the cradle to the grave," this slogan has become a reality in Israel. A baby is born in Israel under the auspices of a maternity insurance scheme that covers the cost of the mother's stay in a hospital, wages lost during maternity leave, and the costs of a layette. Other programs provide for a minimum income, as a last resort or safety net, throughout the life cycle, and at its end, national insurance pays for the costs of burial. Moreover, the right to a minimum level of economic security has fulfilled an important integrative function in the highly segmented and stratified Israeli society. By granting everyone—native and immigrant, Jew and Arab—the "social rights of citizenship" as defined by T.H. Marshall,[10] social security has made it possible for everyone to participate at least nominally in the society and polity.

Although the social security program provides social protection and integration, the program is admittedly weak in its redistribution function and in its contribution to equality. For example, the Israeli social security system in its formative years, like those of some European countries, was strongly influenced by the Beveridge Plan and its operating principles. Though it escaped some of Beveridge's flat-rate pitfalls by immediately providing for wage-related contributions, it still retained the principle of flat-rate old-age pensions with the result that large numbers of elderly persons have a retirement pension that is inadequate even for a subsistence level of living.

Two far-reaching and largely unintended social and political consequences flowed from this adoption of a British principle. First, it became necessary to establish an income-conditioned scheme to supplement the inadequate old-age pensions, which has made it inevitable that many elderly are dependent on an income-tested assistance program for their basic livelihood. This means that national insurance could not achieve one of its basic goals: namely, that after a lifetime of work, an elderly person should not have to apply for assistance. Second, by both design and default, the system has provided an impetus for the growth and development of private occupational pension schemes that can undermine the existing old-age insurance program. With the growth and maturation of private pension plans, the small, old-age insurance pensions have become almost superfluous for the middle classes in Israel. This serves as justification for the Treasury's periodic recommendation to abolish the scheme and transform it into one designed for the needs of only the poor. This policy objective was not foreseen by the original planners of national insurance or by the Histadrut, which initially supported the two-tier system of income provision for the aged.

Similarly, the adoption of Beveridge's insurance philosophy as a way of avoiding stigma meant that a heavier burden was placed on low-income persons because of the regressive nature of the taxes that financed the old age pensions. Only in the later years of the program when the insurance principle was somewhat relaxed was it more accessible to large, underprivileged groups and able to have a more significant integrative and redistributive effect.

There were two aspects of the original policy objectives that related to redistribution: from the higher to the lower income groups and from those still active in the labor market to those who were no longer part of the employed population. After forty years, the system had brought about a substantial intergenerational redistribution of income from the adult population to the elderly, to children, and to those groups outside the labor market such as the disabled, chronically ill, and the unemployed. But, as in most other social security systems, there has been little redistribution from the rich to the poor.

This case study of Israel also has some implications for the political economy of social policy, mainly regarding the role of trade unions and politics in the development of social security. The Israeli Labor parties—like their social-democratic counterparts elsewhere—though they remained ideologically committed to progressive social policies, became hesitant and vacillated about implementing their beliefs once they obtained power. Although in theory, social-democratic Labor parties are more willing than their opponents to introduce new social benefits and to reform existing ones, in practice they usually choose the more cautious and conservative measures and rarely venture into new social experiments. It cannot be said of the Histadrut, as some have noted about the trade union movement in Sweden, that it played a comparatively creative and constructive role in the development of social policy.[11]

The question raised by many researchers—does politics matter?—does not have a clear-cut answer in the case of Israel. Although politics obviously does matter, it does so only to a limited degree. It seems that the structure of the polity as a whole, and the flexibility or rigidity of its social institutions are, in the end, more important factors in determining a country's capacity to respond to changing social circumstances and initiate necessary social reform. Politics can facilitate or retard that process. There is little doubt that the dominance of the labor movement in Israeli politics in the formative years of statehood greatly facilitated this process, and it is questionable whether a more conservative coalition would have done the same. In view of the complex and unique social conditions that existed in Israel, the modest social reforms carried out chiefly by the Labor Party through social security in general and national insurance in particular should not be underestimated. These reforms, though often far short of what was necessary and often long-delayed, nevertheless played an important part in improving the circumstances of the majority of Israelis and in changing the face of Israeli society.

Prospects for the Future

After more than forty years of statehood, what are the future prospects of the Israeli welfare state and its social security system? As in many other countries in Europe and North America toward the end of the 1980s, Israel found itself in the midst of a prolonged debate about the future of its social security arrangements. The country is in the midst of a "reframing of the intellectual discourse"[12] about the future of these social policies, which is a process that is occurring in a climate of persistent stagflation for more than a decade, drastic upheavals in the Israeli economy, and significant changes in the Israeli polity. In this context, social security—the core of the welfare state in Israel—has become a target of intense political attack. The attack is not a simple reaction to the limits of economic capacity but reflects the pervasive political and ideological changes in Israeli society.[13]

The two principal factors in this changing scene are the almost complete collapse of the Socialist Zionist ideology that guided the social and political thinking of the leadership of the state from its inception and the rise of conservative political groups aggressively promoting an unrestrained, competitive free market. These trends, which are at the heart of the current reframing of the intellectual discourse on future social policies, are critical of governmental intervention to promote redistribution of income; conservative political groups demand the reduction of public spending on social programs and advocate the "targeting" of benefits for the poor alone or for the truly needy.[14]

There were many elements that contributed to the deradicalization and embourgeoisement of Israel's labor movement and the Histadrut. It remained in large part a prisoner of its pre-state, predominantly Marxist ideology, with its negative attitude toward social welfare policies designed to assist weaker members of the population: low-wage earners, elderly, disabled, and so on. Acquiring an enormous amount of economic power through its own enterprises, the Histadrut succeeded in dictating Labor Party policy more often in the interests of its own organization than in those of the working population. To the extent that there was a social-democratic trend within the labor movement, it eventually ceased to represent the aspirations for a more just and equal society. The technocrats and managers who gained positions of power in the Labor Party openly supported a hierarchical society—at best, meritocratic in nature and at worst, a stratified class structure. Those who have gained supremacy in the labor movement have thus few incentives to promote distributive social policies and, in effect, support increased differentials in wages, incomes, and allocating social security benefits on the basis of individual achievement.[15]

The Israeli labor movement, which played such a substantial role in shaping the country's social security system, was also influenced by changes that have occurred in the economies and labor markets of the advanced industrial societies. For example, the diminishing size of the industrial working class and the increasing marginalization of labor inevitably affected the size and political strength of labor parties. This process was exacerbated by the division of postindustrial economies into two quite separate populations: a highly skilled minority of service, technical, and research personnel and the nonskilled and semiskilled workers in the traditional industries.[16] The Israeli labor movement suffered an additional and major setback when large numbers of its members abandoned their traditional allegiance to their party and transferred their political support in 1977 to the right-wing Likud bloc.

Part of the vacuum created by the crumbling of socialist beliefs and the weakening of the power of labor was filled by economics—a recurring secular theology. The principal school of classical economical theory that flourished in Israel since its inception and has exercised considerable influence in many spheres of national life is strongly opposed to redistribution or any form of social policy associated with egalitarianism. Paradoxically, important segments of the labor leadership have adopted these views, apparently without recognizing the contradiction between them and the goals of their labor movement—of which a progressive social policy is an integral part. To the right-wing Likud bloc there is, of course, no problem in subscribing to these economic theories.

As in many other countries, the earlier political consensus that supported the welfare state has also broken down in Israel. This loss of support has been aided by the development of private welfare states throughout the economy favoring the better-off workers as well as the absence of an articulate constituency in support of social security.[17] Many Israelis increasingly have questioned the general assumption, which was shared in the past by labor and non-labor parties alike, that the state must intervene in the operations of the market and take some responsibility for the economic security of individuals. In part, this grew out of cross-national learning whereby small countries tend to look to the United States or United Kingdom as reference groups for appropriate policies, regardless of their suitability. In this context, the debate turned on the legitimacy of the role of government in the field of social security.

Despite these inroads, there still remains a considerable measure of agreement on the need to maintain the social security system as the primary means of providing income security and supplementation for large population groups. Although the voices of the supporters of redistributive social policies have been seriously weakened, they are still heard. At the very least, parts of the Israeli labor movement and some important populist groups within the Likud right-wing alignment are acutely aware of the danger in reducing even further the modest level of income protection provided to large numbers of people. There is recognition that the delicate balance between social integration, prevention of poverty, and a more equitable distribution of income that has been achieved over the years can be unsettled with grave consequences; namely, the resurgence of those deep ethnic, class, and religious cleavages that still divide Israeli society and could threaten the stability of its democratic institutions.

The resilience that social security systems have manifested in other countries, despite the obstacles encountered during the 1980s, also has been in evidence in Israel. As we have described, most attempts to cut or downgrade existing provisions by reducing public expenditures on social security in Israel failed. The universalistic character of the system has remained largely intact, although by introducing or increasing the number of income-conditioned elements, selectivist inroads have been made. There is, of course, the danger that, over time, this tendency could erode the universalism of the system and transform it into one that serves mainly the poor.

One of the most important factors operating in favor of continuation of the existing social security system and even strengthening it is the NII itself. As one of the more significant social institutions in Israel, the NII has helped insure the effectiveness and political acceptability of many social policies. From its inception, the NII enjoyed a high degree of autonomy within the national government. In recent years, however, there have been a succession of political attempts to reduce the degree of freedom of the NII and to subordinate it more and more to control of the Treasury. Opposition to these efforts to encroach on the independence of the NII has come from its broad constituency, which has been developed over the years and includes client groups, members of the Knesset, political parties, the leadership of the Histadrut, mass media, and the universities. If the promises of recent ministers of Labor and Social Affairs to maintain the special status of the NII are reliable, then the NII will be able to continue advocating and promoting social reform. With all the changes in the top leadership of the NII, it has retained the spirit of the earlier, reform-minded policymaking network and has used its expertise not only to implement benefit programs in an efficient way, but also to introduce innovation and needed improvements when political opportunities presented themselves.

In summing up, it is obvious that Israel's social security policy, at the end of the 1980s, was vulnerable. The ruling political and economic establishment was in the process of adopting policies involving institutional changes that could gradually, if not entirely, dismantle the country's social security system—the core of the Israeli welfare state. Implementation of these policies would be a triumph for neoconservative political ideas, which have gained wide support among the new Israeli managerial classes across the entire political spectrum.

At this junction, the most difficult task in preserving the social security system in Israel is more in the realm of ideas than in institutions. The central question is whether the country will be able to revive the moral justification for a more equitable, distributive social policy. The collective vision of Israel as a model state—"a light unto the nations"—and a just society has suffered serious erosion during the 1970s and 1980s. The self-image of the people of Israel as members of a caring society has undergone a major metamorphosis with the rise of consumerist and individualist values and the failure to progress toward a peaceful solution of the Arab-Israeli conflict. The question remains whether Israel will once again demonstrate its capacity to generate new moral values that might capture the imagination of its people and provide a new impetus to its earlier pioneering spirit.

Notes

1. Douglas E. Ashford, *The Emergence of the Welfare States* (New York: Basil Blackwell, 1986), pp. 27–28.

2. Yoram Ben-Porath (ed.), *The Economy of Israel: Maturing Through Crisis* (Cambridge, MA: Harvard University Press, 1986).

3. The relationship between the development of social insurance and economic growth is discussed in most comparative studies. See, for example, Ashford, op. cit.; E. Oyen (ed.), *Comparing Welfare States and Their Futures* (Aldershot, England: Gower, 1986).

4. Hugh Heclo, *Modern Social Politics in Britain and Sweden: From Relief to Income Maintenance* (New Haven: Yale University Press, 1974), pp. 308–320.

5. Ashford, op. cit., Chapter 1.

6. G. Esping-Andersen, *Politics Against Markets: The Social Democratic Road to Power* (Princeton: Princeton University Press, 1985), pp. 146–147.

7. Arnold J. Heidenheimer, Hugh Heclo, and Carolyn Teich-Adams (eds.), *Comparative Social Policy: The Politics of Social Choice in Europe and America* (London: Macmillan Press, 1975), p. 76.

8. Bentley B. Gilbert, *The Evolution of National Insurance in Great Britain: The Origins of the Welfare State* (London: Michael Joseph, 1966), p. 256.

9. Ashford, op. cit., pp. 300–318.

10. T.H. Marshall, *Class, Citizenship, and Social Development* (New York: Anchor Books, 1965).

11. Heclo, op. cit., pp. 301, 311–312; Joan Higgins, *States of Welfare: Comparative Analysis in Social Policy* (London: Basil Blackwell and Martin Robertson, 1981), pp. 122–128.

12. M. Rein and L. Rainwater, "From Welfare State to Welfare Society," in M. Rein, G. Esping-Andersen, and L. Rainwater (eds.), *Stagnation and Renewal in Social Policy: The Rise and Fall of Policy Regimes* (Armonk, NY: Sharpe, 1987).

13. Lev Grinberg, *Split Corporatism in Israel* (Albany: State University of New York Press, 1991).

14. P. Ruggles and M.O. Higgins, "Retrenchment and the New Right: A Comparative Analysis of the Impacts of the Thatcher and Reagan Administrations" in M. Rein et al., op. cit.

15. Michael Shalev, "Israel's Domestic Policy Regime: Zionism, Dualism and the Rise of Capital," in F.G. Castles (ed.), *The Comparative History of Public Policy* (Cambridge: Polity Press 1989), pp. 100–198.

16. U. Himmelstrand, "The Future of the Welfare State: A Question of Holistic Diagnosis and Structural Reform," in Oyen, op. cit.

17. Abraham Doron, "The Histadrut: Social Policy and Equality," *Jerusalem Quarterly* 47 (Summer 1988), 131–144.

Index